"In *The Church as Movement* White and Woodward rewrite what it means to cultivate and grow churches in the mission fields of post-Christendom. Accomplishing the impossible, they provide an exhaustive preparation for those who dare to navigate this terrain. It's a learning experience enormous in its aspirations yet so necessary for the task that lies ahead for the church in mission."

David Fitch, B. R. Lindner Chair of Evangelical Theology, Northern Seminary, author of *Faithful Presence*

"This is a book of wisdom by thoughtful practitioners, experienced and mature in their own leadership. It provides valuable help in an integrated approach that many will find inspiring and, most of all, truly helpful."

Mark Labberton, president, Fuller Theological Seminary

"JR and Dan have produced a simple, intensely practical guide for those of us who want to shift from merely sustaining the 'religious industrial complex' to unleashing a dynamic missional church planting movement. *The Church as Movement* is full of ideas on missional discipleship, rhythms of life, cultural exegesis, fivefold leadership models and more, all anchored in a beautiful biblical vision of the sent-and-sending God."

Michael Frost, author of *The Shaping of Things to Come, Exiles* and *The Road to Missional*

"Theologically and theoretically complex and robust, yet practically so transferable in its attentiveness to movement dynamics and awareness of place-based disciple-making. This is a book that will surprise and challenge trained practitioners while offering tools that are adaptable enough for real movement. I believe even the title is a phrase that will become integral to the new vocabulary of church multiplication. I honestly wish I had written it myself!"

Linda Bergquist, church planting catalyst and coach, coauthor of *Church Turned Inside Out*

"A church building or sign is no indicator that the community of God is truly present as a transforming force in any particular place. This book pushes us to see the church as it was meant to be biblically and as it needs to be today in order to advance the kingdom of God. Missional, incarnational movement and discipleship cannot be optional ideas for the church but must be core essentials so that the justice and truth of God is experienced in a broken world."

Efrem Smith, president and CEO, World Impact, author of *The Hip Hop Church* and *The Post-Black and Post-White Church*

"*The Church as Movement* is a book I wish I'd been able to get my hands on twenty years ago. I got into church planting because I wanted to be a disciple and make disciples of Jesus. Instead, I encountered a system that largely measured success in terms of attendance, budgets, and buildings. Woodward and White not only offer an alternate transformational vision, they have created an immensely practical resource. I've seen their work firsthand and am deeply encouraged by their ability to come alongside leaders and equip them to embody the way of Jesus in their local communities."

Mark Scandrette, founder, ReIMAGINE, author of *Practicing the Way of Jesus, Free*, and *Belonging and Becoming*

"What I love about JR and Dan is that they don't just write about the stuff of missional discipleship, they live it! *The Church as Movement* is a real gift to the church. It is not only crammed full of practical wisdom, but is written in a way that is accessible to everybody."

Debra Hirsch, author of *Untamed* and *Redeeming Sex*

"JR and Dan use their wisdom and experience to help churches plant churches that better reflect the effectiveness of the early church, emphasizing the importance of community and discipleship."

Ed Stetzer, executive director of the Billy Graham Center for Evangelism at Wheaton College

THE CHURCH AS MOVEMENT

**Starting and Sustaining
Missional-Incarnational Communities**

JR Woodward // Dan White Jr.

Foreword by Alan Hirsch

IVP Books

An imprint of InterVarsity Press
Downers Grove, Illinois

InterVarsity Press
P.O. Box 1400, Downers Grove, IL 60515-1426
ivpress.com
email@ivpress.com

InterVarsity Press® is the book-publishing division of InterVarsity Christian Fellowship/USA®, a movement of students and faculty active on campus at hundreds of universities, colleges and schools of nursing in the United States of America, and a member movement of the International Fellowship of Evangelical Students. For information about local and regional activities, visit intervarsity.org.

All Scripture quotations, unless otherwise indicated, are taken from THE HOLY BIBLE, NEW INTERNATIONAL VERSION®, NIV® Copyright © 1973, 1978, 1984, 2011 by Biblica, Inc.™ Used by permission. All rights reserved worldwide.

While any stories in this book are true, some names and identifying information may have been changed to protect the privacy of individuals.

Material taken from JR Woodward, Creating a Missional Culture, is copyright © 2012 by JR Woodward. Used by permission of InterVarsity Press, P.O. Box 1400, Downers Grove, IL 60515, USA. www.ivpress.com.

Material taken from Dan White Jr., Subterranean: Why the Future of the Church Is Rootedness (Eugene, OR: Cascade Books, 2015) is used with permission from Wipf and Stock Publishers, www.wipfandstock.com.

The Baptism of Christ and The Last Supper images by Martin Erspamer in chapter five are reprinted from Clip Art for Year A by Martin Erspamer, OSB, © 1992 Archdiocese of Chicago: Liturgy Training Publications. All rights reserved. Used with permission.

Cover design: Chris Diggs @ dribble.com/chrisdiggs and Dan White Jr.
Interior design: Beth McGill
Images: esdrop/Fotolia.com

ISBN 978-0-8308-4133-2 (print)
ISBN 978-0-8308-9362-1 (digital)

Printed in the United States of America ∞

InterVarsity Press is committed to ecological stewardship and to the conservation of natural resources in all our operations. This book was printed using sustainably sourced paper.

Library of Congress Cataloging-in-Publication Data

Names: Woodward, J. R., 1963- author.
Title: The church as movement : starting and sustaining
  missional-incarnational communities / JR Woodward and Dan White Jr.
Description: Downers Grove : InterVarsity Press, 2016. | Includes
  bibliographical references.
Identifiers: LCCN 2016010703 (print) | LCCN 2016013160 (ebook) | ISBN
  9780830841332 (pbk. : alk. paper) | ISBN 9780830893621 (eBook)
Subjects: LCSH: Church development, New. | Discipling (Christianity)
Classification: LCC BV652.24 .W66 2016 (print) | LCC BV652.24 (ebook) | DDC
  254/.1--dc23
LC record available at http://lccn.loc.gov/2016010703

| P | 24 | 23 | 22 | 21 | 20 | 19 | 18 | 17 | 16 | 15 | 14 | 13 | 12 | 11 | 10 | 9 | 8 | 7 | 6 | 5 | 4 | 3 | 2 |

| Y | 37 | 36 | 35 | 34 | 33 | 32 | 31 | 30 | 29 | 28 | 27 | 26 | 25 | 24 | 23 | 22 | 21 | 20 | 19 | 18 |

To the church planters and teams in the V3 Church Planting Movement—

Your faith to plant place-based, community-forming, discipleship-fueled, movement-oriented, missional-incarnational churches is an inspiration to us.

Contents

List of Figures and Tables

Tables

Foreword

Alan Hirsch

People in any organization are always attached to the obsolete—the things that should have worked but did not, the things that once were productive and no longer are.

PETER F. DRUCKER

If we can accept Einstein's dictum that insanity is doing the same thing over and over and expecting a different result, and then use it as a lens to assess the prevailing organizational habits of the church, we can actually shed light on a fair bit of "organizational insanity" laced into the prevailing practices of most contemporary and historical expressions of church. It always astounds me that many leaders seem to think that simply repeating and optimizing the inherited habits of church will eventually deliver paradigm-shifting results.

Part of the problem we face in the twenty-first century church is that most churches operate out of a largely obsolete understanding of the church that was developed in a completely different age and for a completely different set of cultural and social conditions—largely that of European Christendom. This is like trying to negotiate New York City with a map of Paris or Rome. We can all spot the insanity of this with regard to geographical maps, but we persist in doing this with our ecclesial ones. The very marginalization of the contemporary European church itself is a tragic witness to this obsolescence. This alone should shock us into reality and yet, in the name of some absurd commitment to long-hallowed church habits, we persist in using outworn ecclesial maps to negotiate new cultural territories.

My own writings have concentrated on helping us to think about our situation with a different paradigm and with the view of activating a different form of the church, one that is equal to the task of advancing Jesus' cause into this century in which we are called to be faithful witnesses. I speak of the paradigm of missional or *apostolic* movement. I believe that the apostolic movement paradigm provides us with the appropriate frameworks that will enable us to reorient the church to the massively changed, and constantly changing, conditions of the twenty-first century. As uncomfortable as it is, it is necessary for us to consider that when there is a fundamental paradigm shift, everything must go back to zero.

But changing the paradigm or metaphor of the church is only half the battle. Having won hearts and minds, the battle for change shifts to changing the now-outdated habits of organizations that accompanied the old paradigm and developing new practices that conform to the new. We need to recalibrate the church based on the new paradigm and the new set of conditions. This is the subject of all my writings, but especially in *The Forgotten Ways*, where I articulated the movemental paradigm, and in *On the Verge*, where I suggest a model for recalibrating the church along the lines of missional movement paradigm.[1] In the last few years there has been a widespread adoption of the missional paradigm, however our practices lag way behind. This is where JR Woodward and Dan White's revolutionary new book comes in—it's all about developing disciplined practices that are consistent with movement.

For one, I like the way they describe *movement*. Citing Scripture, current movement thinkers and critics of some movement literature, they see missional movement as flowing from being rooted in the depth, width, length and height of God's love. You will find their description in table 1.1.

One of the strengths of the book derives from the fact that JR and Dan are reflective practitioners; both have planted churches, are leading a wonderful new movement called V3 and have been training planters all across North America. As a result, this book reflects the many lessons learned in ways that are accessible not just to the professional church planter but especially to the everyday Christians who desire to get into what God is doing to change the world in the Way of Jesus. Furthermore, their understanding of movement is wonderfully minimalist without being reductionist. The result is that it can be practiced by ordinary, everyday Christians. Here they activate the essence of movement—where *everyone,* regardless of race, gender and class, is an active agent in the game. The Jesus movement is a people movement!

The Church as Movement is a thoroughly practical but theologically rich guidebook for starting real-time, local, missional, incarnational communities. It is written in a popular tone and uses simple tools and pictures to synthesize large concepts. It starts from the key grounded practice of discipleship and expands from there into other vital areas of mission. The tone is revolutionary without being alienating, and is constructive in providing a tangible way forward.

Here are some other highlights as I see it:

- JR and Dan flip popular (mis)conceptions of mass movements on their heads by intentionally focusing on what it means to catalyze smaller ecclesia, and then indicate what it will take to go to scale through multiplication.

- This book is unapologetically a journey through the basics, giving it wide accessibility to everyday practitioners and to leaders seeking to help transition ordinary parishioners to become missionaries in every context of life.

- The material on incarnational practices and community formation takes complex ideas and simplifies them into hands-on tools that can be applied in groups.

- JR and Dan give us dozens of transferable tools that are simple, sticky and scalable.

- The formational learning approach can break new ground and pioneer a clear pathway forward in shaping our habits and process for discipling people into more missional postures.

- Their definition of *movement* builds on best thinking and develops it further.

- As they say, while some church planting books implant a desire in people to be on the stage, *The Church as Movement* creates a desire in people to want to be on the streets.

- This book will help train people in place-based, discipleship-focused, community-building, movement-oriented, missional-incarnational church planting. This in my opinion is precisely the kind of church that will advance Christianity in the twenty-first century.

- This book prepares people for mission by helping them understand how God re-shapes us for mission in very concrete and eminently *doable* ways.

I am absolutely thrilled that my good friends have labored to produce this much-needed book. It deserves to be widely used in the broader missional movement to which they belong. I will use this book in the many forums I work in and will refer other practitioners to it along the way.

Introduction

· ·

Why This Guidebook?

Many recognize the need to recalibrate what it means to be the church in today's world, in our local places. A growing number of people are starting new communities because they hope to be the people of God in a fresh way. People have been trained how to draw a crowd, create an event or preach a good sermon. However, few have been equipped for incarnational approaches to mission. Many are starving for wisdom, guidance and grounded tools on how to cultivate new types of church bodies.

This book is an attempt to help people plant the kind of churches that reflect the viral movement of the early New Testament, fueled by the values of tight-knit community, life-forming discipleship, locally rooted presence and boundary-crossing mission. This is "church as movement."

How to Use This Guidebook

This book was birthed out of training with church planters, leaders and disciplers who have started and are starting new communities all over North America, from LA to New York, from Seattle to Miami and from Honolulu to Toronto. The training has been used in diverse contexts with diverse people who share a dynamic vision for seeing God do something new in their cities and towns.

This guidebook approaches starting new communities from a *discipler* mentality. A discipler is one who invites others on the journey of starting a fresh missional-incarnational community. The discipler senses and responds to a call and breaks open space for others to walk with them. This book is best used with a group of four to twelve people. We call this cluster of people who gather to work through this guidebook for starting and sustaining missional-incarnational communities the "discipleship core." This requires an invitation to relearn what it means to be the church and apply a missional-incarnational, place-based, discipleship-focused approach to being the church through a movement lens.

Formational Learning

It is important to work through this material with others, since it was designed for a group rather than to be digested alone. On our website (churchasmovement.com) we have a sample group covenant you can download to help your group set out the commitments to a mutual path of discipleship.

The journey together is one of engaging in *formational learning*. Formational learning involves more than passing along information or increasing intelligence. Formational learning is passionate about the active shaping of our minds (meta-learning), our souls (reflective learning) and our bodies (experiential learning); we'll dive deeper into this in chapter four, but the following is a quick introduction.

At the end of each section there are formational learning questions that combine the three levels of learning for your group.

Meta-learning. Have you ever had a moment when you've been forced to stop and think about what you're doing? Maybe you've been surprised. Maybe you've stumbled across something that captures your attention and gets the gears of your mind moving in new ways. These experiences are called "meta-moments": moments of discovery that have the possibility of shaping you in a significant way if you become mindful of them.

Meta-learning is the effort of exposing a learner's *mind* to a new reality through communication and information that brings sudden awakening. It is the work of getting at the big idea: What is the significant shift, truth, story, concept that you are now seeing? Meta-moments often happen when we're contemplating something we've heard a thousand times before that we now deconstruct to reveal a new meaning that was hidden in plain sight.

In the meta-learning exercises we will ask you to process and write down the over-arching but deepest meaning of each section for you personally. This is not necessarily about questions of application, which you will get to in the experiential learning exercises. Instead, consider, what is the vital, essential truth you are now faced with?

Reflective learning. Reflective learning excavates what is in the *soul* through good questions and conversation. It's taking a magnifying glass to explore what's below the surface. God made us as relational beings, and he brings understanding through interaction and reflection.

After focusing on meta-learning we invite you to reflect on how it makes you feel (e.g., conflict, clarity or confusion). This is the process of becoming conscious of how something connects with you, writing down your observations in descriptive language rather than abstract or general language. In discipleship we must cultivate space for questions that seek not the regurgitation of information but the processing of meta-learning's implications. In the reflective learning exercises we invite you to write down where you feel some rub, a bit of fear or even an allergic reaction.

Experiential learning. Experiential learning comes by creating movement in the body through real-time experiences, taking active steps. Experiential learning comes into its fullness when we learn to take a risk, experiment and practice. It is best catalyzed in a group that seeks to make an attempt at the discipleship journey together.

Experiential learning is a process by which we develop deeper understanding through a direct experience outside a traditional meeting or academic setting. Journeying through this book, a group should see its neighborhood, relationships and everyday world as their laboratory. Group members should seek to support each other as they apply their conceptual understanding of the real world through concrete practices. In the experiential learning section we will encourage you to write down a goal, a step, and follow through for the next week or two. This is often the hardest but most important level of learning.

Because this book is designed for formation and transformation, we have purposely broken the book into bite-size sections (labeled 1.1, 1.2, etc.) so that you and your discipleship core can digest the big idea, reflect on how this idea can transform your community and then practice what you are learning. You can download a notebook with all the formational-learning questions and space to answer them free from our website (churchasmovement.com).

Ways to Enact This Guidebook

- Weekly (for eight months): Read one section (e.g., 2.1 or 2.2 weekly), gather for reflection, brainstorm some possibilities for practice and then repeat. This is the way we've used the training thus far.

- Twice a month (for four months): Read one whole chapter, gather for reflection, brainstorm some possibilities for practice, take a week off and then repeat.

The Basics for Climbing

We need to return to the essentials, the most vital practices of starting and sustaining the church, and become proficient in the basics. We often relegate the basics to children, yet the basics are foundational moorings and habits we need to survive in the world.

The preparation in starting and sustaining missional-incarnational communities is akin to learning how to climb a mountain. On a mountain-climbing expedition, climbers must develop certain life-saving and life-giving skills for the trek ahead. Many people who hike the Himalayas are ordinary people with great passion and who underwent great preparation. No one wakes up one morning and decides to scale Everest that day.

Mountaineering in the Himalayas is not for the halfhearted. Everyone who has a vision for climbing Everest must accept the terms of physical and mental preparation. The rigors of hiking at such altitudes calls for focused development in cardiovascular, strength, technical and mental conditioning. This is where Sherpas come in.

In the Everest region of Nepal, there is the Khumbu Climbing School, which is a training organization that teaches people to climb mountains by giving them concrete tools and opportunities to practice in real-life situations. They familiarize people with competencies of equipment inspection, rope management, high altitude protection, wilderness first aid, risk avoidance and camp hygiene. In other words, they have discerned the essential competencies needed for people to climb mountains well.

Sherpas are highly regarded as experts in their local terrain because of their familiarity with the peaks and passes in the region. Today, the term *Sherpa* is often used to refer to almost any guide hired for mountaineering expeditions in the Himalayas. It has become slang for a mentor-guide hired to coach a team for a climb. Sherpas have one goal in mind: to help condition rookie climbers to thrive on the path ahead. The right tools and competency with those tools are necessities.

Starting and sustaining a missional-incarnational community is simple, but not simplistic. This book is unapologetically basic, but we hope it's what you find crucial for being the church seeking the manifestation of the kingdom of God. We want to offer our humble Sherpa experience. We understand there are various methods for climbing the mountain of starting and sustaining missional-incarnational communities. These are the competencies and tools we sense are essential for disciples to make the missional trek.

As you work through this book with your discipleship core, you will

- learn how to put discipleship at the center of the church instead of the periphery;

- develop self-awareness about how your strengths and weaknesses shape the heart of your own discipling;

- learn how to craft a communal rule and rhythm of life that reshapes your desire for God and his mission in the world;

- discover how the social and sending nature of God informs our way of being the church;

- learn sticky practices that help sustain life-giving community;

- explore what it means to exegete and map out a neighborhood and network within the city;

- learn how to share a holistic gospel that invites others to participate in the renewal of all things;

- participate in an incarnational process that leads you and your community to live

in and among the people to whom God has sent you;

- activate the five vocational intelligences for sustainable movement; and

- explore how a polycentric approach to leadership stewards power and influence in distributive ways.

The Trek Ahead

We will explore eight competencies vital to starting and sustaining missional-incarnational communities. We've organized these competencies under the four themes of distributing, discipling, designing and doing.

In *distributing* we start with the end in mind. We learn how to start and sustain missional-incarnational communities by seeing the church through a movement lens. In *discipling* we will learn what it means to be and make disciples in the way of Jesus and place it at the foundation of being the church. In the *designing* section we look at what it means to develop a missional framework and missional theology for the people of God. After thoughtfully considering the whole, we finally get down to *doing* the work. This is where we move into the significant work of community formation and incarnational practices in the neighborhood.

We will take time to unpack the tools that will equip you in the grounded work of planting missional-incarnational churches. These tools are crafted to help shape us for transformation and in ways that can be remembered, applied and passed on to others. We have no illusions that the tools by themselves create success. We don't think we've cracked the code. We simply want to pass on what has meaningfully strengthened and supported us on the precarious journey of climbing the mountain.

While this book was written with church planters in mind, it was also written for the whole priesthood of believers. Thus it can be used by ordinary Christians who seek to start and sustain missional-incarnational communities, which is why we identify those using this book as *disciplers* instead of *planters*. All of us who self-identify as Christians are called to make disciples of Christ, not just a special professionalized group of people.

Jesus as the Founder of Movement

Before diving into our first competency, let's reflect a moment on the founder of *movement*. At first glance, the fruit of Jesus' ministry might seem unimpressive. After three and a half years of ministry, the crowds who initially wanted to make him king called for his crucifixion. Judas betrayed him, Peter denied him and the rest of the disciples deserted him.

While his resurrection brought eleven of his disciples back into the fold, several weeks later he had a mere 120 followers (Acts 1:14-15).

I (JR) sometimes imagine Jesus filling out a monthly report with a church-planting organization. At the time of his crucifixion he would have to say, "My core team has deserted me, the crowds want to kill me, but I do think my mom is still on board."

Consider the conversation among the denomination executives: "Yeah, the last time I met with Jesus I told him he shouldn't have hung out in the Nazareth neighborhood for thirty years; that's too long. He should stop sharing so many confusing parables and be more clear when speaking to the crowds, but

he didn't seem to listen. If he had spent more time working on his sermons and having an excellent large gathering and less time hanging out with his twelve friends at weddings and parties, he would have more people coming to his service after three and a half years."

But God's foolishness is wiser than our wisdom. His approach is typically counterintuitive. While there are different views on Jesus, those who have studied his life have come to the common conclusions that Jesus' main message centered on the kingdom of God and his primary way of creating movement was confiding in the three, training the Twelve and mobilizing the seventy.[1] This is the grassroots part of movement.

The Core of Movement

We agree with Dallas Willard's diagnosis of why we don't see movement taking place in the West today: we have failed to *be* and *make* disciples of Jesus.[2] The cost of nondiscipleship is the irrelevance of the church. People run here and there seeking true transformation, trampling on the church to get there.

While we are chasing the latest methods and models, God is seeking to transform us for his mission in the world. For the One who made us has clearly revealed that movement starts with our imitation of Christ, the person in whom all wisdom abides. From Jesus we learn why we live, how to live and how to involve him in our everyday living. Transformation comes by following Christ through the Spirit with others. We must die to our self, our infatuation with speed and size, and devote ourselves to the work of making disciples, training the few.[3] Robert Coleman observes, "When [Jesus'] plan is reflected upon, the basic philosophy is so different from that of the modern church that its implications are nothing less than revolutionary."[4]

It is clear that Jesus had a public ministry. What he did was not done in a corner. He was an itinerant preacher who went all around Israel proclaiming the good news. We too must share the message in public spaces all around our cities. But Jesus seemed to view and use public space in a different way than the church does today. While we think the church needs to reexamine how we understand and use public space, this is not the focus of this book. In fact it would require a book in itself.[5]

This book focuses on the social, personal and intimate spaces, where grassroots movements live or die. While Jesus spoke riddles and parables to the crowds, he offered explanations to his disciples. While he ministered to the crowds, he called his disciples to be with him. While he fed the crowds, he dedicated much of his energy and time to live with and train his disciples. While focusing on the few may seem counterintuitive, it is necessary for movement.

Jesus used common people to see the world reconciled with God, and he kept the group small enough that he could work deeply with them.[6] If we fail to disciple the few, we will continue to foster the irrelevance of the church. Though Jesus' way looked unimpressive in his lifetime, his focus on the Twelve eventually turned the world upside down.

Let's remember what Jesus co-missioned us to do:

> God authorized and commanded me to commission you: Go out and make disciples, far and near, in this way of life, submerging them in trinitarian presence. Then instruct them in the practice of all I have commanded you. I'll be with you as you do this, day after day after day, right up to the end of the age. (Mt 28:18-20 *The Message*)[7]

Take a moment to reflect on this co-mission. Then be still and know God is with you. Take a deep breath and then exhale. You are starting a grace-filled journey up the mountain full of wonder and discovery in what it means to be "the church as movement."

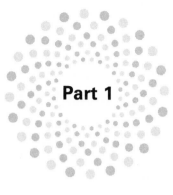

Part 1

//DISTRIBUTING

1

Movement Intelligence

· ·

The kingdom of heaven is like a mustard seed, which a man took
and planted in his field. Though it is the smallest of all seeds, yet
when it grows, it is the largest of garden plants and becomes
a tree, so that the birds come and perch in its branches.

JESUS CHRIST, MATTHEW 13:31-32

Movement occurs when we answer our call to live in *communion* with God, and out of the overflow of our life with him, we live into our sentness as a *community*, carrying out his *co-mission* to be a sign, foretaste and instrument of his kingdom in ever-expanding geographical areas (Acts 1:1). Movement occurs when the making of mission-shaped disciples—who live in the world for the sake of the world, in the way of Christ—goes viral. Movement is about developing structures and systems that catapult people into mission, where reproducing discipleship groups, missional communities, churches and networks of churches is a natural part of its DNA. It's the ripple effect: throwing a rock into a pond creates one ripple and then another and another, till ripples cover the whole pond.

Connecting to Movement

Jesus' metaphors and parables of the kingdom describe the nature of movement. It starts small and becomes significant over time. It starts with a mustard seed and ends with a tree. In our current culture we mock and are unimpressed with the small. We'd rather have fast, furious, fantastic growth. Yet we must pay attention to the small if we want to recover our movemental beginnings. It's within the small that disciples are formed and are sent into neighborhoods for the sake of God's mission. Within the small, communities learn to gather under the essentials of being the church. We need to water the small, over and over, and allow God to bring fruitfulness. The power of movement is in the power of God's Spirit blowing on the smallest embers.

1.1 Gaining New Eyes to See

It takes me (Dan) a while to buy something new. I often push things I own to the brink of being unusable before I use my hard-earned cash to replace them. I'd like to think it's because I'm not materialistic, but it might be because I'm cheap. This recently happened with my glasses. I've been wearing the same glasses for a few years and have been complaining about them for a while, but I've refused to get new ones.

Everything seemed foggy and unclear. These glasses became so bad that driving at night was probably not wise. Eventually I surrendered and got a new pair. I remember the first time I put them on; it was as if someone gave me new eyeballs. I could see! The coating on my previous lenses had eroded so much and had accumulated so many scratches that the world looked different. My new lenses gave me a different, clearer perspective.

We all have a set of glasses that affect the way we see the world. Each of us has preconceived notions of what *church* means. To awaken and embrace the dormant *movemental* impulse of the church we must explore and evaluate the inherited way that we see the church.

All Christians have been given the same co-mission from Jesus, to go and make disciples of all the nations. Yet over time, the co-mission has gotten fuzzy. When our vision has been clear, we see the church as movement. This has produced bright moments in our history. The *Devotio Moderna* movement, which produced *The Imitation of Christ* by Thomas à Kempis, is an example. The Franciscans, the Anabaptists, the Moravians, the Wesleyans and the Pentecostal movements are other examples. But when our vision gets fuzzy, we distort the way we understand the Great Commission and how we see the church.

Where did the primary lens come from that dominates our vision of the church in the United States?

The church as industrial complex. In a farewell address to the nation in 1961, President Dwight Eisenhower gave a speech that became famous because it used the expression "military-industrial complex."[1] In it, Eisenhower warned of the growing danger of our nation stockpiling weapons, expanding its investment in defense spending and increasing the size of our government. This term, *military-industrial complex*, was coined to explain the excessive push to weaponize our country to ensure its security and safety. Eisenhower viewed our relationship with the military as increasingly unhealthy. Over the years, the military was demanding more money, was taking our best people and was becoming dominant in the public consciousness. It was consolidating and consuming all our resources.

Authors Skye Jethani and Scott Bessenecker have borrowed Eisenhower's terminology to describe the current cultural lens by which we see the church, calling it the "Christian-industrial complex."[2] The Christian-industrial complex is a mindset and way of thinking about the church. There is an unquestioned, undergirding concept of the church that is highly informed by the United States' ideas of success.

In our American imagination success means growing bigger, collecting more resources, consolidating power, creating strong hierarchical structures and growing rapidly.

These are the most obvious, simplistic cultural signs of success. The same is true of the church, whether we serve in small or big churches. American church leaders' imaginations and metrics for success are increasingly shaped by the things they can count. But, as Albert Einstein said, "That which counts is often the most difficult to count."

We need a new lens through which to view the church if we want to live into the reality of the church as movement. The church-industrial complex has become the dominant lens for the church. Today, many churches believe their survival and success depends on collecting and consolidating more resources, programs, paid staff, property and people in attendance.

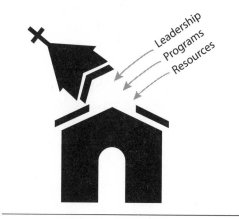

Figure 1.1. Church as industrial complex

A natural impulse for an organism is to collect resources into its own center of gravity. This is especially true for the church in the United States because of its large-scale rejection in society. The church as industrial complex unintentionally turns spirituality into a product, church growth into a race, leadership into a business and members into consumers. Through this lens, more is better.

For the church to become a movement again we need to see differently, and heed God's caution: "The LORD does not look at the things people look at. People look at the outward appearance, but the LORD looks at the heart" (1 Sam 16:7). God compels us to look further than the cultural signs of visible church success.

In seeing the church as movement rather than the church as industrial complex, we must allow ourselves to be interrupted. At one point Jesus performs an odd two-stage miracle. Jesus spits in some dirt, makes mud and puts it on a blind man's eyes—"'I see people; they look like trees walking around.' Once more Jesus put his hands on the man's eyes. Then his eyes were opened, his sight was restored, and he saw everything clearly" (Mk 8:24-25). At first the man's vision was hazy. Only when Jesus touches him a second time can he see clearly. What is going on here? Was Jesus losing his power? Obviously not.

Earlier in the same chapter, Jesus had warned his disciples to beware the yeast of the Pharisees (Mk 8:15). Yeast is necessary for baking bread, but in this case it refers to the bankrupt teaching of the Pharisees. The disciples wondered why Jesus was talking about bread. Jesus was upset and responded, "Do you have eyes but fail to see?" (Mk 8:18).

Jesus is genuinely aghast that his disciples have spent so much time with him but are still blind to his ways. Jesus is making a statement with the healing—even though we may have encountered Christ, we still are nearsighted to some degree or another. Our own experiences and knowledge smudges our vision.

We are like the blind man who now can see, but only partially. We must recognize our vision for being the church as movement is clouded by the church as industrial complex, which has led to the static state of the church today.

The static state of the church. We're in a predicament. While the church in some places in the world is thriving, the church as a whole in the West (especially the Euro-tribal denominations) is increasingly viewed as irrelevant to the pursuit of spirituality and life transformation.[3] We are swimming in resources, ministry real estate and fast-growing churches, but little of this seems to resonate within the wider culture.

Are people still going to Sunday worship services? Of course. But here's a challenge: Ask the people of your city their thoughts on church. You will need thick skin because the responses will be disheartening. It is estimated that only 3.5 percent of my (Dan's) city attend church on a regular basis. We're a minority—not an oppressed minority, but a largely irrelevant minority. Not every city is as dechurched as mine, but this is a growing reality. A sizable chunk of every city's inhabitants have experienced the church and found it unhelpful for being a whole and healthy person. We believe the way of Jesus is the ultimate road to wholeness and healing, but somehow that isn't the word on the street when it comes to the reputation of the church.

We have few options in the face of this reality. The first is denial. Denial uses excuses to justify that all is good. This is certainly an option, but denial is more painful than dealing with the writing on the wall. Missiologist David Bosch says, "The Church is always in a state of crisis and . . . its greatest shortcoming is that it is only occasionally aware of it."[4]

The second option is to give up and take a long break on the organization of the church. We have probably all had moments when we have wondered if it was worth the energy. Still, the resurrection of Jesus inaugurates a breathtaking vision of Jesus' own words, "I will build my church, and the gates of hell shall not prevail against the kingdom of God, and the boundaries between heaven and earth are being removed"(Mt 16:18 The Kingdom New Testament).

There's something tectonic about this; it rattles our bones every time we wonder about the future of the church. Rather than letting the predicament we're facing in the West call us into quitting, it compels us into faithfulness. Encountering this crisis raises the possibility of truly being the movemental church. The problem is big, but the kingdom of God is much bigger. Our cultural irrelevance is an opportunity to recognize that it's time to get a new set of glasses.

There is something timeless and primal about the supernatural movement started by Jesus and his disciples two thousand years ago. Alan Hirsch calls this "the forgotten ways."[5] We need to recover and reignite the axioms of disciple making, incarnational practice, community formation, neighborhood presence and boundary-crossing mission. These attributes are as old as the church itself, but we need a fresh expression of them today. This book is an attempt to help disciples start communities that echo these values. We didn't invent these movemental values. Jesus the founder of the church did.

The church as movement. So what do we mean when we refer to the church as movement? Why is it better to see through the lens of the church as movement as opposed to the church as industrial complex (see fig. 1.2)?

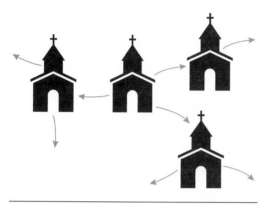

Figure 1.2. Church as movement

Scripture never defines church-planting movements, yet those who study the New Testament and observe the movements of God taking place have sought to bring greater clarity to defining and identifying movements. So while every definition is extrabiblical (as opposed to nonbiblical), we are seeking to provide a definition of *movement* based on Scripture, various students of movements and critics of current literature. Greater clarity on the nature of movements will help us to faithfully fulfill the commission Jesus has given us.

All church-planting movements start with life in God. They are rooted in God's love. "We love because he first loved us" (1 Jn 4:19). When we learn to live into the height, depth, length and width of his love (Eph 3:17-19), we, like the apostle Paul, are compelled to live and share the good news, and it goes viral. Church-planting movements start when we as God's people develop deep roots in the love of God, and as we live into the four dimensions of his incomprehensible love, we gain some clues to the four dimen-

sions of fruit that movements tend to bear (see table 1.1).

Most who study movements would say that one element of movement is depth. In other words, you have the beginning of movement when you have gone three to four levels deep (see fig. 1.3). There are four generations of disciples in Paul's second letter to Timothy. See if you can identify the depth of discipleship Paul is advocating: "The things you have heard me say in the presence of many witnesses entrust to reliable people who will also be qualified to teach others" (2 Tim 2:2).

Table 1.1. Defining church-planting movements

Deep	Movement is taking place when Spirit-filled discipleship and church planting goes three to four generations deep, with at least as many new births as transfer growth.
Wide	Movement seeks to expand into four spheres; from city, state and people groups to the ends of the earth, in a posture of listening, where we learn to be more like Jesus.
Long	Movement can be long lasting and has the potential to become a permanent revolution with a commitment to shared leadership, faithfulness and sustainability.
High	The cost of movement is high and takes faith-filled people who live risk-taking, intentional, sacrificial lives, finding our identity in God, not our image or reputation.

Here are the four levels: Paul, the author of the letter, is the first generation. Timothy, who Paul often calls his son in the faith, is the second generation. "Reliable people" who Timothy is to discern from the crowds is the third level. And those who the reliable people will disciple, the "others," are the fourth generation. This constitutes a movement of disciples. In a Facebook post

Alan Hirsch gave us a lesson in apostolic math: 12 > 12,000. In other words, you can do more with twelve disciples than with twelve thousand religious consumers.

generations deep, but it is four spheres wide. The co-mission that Jesus gave the church was not merely to make disciples in our hometown (Jerusalem) or our own state or

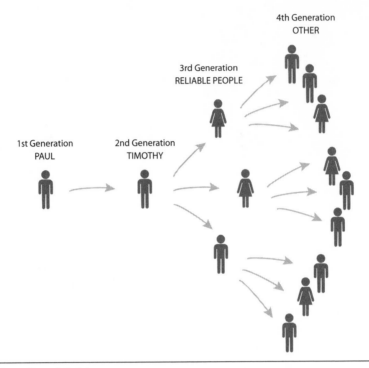

Figure 1.3. Four generations of disciples

While discipleship has a slow beginning, multiplication trumps addition in the long run. We are not in a sprint but a marathon. In the same way, church-planting movement is taking place when we go three to four church plants deep, seeing at least as many new births as transfer growth. The church as movement moves discipleship from the periphery of the church to the center. The church as industrial complex creates a desire to be on stage. The church as movement fosters a desire to be on the streets. Not only is *movement* four

> The church as industrial complex creates a desire to be on stage. The church as movement fosters a desire to be on the streets.

geographical region (Judea), where we can become quite comfortable. He calls us to cross boundaries, bringing the good news to "despised people," people different from us (Samaria) and people far away (the utter ends of the earth). Movement is when the good news becomes so contagious that it spreads four spheres wide.

While the church as industrial complex seeks to go wide, it typically does so in a way to franchise its brand. Knowingly or unknowingly, it tends to meld mission with colonialist triumphalism. The church as movement understands the reason Jesus wants us to go wide differently. It's not about the McDonaldization of the church but carefully incarnating the good news locally.[6] When we see the co-mission through the lens of the church as movement, we realize that Jesus calls us to go wide to unmask the way our culture has squeezed us into its mold, how the empire has demonized "the other" Jesus has called us to be reconciled with.

We are not told to go and colonize the nations. We don't bring the image of God *to* other people, we identify the image of God *in* other people. We go, knowing that our missionary God has already gone before us. We go with a listening and learning posture, so we see the good news incarnated in another culture and better understand our own cultural baggage in the process. Going wide allows us to better expose how our own culture of success and power has misshaped us. We go to learn how to be more like Jesus.

I (JR) have had the privilege of traveling to thirty-nine countries. While I was asked to come teach in many of these countries, I ended up learning more from them about how to be like Jesus. When I visited Kenya I learned joy in simplicity and what it means to live as a rich, interdependent community. I've learned the meaning of the holy kiss from my visits to Italy. People in Latin America, China and the Ukraine have taught me about radical hospitality, giving out of their need, not their excess. I've learned that Jesus has called us to go wide because other cultures help us differentiate the good news from our own cultural baggage. We don't colonize or capitulate to culture, we contextualize the good news.

The incarnation teaches us *how* to go wide. Hudson Taylor was an early pioneer in this, recognizing that when we seek to share the good news with other people, we need to strip away our cultural clothes and comforts, take off our shoes and learn to put our feet in the shoes of those we are sent to. Peter thought that Cornelius was the one who needed to be converted, but God showed Peter that he also needed conversion (Acts 10). While new birth is a distinct form of conversion, anyone who is not living under the reign of God is in need of conversion.

The church as industrial complex seeks to go wide with a sense of pride and triumphalism, seeking to build its own brand. When the church as movement goes wide, it goes in humility and weakness, seeking first God's kingdom. The church as movement crosses boundaries in order to be present and listen, joining what God is already doing. As we leave our families and cultures to bring the good news of the kingdom, we learn more about the nature of that kingdom, and those the empire demonized as enemies become our mothers, brothers and sisters, giving us a glimpse of the reconciliation of people from every tribe, tongue and nation.

Movement goes four levels *deep* and four spheres *wide*, and has the potential to last a *long* time—at least four generations long. Moses writes, "These are the commands, decrees, and regulations that the Lord your God commanded me to teach you. . . . And you and your children and grandchildren must fear the Lord your God as long as you live" (Deut 6:1-2 NLT). Notice the four generations. Moses is the first generation, the children of Israel the second, their children the third and their grandchildren the fourth. Movement is not meant to be short lived.

The church as industrial complex often puts greater value on the personality of the senior leader, sizable impact and rapid growth, desiring an immediate return on their "investment," while the church as movement values shared leadership, sustainability and faithfulness, leaving fruitfulness to God. When the church is built around a personality, the movement comes to an end as soon as the personality leaves. We've seen many cases of this in our day: the seed fell in the rocks, sprouted quickly (we too easily idolize speed) and soon withered in the sun because the soil was too shallow.

If, for the sake of movement, one sacrifices family on the altar of immediate impact and rapid growth, it often results in the next generation becoming tragically lost. The church as movement is mindful that what we do now shapes the future for those who come after us. In their desire for immediate impact and rapid growth, corporations in the Industrial Age (and our time) have left us with polluted waters and skies; similarly in our approach to movement, putting greater value on immediate impact and rapid growth instead of sustainability and faithfulness creates unintended consequences.

Missionary-theologian Lesslie Newbigin gives us insight into the dangers of seeing the church through the lens of the Christian-industrial complex:

> We have to ask whether the church is most faithful in its witness to the cru-

cified and risen Jesus and more recognizable as the community that "bears about in the body the dying Jesus" when it is chiefly concerned with its own self-aggrandizement. When numerical growth is taken as the criterion of judgment on the church, we are transporting with alarming ease into the world of the military campaign or commercial sales drive.[7]

Newbigin reminds us that we must never forget that "mission is not essentially an action by which the church puts forth its own power and wisdom to conquer the world around it; it is, rather, an action of God, putting forth the power of his Spirit to bring the universal work of Christ for the salvation of the world nearer to completion."[8]

Because the church as industrial complex worships speed and rapid growth, too often our neighbors become objects of mission. With a focus on faithfulness and sustainability, the church as movement sees our neighbors as fellow subjects in the story of God, pointing people to the center of that story, Jesus, who is not an imperial power but a slain Lamb.

As we understand the depth, width and length of movement, we also need to remember that genuine movement has a *high* cost. Some of the highest costs we pay are the emotional hits we face when we seek to live into the church as movement.

The first hit is in the area of expectations. While those in the Christian-industrial complex tend to like big launches, often allowing the tail (large gatherings) to wag the dog (the work of disciples in social, personal and intimate space), the church as movement focuses on the "small" grassroots work of developing a discipleship core that builds a missional community together. In this way we will be tested. But while addition looks impressive, a commitment to multiplying disciples is far better in the long run. Patience is needed.

There are also the hits in the area of finances, unsafe people and ministry crises. Some of the most difficult emotional hits we will take in ministry are enduring the pain of being deserted by those we love. It is especially hard when some get sucked up into the Christian-industrial complex. In resisting the ideology of the Christian-industrial complex, our progress will likely feel a lot slower than expected, which is why it is important to develop our inner life in God, finding our identity in God, not in our image or reputation.

When we are in emotional pain, we need to take heart and look to Jesus, the founder of our faith and the pioneer of the church as movement, who understood the priority of training the Twelve. Sometimes the early church got caught up in the Christian-industrial complex. We see this happening in Corinth as well as in Philippi. We can deduce from Paul's letter to the Philippians that two leaders of the church were thinking more about how others saw them than how God saw them. So he writes to them,

> Don't be selfish; don't try to impress others. Be humble, thinking of others as better than yourselves. Don't look out for your own interests, but take an interest in others, too.
>
> You must have the same attitude that Christ Jesus had.
>
> > Though he was God,
> > he did not think of equality with God
> > as something to cling to.
> > Instead, he gave up his divine privileges;
> > he took the humble position of a slave
> > and was born as a human being.
> > When he appeared in human form,
> > he humbled himself in obedience to God
> > and died a criminal's death on a cross.
> > Therefore, God elevated him to the place of highest honor
> > and gave him the name above all other names,
> > that at the name of Jesus every knee should bow,
> > in heaven and on earth and under the earth,
> > and every tongue declare that Jesus Christ is Lord,
> > to the glory of God the Father. (Phil 2:3-11 NLT)

Now that we are looking through the lens of movement, let's unpack how ordinary Christ-followers can live into the church as movement.

FORMATIONAL LEARNING

 Meta-Learning

- What are the biggest differences you see between the church as movement mentality and church as industrial complex?

 Reflective Learning

- How have you personally contributed to the church as industrial complex in your own life?

- What part of movement do you resonate with the most: deep, wide, long, high? Why?

 Experiential Learning

- What is the first step for you to take to live into the church as movement?

1.2. The Anatomy of Movement

Throughout church history it seems that some of the brightest spurts of genuine growth occurred in times of persecution, weakness and suffering. Genuine flourishing seems to come

when the church is in a place of vulnerability rather than strength. Africa and East Asia are seeing remarkable growth with few resources. Roland Allen observes, "In Madagascar for twenty-five years all missionaries were driven from the island and a severe persecution of the Christians was instituted. 'Yet,' we are told, 'at the close of a quarter of a century of persecution the followers of Christ had multiplied ten-fold.'"[9]

Alan Hirsch writes that when Mao Zedong took power in China in 1949, the Chinese church, modeled on Western forms, was estimated to be two million people. "As a part of this systematic persecution, Mao banished all foreign missionaries and ministers, nationalized all church property, killed all senior leaders, either killed or imprisoned all second- and third-level leaders, banned all public meetings of Christians with the threat of death or torture, and then proceeded to perpetrate one of the cruelest persecutions of Christians on historical record."[10]

Mao's reign ended when he died in 1976, and the so-called Bamboo Curtain was opened in the early 1980s. What happened to the church? Was it decimated? No. There was a thriving church estimated at 60-80 million Christians. This explosive growth came about with none of the resources we think are necessary for movement to take place.

They believed that every believer is a church planter and every church is a church-planting church. In other words, the seed has the potential of becoming a tree and a tree has the potential of becoming a forest.

The early church, with little resources and under persecution, also flourished. Paul typically only spent a couple of years in a city before planting a church in another city. When did he know it was time to move on? According to Roland Allen, it was when a church community was dependent on the Holy Spirit in the same way the apostle Paul was dependent on the Holy Spirit. According to the book of Acts, while Paul seeks to make plans, he often is redirected by the Holy Spirit in spontaneous ways.

God is building his church. Looking at these examples, we are reminded that our triune God is building the church, and the gates of hell will not prevail. When we try to take charge and manufacture growth, numerical growth might occur, but not genuine growth. Some churches seek to manufacture growth through pragmatism and business practices or through the ten secrets that will guarantee success. This is not what we mean by movement. Being movemental is recovering a way of being the church of God in the way of Christ and in the power of the Spirit, and allowing God to bring fruit in whatever way he sees fit. Our focus is being faithful and joining God's mission, trusting him for fruitfulness.

Jesus didn't say, "Well done, my good and *fruitful* servant." He said, "Well done, my good and *faithful* servant" (Mt 25:23). When we try to control how fruitful we are (which is not possible), it leads to surface-level growth and passive, consumptive disciples. Our job is to be faithful in the way of Jesus Christ, and as we do that God will make us fruitful (Jn 15). We plant and water, but God causes the growth in his time and his way. What is God calling us to be faithful to?

What is the *anatomy* of movement that we observe from the early church and from stories throughout church history, like the movements in China and Madagascar? We discern that the *how* of the church as movement requires *dogmatic depth*, *ecclesial essentials*, *minimalist methods* and *transferable tools*.

Dogmatic depth. There are many areas of theology where it is important to engage with a critical openness, giving room to freely explore the truth under the vast umbrella of God's grace, not naively but with intelligence, wisdom and love. Yet it is also important to have convictions, to be able to articulate what we believe deeply so we can embody that reality. Paul was convinced that nothing could ever separate us from Christ's love (Rom 8:31-39), that he died for all and that God reconciled us to himself through Christ. Thus we have the ministry of reconciliation (2 Cor 5:19-21). This is dogma for Paul. Where else should we have dogmatic depth?

When it comes to the missional church and movement, we can have dogmatic depth in the theological convictions that the church worldwide has been developing over the last century.[11] This dogma is contextual, timely and tested.

While we will expand on these, especially in the chapter on missional theology, here is a brief overview of some dogma we need to hold fast to if we want movement.

- *Trinitarian missiology.* The social nature of God as evident in the relationship of the Father, Son and Spirit helps us understand what it means to live as community. The sending nature of God, as evident in the Father sending the Son, and the Father and Son sending the Spirit, help us understand how to live on mission.

- Missio Dei. God is a missionary in his very nature. We join God's mission in the world; we don't ask him to join ours. God in Christ came as one who appeared weak, as a servant washing the feet of the world. This should lead to a humble posture, rather than a triumphalist one.

We look for God, listen to the Spirit and seek to bend low to love and serve rather than rule over the world.

- *Holistic gospel.* A reductionist gospel leads to an anemic mission; a holistic gospel leads to a robust mission. When the gospel is reduced to being merely about me, Jesus and going to heaven, it leads to a private, transactional understanding of salvation. Though the good news is personal, it is not private. The good news is social, communal and cosmic, engaging with all these spheres.

The Anglicans are in a season of starting fresh expressions of church that are reaching many new people. No doubt, as they have articulated a clear, simple, holistic mission in an elegant minimalistic way, they are beginning to experience the church as movement. We can learn from how they have defined a holistic mission:

1. Witness to Christ's saving, forgiving and reconciling love for all people.

2. Build welcoming, transforming communities of faith.

3. Stand in solidarity with the poor and needy.

4. Challenge violence, injustice and oppression, and work for peace and reconciliation.

5. Protect, care for and renew life on our planet.[12]

- *Sent people.* Not only is God a sending God, but when we answer the call to follow Christ, we become a sent people. We are all clergy. We are all priests. We are all missionaries. We are all sent.

Having no priestly caste is an original idea with Jesus. The church is not the church if it is not moving deeper into the brokenness of our world.

As Karl Barth wrote,

Theology is not the private reserve of theologians. It is not a private affair for professors. . . . Nor is it a private affair for pastors. . . . Theology is a matter for the church. It does not get on well without professors and pastors. But its problem, the purity of the church's service, is put to the whole church. *The term 'laity' is one of the worst in the vocabulary of religion and ought to be banished from Christian conversation.*"[13]

Regarding Jesus' sacrifice on the cross, missionary and author Vincent J. Donovan writes, "For the first time in the history of religion, . . . an entire people [as] priest. Is this not *one of the biggest differences* between Christianity and all other religions on the face of the earth?"[14]

Yet the sad state of affairs is the clerical captivity of the church.[15] Too often as leaders we have become bottlenecks to movement, instead of helping our fellow priests live out their calling. As theologian Hans Küng writes, "The idea of a Priesthood of All Believers gradually came to be almost forgotten by the faithful and by most theologians."[16]

The continued use of clergy-laity language perpetuates the myth of laity, which typically demeans the majority of the body of Christ by relegating people's function and status to second class.[17] It is interesting that the common element leading to the growth of the church in China and Madagascar was

the removal of the professional clergy. This leads to our final dogma.

- *Missional hermeneutic.* We need to move from a theology of mission to a missional theology. A theology of mission is about going to Scripture to justify our acts of mission. A missional theology looks at the narrative of Scripture, theology and embodied practices in light of the missionary nature of God. From this story we call faith communities into existence to incarnate the good news locally and to join with God in the renewal of all things. Martin Kähler says it with simplicity and clarity, "Mission is the mother of theology."[18]

Ecclesial essentials. While having dogmatic depth enables us clarify our approach to mission, it is also helpful to remember the ecclesial essentials:

1. Communion
2. Community
3. Co-mission
4. Discipleship
5. Leadership

Church is not a building. Our image of what it means to be the church has been stunted by the size of our church buildings, just as a shark will only grow to the size of the tank it is in. When we understand the ecclesial essentials, we have a lot of freedom in what it means to be the church in our local situations.

The first three essentials, *communion* and *co-mission* as a *community* are summed up nicely in this statement by Lesslie Newbigin: "The deepest motive for mission is simply the desire to be with Jesus where he is, on the frontier between the reign of God and the usurped dominion of the devil."[19]

And while the fourth essential, *discipleship*, is included in the co-mission Christ gave us, it's important to reemphasize being and making disciples. This is so essential to movement that Dietrich Bonhoeffer said, "Christianity without discipleship is always Christianity without Christ."[20]

In an article on discipleship, Phil Meadows says we would have more vibrant churches if instead of thinking about how to do church differently, we started with a vision of discipleship. If we first seek to make disciples, he says, we will become vital congregations, have authentic worship, experience real fellowship and develop effective mission.

Meadows goes on to say, if we "start with a mission strategy, we usually end up running programs rather than sharing faith." If we start with community, "we may end up with social circles rather than spiritual communities." If we start with church structures, "they typically become an end in themselves. . . . Discipleship is reduced to serving the structures." And "If we start with church service we are likely to end up as consumers rather than disciples." Changing our services, structures and strategies without changing our lives will not lead to authentic worship, real community and effective mission. Maybe that is why the commission is to "make disciples," not start a church service.[21]

The final ecclesial essential is *leadership*. Every church must have an approach to leadership. And when leadership is approached in a polycentric way (which we will talk about in chapter two), it lends itself to a relational approach to leadership, a communal approach to being the church, and an incarnational and distributive approach to being on mission.

Minimalist methods. Minimalism in design, music, architecture and literature gained momentum in the 1960s and 1970s. "Less is more" is the idea. Minimalism refers to a shift that seeks to pare everything down to the basics, decluttering in order to craft open space. Open space provides more intentional focus on the inhabitants and their relation to each other.

Minimalism allows us to place energy and emphasis on what matters most to us. Minimalism, to quote William Henry Channing, seeks "to live content with small means."[22] In a similar way, Roland Allen notes,

> The spontaneous expansion of the Church reduced to its elements *is a very simple thing*. It asks for no elaborate organization, no large finances, and no great numbers of paid missionaries. . . . The organization of a little Church on the Apostolic model is also extremely simple, and the most illiterate converts can use it, and the poorest are sufficiently wealthy to maintain it.[23]

The key element to the spontaneous expansion of the church is simplicity. Movement requires reproducibility. What we are multiplying should be reproducible by just about everyone. This is no doubt part of what happened in China. If our model can only be reproduced by paid clergy or the most dynamic speakers, it will stunt genuine movement. We often talk so intensely about our buildings, budgets and bands that we have crowded out the minimalism of the first-century church.

But no matter what model we develop or adopt, the grassroots movement of the church is the discipleship core, the mid-sized group and the gathered and scattered rule and rhythm of life. These are explained in chapter six.

The primary minimalist methods revolve around discipleship. In the anatomy of movement, discipleship is the engine for everything. Without it, we drift away from our core DNA. We see discipleship taking place in personal space, where vital theology and practices are passed on to others. This discipleship core is the starting point of the church as movement, getting back to a formational infrastructure with a small band of people.

The next layer is the mid-sized social space (missional-incarnational communities). This is a larger laboratory where disciplers lead others in what it means to live as a community on mission in a particular place. This social space feels like a large family and is the frontier of mission. The discipleship core commits to an intentional rule and rhythm of life, breaking into mutual discipleship triads, all the while living within the larger ecosystem of a mid-sized community. The apostle Paul says, "come follow me as I follow Christ," which the discipleship core models to the missional-incarnational community, inviting them to join them so that others will grow to maturity, living in the world for the sake of the world, in the way of Jesus.

The following figures illustrate that while this approach may have a slow beginning, in time we see how a steady discipleship approach leads to movement. Figure 1.4 shares the heart of what a movemental church is seeking to reproduce. These figures are meant to give a sense of how movement takes place. We must remember that faithfulness is our part, and fruitfulness is God's. He can choose to move as slow or fast as he desires.

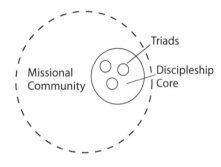

Figure 1.4. Movement year one

In year one a missional community builds a healthy inner culture, and the discipleship core is the nucleus shaping the temperature and direction of the whole. The missional community is situated in a neighborhood or network in which we seek to be missionally present.

In year three we observe a healthy trajectory of multiplication (see fig. 1.5). The original missional community has grown and birthed another missional community, guided by a discipleship core. Typically this second missional community seeks to be a faithful presence within a new neighborhood or network to which they are called.

We've noticed that God tends to do less

> No matter what model we develop or adopt, the grassroots movement of the church is the discipleship core, the mid-sized group and the gathered and scattered rule and rhythm of life.

than we expect in the first three years and more than we expect over ten to fifteen years. Often it is in the first three to five years that he has to do more in us, so that we are better prepared for what he does through us.

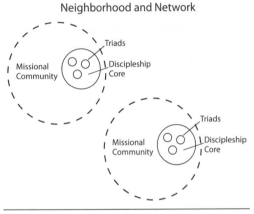

Figure 1.5. Movement year three

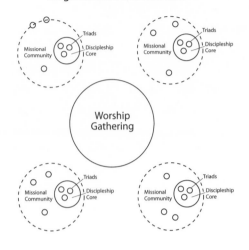

Figure 1.6. Movement year four to five

Another element that tends to shape the speed of multiplication is based on the fivefold vocational gifting of the leader(s). Apostles and evangelists multiply faster on average, while prophets, pastors and teachers tend to be slower, though typically deeper. That is, we plant and water, but God causes the growth.

In year four to five we see multiplication that creates the need for a larger public worship gathering that rallies their missional-incarnational communities together for the purpose of unity and collective worship (see fig. 1.6). This development keeps the movement centered while simultaneously decentralized.

Being the church in this way gives everyone a meaningful way to participate. There is simplicity and elegance to this. The public gathering ought to help, not hinder, the core of what is being multiplied. The next page shows what the church might look like in

ten to fifteen years. As the multiplying effect starts to take hold, there are multiple congregations in various neighborhoods around the city (see fig. 1.7).

Transferable tools. The church as movement has dogmatic depth, ecclesial essentials, minimalistic methods and transferable tools. Tools are necessary for every vocation, whether a doctor, engineer, artist, writer or church planter. Part of discipleship entails being familiar with and passing on some of the most basic tools of the trade. As Eugene Peterson says, "The human, in a classic definition, is the tool-making creature, *homo faber*. We are not animals, living by sheer instinct, in immediate touch with our environment. We are not angels, living by sheer intelligence, with unmediated access to God. We are creatures, heavily involved with tools."[24]

Tools that are *simple*, *sticky* and *scalable* promote movement.[25] *Simple* tools can be used by the educated and uneducated. Everyone can use a hammer and screwdriver. We

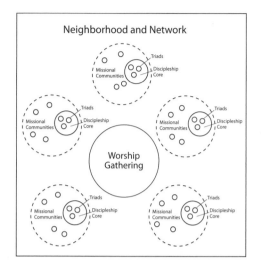

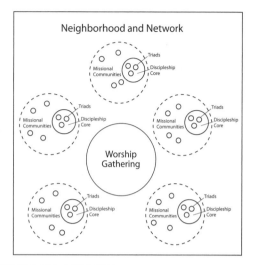

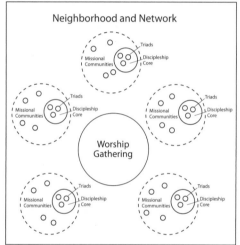

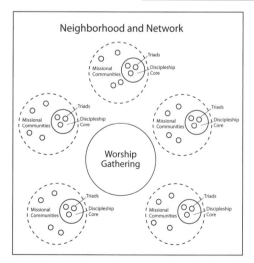

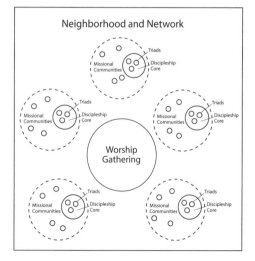

Figure 1.7. Movement year ten to fifteen

need to do the hard work of simplifying the complex without losing depth.

As we make the journey through this book, you will notice that we have sought to make our tools *sticky*. Sticky tools are easy to recall and remember. Stickiness can come through alliteration, rhythm or repetition. While some might feel this is unnecessary, we've discovered that without it vital theology and practice can be hard for people to pass on and share with others.

Finally, tools are *scalable* when they can be used at different levels of the church or organization. For example, the five Cs of team building—character, compatibility, competency, capacity and confidence (which we cover soon)—can be used when developing a discipleship core, choosing leaders for a mid-sized group, selecting elders in the church or picking coaches for church planters in a church-planting movement. Of course the context determines the depth of what we are looking for in each of the Cs.

While tools are needed and useful in every vocation, the problem with tools is that they can have power over us. And like any power, while they are created for the good, they insidiously seek to become idols that possess us. The psalmist said, "Some trust in chariots and some in horses, but we trust in the name of the LORD our God" (Ps 20:7).

Tools seek our devotion. They can subvert our devotion to God. They can be dangerous, so we seek to hold a healthy tension with our tools so that we don't make church as movement about the collection of gadgets. Thus it is important to continually assess how the tools we use are shaping us or mis-shaping us as a community.

The anatomy of movement consists of dogmatic depth, understanding the ecclesial essentials, engaging in minimalist methods and developing transferable tools for mission. These sensibilities inform our recommendations in the rest of the book, helping us to be faithful while trusting God for fruitfulness.

FORMATIONAL LEARNING

 Meta-Learning

- What does it mean to have a movement mentality?

 Reflective Learning

- What do you consider to be a part of your dogmatic depth?

• What are your ecclesial essentials?

• What transferable tools do you use as a community, and how are they shaping you?

 Experiential Learning

• Take some time to work through one or more of the following elements with your discipleship core: dogmatic depth, ecclesial essentials, minimalist methodology or transferable tools.

1.3 The Missional Potential of the Fivefold

Frederick Buechner said, "The place God calls you is where your deep gladness and the world's deep hunger meet."[26] Both of these elements are important when understanding our calling. If we are meeting the world's deepest needs while falling into depression because we lack any joy in our work, we may be missing our calling. The inverse is also true. If our work simply serves our self-interest but doesn't benefit the world's deepest needs, it's just a career, not a calling. To miss out on our calling is to miss out on the reason God put us on earth. To fulfill our calling is to be a blessing to the world and to experience a full life.

Paul starts Ephesians 4 saying, "I urge you to live a life worthy of the calling you have received" (Eph 4:1). What does it mean to discover and live out our calling? A calling is not primarily about increasing our earning potential or gaining a prestigious role or title. A calling refers to the fact that God made us with certain passions and capacities and embedded certain theo-genetic codes in us, and if we are going to partner with him in bringing more heaven to earth, then this world needs us, and those we serve, to fulfill the calling we have been given.[27]

Calling and vocation are synonymous; *calling* derives from an Anglo-Saxon root and *vocation* from a Latin root. Vocation comes from the word *voice* and implies that there is a caller who calls us. So vocation is not primarily a goal we pursue but a calling we hear. As Parker Palmer says, before I can tell my life what I want to do with it, it is wise to listen to my life telling me who I am.[28]

Discovering your theo-genetic code. When Paul urges us to live out our calling, we must remember that we are first called to know God, to know his love, to know his mercy, to receive his forgiveness, to live as his child, to be a part of the new humanity he is creating. This is what Ephesians 1–3 is about.

But God has also embedded a theo-genetic code in every human being. He wired us all for ministry. And as we uncover and awaken the fivefold typology (fig. 1.8) in our missional communities and in our neighborhoods, we will not only be able to live out our calling but also help others discover theirs. Everyone has certain longings and desires. We have a calling. Paul says, "To each one of us grace has been given as Christ apportioned it" (Eph 4:7). And then he says,

> So Christ himself gave the apostles, the prophets, the evangelists, the pastors and teachers, to equip his people for works of service, so that the body of Christ may be built up until we all reach unity in the faith and in the knowledge of the Son of God and become mature,

attaining to the whole measure of the fullness of Christ. (Eph 4:11-13)

Notice in the text that these are not external gifts given to people, but the people themselves are the gifts. These are people gifts, vocational intelligences and theogenetic codes that have been implanted in our DNA. Discovering them makes all the difference in the world.[29]

Three primary gift passages. While other passages speak of gifts, the three key New Testament passages are 1 Corinthians 12, Romans 12 and Ephesians 4. Alan Hirsch and Tim Catchim do a great job in distinguishing how these gift lists differ from one another. Each of the gift lists are preceded by a particular word that helps us understand that unique list.

The key word in 1 Corinthians 12 is *manifestation*, because the initial list of gifts, given by the Spirit at new birth, manifests the power of the Spirit: gifts like healing, speaking in tongues, faith and miracles. While Paul later talks about other gifts (as he helps the Corinthians work through issues regarding the gift of tongues), his initial list comprises manifestation gifts. The key word in Romans 12 is *praxis*, because these are action-oriented skills. And the key word for the Ephesians 4 list is *calling* (Eph 4:1), because these are people gifts, vocational gifts.

APOSTLE   PROPHET   EVANGELIST   PASTOR   TEACHER

Figure 1.8. The fivefold typology

The gifts in 1 Corinthians 12 and Romans 12 are gifts given to us, external to us, while in Ephesians 4, the people themselves are the gift. Why? Because calling is so intertwined with us that God put it in our coding at birth. We find our calling in the fivefold typology, and the other gifts are given to us by God to enable us to live out our vocation.

So if God gives you a *word of knowledge* (a manifestation gift), and your vocational intelligence is a *pastor*, you would likely use that word of knowledge to help people work through past hurts and move toward healing and wholeness. But if you have been given a *word of knowledge* and happen to have the vocational intelligence of an *evangelist*, you are likely to use that word of knowledge to help bring people to Christ or help excite others to participate in sharing their faith. Understand the fivefold topology is essential if we want to understand our calling and help others live into their calling. This is the missional potential of the fivefold.

Everyone made in God's image reflects this fivefold typology, but when we answer our call to Christ, we are set free to serve kingdom purposes, and these theo-genetic codes start to animate our lives.

Created order and redemptive order. Andrew Dowsett shows that a proper understanding of Ephesians 4:8-10 demonstrates that the fivefold topology is reflected in both the created order and redemptive order. Paul quotes from Psalm 68, where God descends from Mount Sinai to deliver his people from captivity, takes them through the wilderness to the Promised Land and then ascends to Mount Zion. Andrew writes,

Paul interprets Psalm 68 as applying to, or being fulfilled in, Christ. The descent therefore refers to his incarnation, to the embodying of the Word of God to dwell among us, to show us how to live-out the freedom he has decisively worked for us. This is followed by his ascent, to where Jesus is over all, and in all—that is to say, that his life is lived out through us as he apportions it. In his ascension, Jesus takes what was held captive and has been set free, and makes it free indeed.... My contention is that he is interpreting it as an image of Jesus' incarnation and ascension, to explain how Jesus has set prisoners free, received them as tribute, and given them to his people, for the purpose of the expansion of his family and extension of his kingdom.[30]

This makes sense because we see the fivefold typology reflected in most any healthy organization. Apostles are like entrepreneurs or pioneers. Do you have to be a Christian to start a company? No. Prophets are visionary activists posing important questions to our world in regard to social justice issues. Some of the most amazing prophets today are making indie films and music, posing important questions to society, yet many are not Christians. Evangelists are recruiters and salespeople. Do we find them in the created order? Pastors are like nurturers, protectors and counselors, and teachers love to gather wisdom, knowledge and understanding and pass it on to others. Our calling is our calling, but it finds its fullest expression as we answer our call to Christ and he gives us to his body for kingdom purposes.

Discovering your vocational intelligence.
Before I (JR) was twenty-five, I worked
twenty different jobs. Some of the jobs I enjoyed, some I could endure for a season, and
some caused me to feel absolutely depressed
when I woke up. In part, I was discovering
my calling in life. In time I learned to honor
the way God had made me.

So let's look at what it might be to discover and live out our calling in a way that
honors what God has planted in us, the raw
material that he has given us as it relates to
the fivefold topology. As we take a look at
each of these vocational intelligences, try to
discern which one you identify with the
most and the second most.[31]

Apostles: Catalyze and co-mission. Apostles
are *catalysts* who start new works, and they
co-mission others to join God in the renewal
of all things (fig. 1.9). They are pioneers,
always moving into new territory. Apostle

Figure 1.9. Apostle icon

literally means, "sent
one." They help to cul-
tivate a thriving envi-
ronment in the con-
gregation and love
crossing boundaries.
We might call them
"dream awakeners" because they help people
discover and live out their calling. They
help cultivate a discipleship ethos in order
to see the multiplication of disciples, ministries, churches and movements. Apostles
help people and communities live out the
answer to Jesus' prayer, "Your kingdom
come, your will be done, on earth as it is in
heaven" (Mt 6:10).

Prophets: Expose and embody. Prophets
expose false claims to authority and power,
demonstrating how they are not able to keep

their promises and uncovering the direction
their claims will take us if there is no repen-
tance (fig. 1.10).[32] They also *embody* a coun-
terculture community, calling people to live
under God's reign. They have a passion for
social justice and seek to cultivate a liberating environment, liberating people from
personal sins, speaking truth to power and
social sins. We might

Figure 1.10. Prophet icon

call them "heart re-
vealers" because they
reveal the heart of
God and the heart of
the people. Prophets
call the church to
God's new social order
and help the congregation to stand with the
poor and oppressed.

Evangelists: Invite and excite. Evangelists
have a knack when it comes to *inviting*
people to live in the kingdom of God, and
they are able to *excite* the people of God to
be witnesses (fig. 1.11). We could call evangelists "storytellers" because they share God's
story in such a way that everybody realizes
they are a part of it, either as villains or

Figure 1.11. Evangelist icon

heroes. They help
people want to be
heroes and heroines.
Evangelists help the
church to proclaim
the good news by
being witnesses and
redemptive agents.
They cultivate a welcoming environment,
helping the community to practice hospitality as a way of life.

Pastors: Guard and guide. Pastors *guard*
the community from the wolves and *guide*
them toward still waters (fig. 1.12). They are

nurturers and protectors. We might call them "soul healers" because they cultivate a healing environment and help us work through our past hurts and move toward a

Figure 1.12. Pastor icon

sense of wholeness in the context of community. They have a deep sense of the brokenness within us and help us to cultivate a life-giving spirituality and embody reconciliation. Soul healers create a sense of family within the group, seeking to protect people and create environments where people can feel safe to be vulnerable.

Teachers: Interpret and inform. Teachers are good at *interpreting* the text and *informing* others (fig. 1.13). They are great at gathering knowledge and passing on wisdom. We could call teachers "light givers"

because they shed light on Scripture and help people understand it in a life-giving way. They help us inhabit the sacred text, immerse people in God's story and teach people how to dwell faithfully in God's story. Teachers cultivate learning environments so that the whole body is growing in knowledge, wisdom and maturity.

So which do you most identify with? Which do you identify with second-most?[33]

Figure 1.13. Teacher icon

If you want to live out God's mission in the world, it is important to grasp and practice your vocational intelligence. In addition, as you grow in understanding the fivefold typology, you can help others live into their calling.

FORMATIONAL LEARNING

 Meta-Learning

- How does a growing understanding of and living into the fivefold typology unlock the missional potential of the church?

 Reflective Learning

- As you reflect on the five people gifts, which one did you identify with most?

- Why did you identify with that particular people gift?

- What in your ministry experience verifies this intuitive hunch?

 Experiential Learning

- Spend some time this week with some people you know well to share the descriptions of the fivefold typology, and ask them which one they think you embody the most.

- Take an online test to get better feedback on your type of people gift.

1.4 Maturing in the Fivefold Typology

When I (JR) became a Christ-follower, I was born as a citizen of God's kingdom within a new church plant and within a new church-planting movement. The culture I grew up in celebrated the apostle, prophet and evangelist, because they sought to start new things and move into new territory. The first church I was a part of was *just one* of fifty churches started that year. Because the apostle, prophet and evangelist are pioneers, we had a culture that celebrated the pioneers in our midst. This is good for getting new things going, but devaluing the developers (pastors and teachers) was bad for sustainability. As a result, some of those who felt less valued departed from the movement. Interestingly enough, they ended up staying in the cities where they felt valued, and in general those churches flourished the most.

While this was going on in my small world, in the larger culture of the Western church, since the Reformation, the pastor and teacher have been valued the most. It is not that the apostles, prophets and evangelists no longer existed; they just found spaces where their vocation would be honored. So they either became missionaries or started ministries that valued apostles, prophets and evangelists. Think of the vocational intelligence of people like Bill Bright, the founder of Cru, and other leaders of parachurch ministries today, and you will see that they tend to be people on the pioneering end of the people gifts found in Ephesians 4.

What I (JR) have learned is that one of the more significant elements to church as movement is an appreciation for all five people gifts Christ has given the church. We need pioneers who will help us cross boundaries and start new churches and movements of churches, and we need developers and settlers who will continue to cultivate a church with movement sensibilities locally. To dishonor or seek to diminish the ministry of any of the five types is to dishonor Christ, who has given these people gifts for the unity and maturity of the body.

Discovering and living into your fivefold type and helping those in your discipleship core and missional-incarnational community do the same is foundational to church as movement. And understanding how the other spiritual gifts enable us to live out our people gift(s) helps to see the beauty and unique contribution of everybody in the body of Christ.

Base gift(s). First we need to understand our base gift(s), the lifelong vocational intelligences we instinctively possess, those intelligences we continually develop due to our internal passions and external circumstances.[34] While there are some fivefold assessments that help us discern our base gifts, one of the best ways to discover our base gifts is by asking ourselves three basic questions. As you think about the description of each of the fivefold, ask yourself the following:

1. Which of these five am I most passionate about, as displayed in my life? Which of the five would be second?

2. In which of these five vocational intelligences do I see the most fruit? In which do I see the second most fruit?

3. Which of these five do people affirm me in the most? Second most?

If you review the nature of each of the people gifts in the fivefold typology, you will recognize that we ought to be living into each of them to some degree. In other words, we are all to teach one another (teacher), care for one another (pastor), share our faith with others (evangelist), live in the Spirit and speak truth to one another and the powers that be (prophet), and live as sent people (apostle). So we are called to live into each one of these people gifts as we fulfill our general calling. As we do this, we start to discover the answer to the three preceding questions and even start to recognize the portion Christ has given us (Eph 4:7).

How I discovered my base gift(s). After my (JR) conversion in college I recognized that one of my base people gifts was that of an evangelist. My life-transforming encounter with Christ took place the summer before my senior year. I was a resident assistant on my hall, and the thing that kept me awake at night, the focus of my prayer life, was each of the people who lived on my hall and the other resident assistants that lived in my dorm. I wanted them to experience the life transformation I was experiencing through Christ. That desire made for a fascinating year. There were many amazing stories of transformation.

I remember the first mid-sized group I helped to form. I noticed fairly quickly that I was always bringing new people into the group, typically people who didn't self-identify as Christians. I would introduce them to some of my friends who were developers (pastors and teachers), and then I went out and met more new people who I eventually invited into our young community. This worked quite well because I was always excited to meet new people, and it was important for me to know that I could introduce them to people who would be community for them. When we move away from an individualist approach to evangelism to a more communal approach, we can see how as each person brings their unique vocational intelligence to the table, we together form a community on mission.

I was invited to restart and lead my first church as a four-year-old Christian. I knew I wanted to plant churches within a month of becoming a Christian. Part of that was probably living into the culture of the group I was a part of, and part of it was an inner passion that was God-given. I dreamed of not only planting a church but planting churches that planted churches that planted churches. As I examined my personal history, I realized that I enjoyed starting new things and persuading people, so my base gifts of evangelist and apostle were evident in my life from an early age and now were becoming more evident in my life as a church planter.

As our first plant multiplied, planting other churches that multiplied and so on, we started to experience the beginning of movement. Planting churches that help people to live into God's story continues to be a burning passion for me, which is why, through my trusted friends' guidance, I am seeking to give all my energy to walk alongside church planters and people who are starting and sustaining missional-incarnational communities. I'm simply living into my base gifts as an apostolic-evangelist. Figure 1.14 shows a Venn diagram of my base gifts, as well as how I reflect the rest of the fivefold typology.

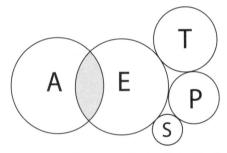

A = Apostle, P = Prophet, E = Evangelist, S = Shepherd, T = Teacher

Figure 1.14. Fivefold Venn diagram

Andrew Dowsett developed a list of twenty primary fivefold combinations to create a multifaceted look at the fivefold typology that rings true to life. For example, some people are apostolic-evangelists, pastor-prophets or prophetic-teachers. In my (JR) twenty years of experience in living into my type and interacting with others who are experientially deep in the fivefold typologies, I found that it is helpful to discern our top two base gifts and recognize the twenty subtypes that these combinations create. Andrew looks at the apostle-prophet as trailblazers and the shepherd-evangelist as healers. As we understand our base gift(s) and corresponding subtypes, and help others discover theirs, we lay a foundation for the church as movement.

Discovering our gifts through the backdoor. Sometimes the way we discover our vocational intelligence is through the back door, understanding the corresponding weakness to our God-given strengths. For example, immature apostles tend to be so goal-oriented that they run over people or run them ragged. Immature apostles find value in achievement, often at the expense of people. I know this from personal experience and I have to repent repeatedly. Adolescent apostles can lack gentleness and patience and tend to be insensitive, because too often mission comes before people instead of mission being for people.

Prophets in the adolescence stage tend to be cynical, angry, judgmental, pretentious, self-righteous and arrogant. In early developmental stages prophets are great at deconstructing everything. And because they see so clearly what could be and how current realities fall short, living in this tension squeezes out a bit of anger. As prophets grow in maturity they start to appreciate the rest of the fivefold typology, seeing what others bring to the table; then prophets move from deconstruction to reconstruction, inspiring people to live toward God's future.

Evangelists in their early stages of development can be so enthusiastic that they are unwise, unstable and consciously or unconsciously manipulative, sometimes seeking to capitalize on emotions. They have tendencies to exaggerate and engage in selective hearing and selective sharing. With a passion to get the good news out, evangelists can justify the means to reach particular ends, without understanding that the means *lead* to particular ends.

Immature pastors can be so sensitive to the feelings of people that they can be driven by fear, panicked at offending anyone and unable to live with disappointing others. With a desire to build a sense of family, they can create a false dichotomy between community and mission instead of building a community for mission.

Teachers at early stages of development can be so exacting and obsessed with accuracy that they project right and wrong dogmatically, which gives no space for others to journey and discover. With the ability to collect vast amounts of information and systematize it, they can be dogmatic in areas where they have little practical experience. Thus knowledge can be valued over wisdom. Teachers can value their relationship with information over their relationship with people; this lack of emotional maturity and arrogance can stunt their ability to pass on knowledge to others.

> Each of our God-given strengths has a dark side, and our vocational callings as apostles, prophets, evangelist, pastors and teachers can be used to build up or damage others.

Each of our God-given strengths has a dark side, and our vocational callings as apostles, prophets, evangelists, pastors and teachers can be used to build up or damage others. But understanding the dark side of the types can be used as a back door to discovering our vocational intelligence. As we discover how

God has wired us for mission, all of us must enter into weakness (death) in order for strength (life) to mature in us. In our weakness and humility the Spirit of God meets us. In our nakedness, Christ will clothe.

Phase gifts. One of the ways God grows us to maturity is by allowing the other people gifts to shape us. If we are to become more like Jesus in character and competency, we need to grow in our intelligences. While each of us has our base gifts, God gives us times in our life when he calls us in concentrated ways to mature in our phase gifting by living into the other parts of the fivefold typology, which are not part of our base gifting.

The process of maturing is a movement toward humility. The Greek word for humble is *tapeinoō*, "to make low." There is a pattern being set, and if we are going to participate in the fullness of these people gifts, descending needs to occur. Dietrich Bonhoeffer calls this a death to self. The most fruitful things grow out of dead stuff. Those who belong to Christ Jesus have crucified the flesh with its passions and desires (Gal 5:24). Participating in our vocational intelligence will require us to walk the same path. Before our people gifts become a mature act of self-expression they must continue to go through a self-emptying process, allowing God to fill us.

Too many have prolonged their adolescence (Eph 4:14-16). God wants us to grow up, to know the whole truth and to model it in love, like Christ, in everything. We take our lead from Christ, who is the source of everything we do. He keeps us in step. His breath and blood flows through us, nourishing us so we will mature into the fullness of God's love. To embrace our gift is first to embrace our need to grow up.

God uses people who have different gifts from us to shape us, and through people and circumstances he helps us become more well rounded by having us experience the parts of the fivefold typology that are not our base gifting.

For example, while prophet is not part of my (JR) base gifting, living deeply into the prophet type during a two-year season helped me to appreciate the necessity of the prophets in my life and in the life of the church. This phase started when I met a bishop from Kenya who shared about his people living in deep poverty. This encounter started a phase in my life that helped me grow in prophet sensibilities.

As you can see from figure 1.15, while God called and gave grace to me to operate in the prophet role, I eventually moved back to operating out of my base gifts, but as a more fully developed apostle-evangelist. Now I am more inclined to be sensitive to the Spirit as well as see the vital role of exposing false claims to authority and power,

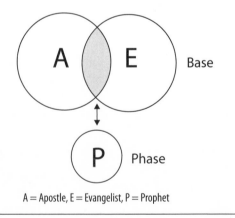

A = Apostle, E = Evangelist, P = Prophet

Figure 1.15. Base and phase

and how embodying God's new social order and standing with the poor and oppressed demonstrates how the reign of God has broken into our world. It's easy to recognize how growing in my prophetic sensibilities (standing with the poor and oppressed) strengthens my calling as an apostle-evangelist and propels holistic movement.

Dan happens to be prophetic-pastor, so we complement each other and appreciate what we bring to the table as we seek to live into the trinitarian presence and see the V3 church-planting movement grow and flourish. Understanding our base gifts helps shape the roles we live out as we build movement together. Answering God's call to live into our phase gifts has helped us to appreciate the strengths God brings through the other person and to lean on each other's strengths in moments of discernment. As we learn to appreciate and cultivate the fivefold typology within our missional-incarnational communities, we will move a step closer in living out the church as movement.

FORMATIONAL LEARNING

 Meta-Learning

- How does God help us to mature and grow in unity as we reflect on the five different people gifts that Christ has given the church?

 Reflective Learning

- What are your base gift(s), and what is the latest phase that God has called you to live into?

- How are you helping your discipleship core discover and cultivate their base gifts?

 Experiential Learning

- Take time to identify your base gifts and the base gifts of your discipleship core, and consider which people gifts you have among you.

2

Polycentric Leadership

· ·

Our cultural norms set us up to look for the visionary, the CEO, the charismatic leader. . . . When we challenge these cultural norms about leadership, we want to be clear that we do not believe leadership should be eliminated. However, we want to emphasize that as God is shaping the church, the Spirit is inspiring, forming, and motivating a cluster of people to provide leadership.

MARK BRANSON

It's been said that Christianity started out in Palestine as a community, moved to Greece and became a philosophy, went to Rome and became an institution, and went to Europe and became a government. Finally, it came to America and became an enterprise. What might it take for us to return to community? One way it can return to community is by the fellowship of church leaders sharing leadership under the direction of our head, Jesus. Polycentric leadership requires that we know how to both lead and follow. We say that all good leaders know how to follow, but when people are in roles where they rarely have to follow, they lose their follower instinct. We need to create leadership structures that model the kind of mutual community we're seeking to form.

Connecting to Movement

Movement requires leaders, but not just any leaders. The church as movement requires humble leaders, people who find their primary identity in Christ, not a particular title. They are people who bring their full self to the table, their gifts, their passions and their experience, to equip others. These leaders learn to recognize the work of the Spirit in emerging leaders and give them space to spread their wings. In the polycentric approach we move from solo leadership to team leadership—people with mutual authority leading together and submitting to one another, thus serving as an example for the entire community.

2.1 Introducing Polycentric Leadership

As I (JR) travel around the United States, I recognize that God is stirring a desire for a fresh approach to leadership and power in the hearts of many, especially young people. Instead of taking the approach they see in most churches today—a hierarchical structure with a senior pastor, assistant pastors, staff and congregation—they desire to lead *as* a community from *within* the community. Something deep within them says leadership should be different.[1]

Some young people in or moving toward Christian leadership positions say they are a part of churches that are "successful" by many people's standards. While the church is growing, meeting genuine needs and seeing people start a relationship with Christ, for them it feels as if the church has become a big machine. Maintaining programs has trumped making disciples, and breadth has been honored over depth. Staff meetings feel more like Fortune 500 meetings, with the senior pastor as the CEO, than a family meeting with a community of leaders in the upper room.

Church members and even leaders often feel like cogs in a wheel or workers on an assembly line, each doing a particular part to keep the machine running. Everyone is playing their role well, and the ministry is experiencing "success," but something seems to be missing. When someone pulls out of the machine for a season, the church community realizes that the sense of community and realness that was initially there has vanished. It is as if they have gained the world of ministry success but somehow lost their souls (the most real part of us) in the process. If everything meaningful about a church seems to disappear with one key person, *leadership should be different.*

People have seen and experienced how power can turn a godly leader into a control freak, stifling any kind of creativity and innovation that develops within the community. And when the news comes out that this person has experienced a moral fall, most are not surprised. In this case, it is clear: *leadership should be different.*

Some young leaders stay in their current situations hoping to change them. Some stay because it puts bread on the table and provides stability for their family. But as I talk with some who stay, it seems as though they are dying a slow death.

Others are taking risks and venturing out by planting new churches, where they seek to approach leadership in fresh and different ways. They are living by faith. They are chasing their God-given dreams. They are also facing the realities of their decision. It's not that they thought life was going to be easy, they just didn't have any idea how tough things would get. They were unprepared for the financial strain and the emotional hits they have endured from people they considered friends. Sometimes, like the Israelites who followed Moses in the exodus, life back in Egypt under traditional, hierarchical church leadership seems much better. "At least there we had meat to eat."

In addition, while some have a clear idea of how they *don't* want to lead, their picture of how they want to lead is foggy. They look at those who are suspicious of all structure and who attempt to have a flat leadership structure, and they see them falling flat. Others have clear ideas about how they want to lead, but when they seek advice from others, they don't find many working models to imitate. Often, their current coach or mentor follows the traditional approach to leadership and tells them they need to "get real" and give up their idealistic thinking.

If the church at large continues on its current path, we doubt it will make the kind of progress we need. But if more people start living out what has been placed deep within them, the church has a chance to thrive again. It is better to live by faith and "fail" than to allow our fears to win the day and slowly die in the process.

We are convinced that if the church is going to be reborn and cultivate a fruitful, missional ethos, it must have a well-developed theology of the powers (the "principalities and powers" language in Scripture) that can inform how missional leaders approach structures and power. For as theologian and author Marva Dawn reminds us, the church is not immune to the fallen principalities and powers.[2]

I (JR) have a confession to make on why this topic has become so important for me. I became the "senior" pastor that I didn't want people to imitate. It's not that people didn't want to imitate me. They did. It's not that I had gone off the deep end. I hadn't. It's not that people didn't want my role. There were many who desired it. It's not that there weren't many good things in my life worth imitating. There were.

But I got to the point where I didn't think it was good for anyone to be in my role, including myself. Because we had become one of the largest collegiate churches in the country, I was often asked to share at pastor gatherings and speak at conferences. Life had degenerated into an endless series of meetings. It was as if Jesus had said, "I have come to give you meetings, and meetings more abundantly." I enjoyed many of these meetings, felt God at work through them and saw lives being transformed. However, gradually—almost imperceptibly—I sensed changes in me that weren't helpful or good. I felt I was becoming less like Jesus and more like a CEO of a fast-growing company.

While most of the time I felt my heart was in the right place, God showed me times when my motives were mixed, and on one occasion he showed me with great clarity that sometimes my chief concern wasn't my relationship with him, nor was it about seeking first his kingdom. My chief concern was *my* own image and the building of *my* kingdom. Most of the time this was not my primary *conscious* motivation. When I was unsure of my motives, or just wanted to understand them better, I would fast. On three separate occasions I fasted for forty days, only drinking grape and apple juice daily, and at times having tomato soup.

I began to realize that there was something about the ministry structure, the very one that I had helped to set up, that gave me an ever-greater temptation to shift my heart from God and his kingdom to *my* image and *my* kingdom. And I'm convinced that being the solo senior leader was a large part of my problem.

Not only did I notice this problem in myself, but I started to see many situations in which this structure—solo senior leadership in particular—seemed to be a primary reason why a godly person became increasingly less godly or in some cases outright wicked. Through these experiences I realized that *structure is not neutral.* This led me to explore the biblical basis of New Testament leadership, which led me to write *Creating a Missional Culture,* where I argue that both the text and our context call us to shared leadership.

As you consider your leadership approach, we want to ask, What is your ultimate goal? Do you see the church as an industrial complex or as a movement?

How we approach leadership shapes the ethos of the congregation and our neighborhood in powerful ways. Different approaches to leadership tend to create different kinds of people. Let's look at the hierarchical approach.

Hierarchical approach to leadership. Let's try to paint the typical approach to church leadership today in the United States. We'll be painting a caricature of sorts, since real life is always nuanced, but follow along and see if you find it helpful.

The senior pastor receives a vision and then works to get people on board with it. One of the primary tasks is getting people to worship services (or other programs) so they can grow and become more like Christ. As a result, the church often seeks to meet the needs of the neighborhood in some way, but often from a distance. Knowledge and truth tend to reside in the senior leader. People get a sense of belonging from church attendance or by serving the church in some capacity. The primary language in these situations is "We *go to* church." The basic measurement of success tends to be counting people, money

and the size of the building. The more people, the more money and the larger the building, the more "successful" the pastor.

What is the source of this leadership approach? It looks strangely similar to the CEO business model. What kind of people does this produce? Or what do businesses seek to create? Consumers! That's how they stay in business. So, is it any wonder why our churches are filled with passive, needy, consumeristic people? Do we think we can baptize the CEO approach to leadership and expect a different result?

We suggest that a hierarchical approach to leadership lends itself to controlling leadership, a programmatic and individualist approach to spiritual formation, and an extractional approach to mission. That is, mission is often defined as inviting more people to church, which has a tendency to extract people out of their local context and often disconnects their contribution from their everyday context. This fosters the perpetual adolescence of the congregation and job security for the pastor. Obviously this is a caricature, but we'll let you be the judge of how accurate it is.

A hierarchical approach to leadership works, but to what end? We suggest that it often leads to a more passive, needy, consumeristic people and often a less Christlike leader in the end.

Is it possible to have benevolent dictators? Sure, there are examples of this. When the people of God had been in slavery for four hundred years they lost the understanding that they were made in the image of God and needed Moses to lead them.

But as a whole, we think human hierarchy is like the kings in the Hebrew Scripture.

The people of God wanted a king like the other nations, yet God wanted to be their king, so he says to Samuel, "It is not you they have rejected, but they have rejected me as their king. . . . Now listen to them; but warn them solemnly and let them know what the king who will reign over them will claim as his rights" (1 Sam 8:7, 9). Samuel warned Israel that the king would create a powerful centralized government, send their sons to war and take the best of what they created for himself. He warned them that as this happens, they would come running back to God, but God would not answer them.

In spite of this warning, the people insisted on a king, so God allowed it. And sure enough, there weren't too many good kings. They were never meant to "wear the ring." Only a holy God can handle that kind of power. We aren't designed to sit on God's throne; we were designed to be God's vice regents, acting together as his stewards and reflecting this in our approach to leadership.

Leaders create culture, and our approach to leadership and structure is not neutral. So again, the question is, What is your ultimate aim?

Flat approach. Some people have reacted negatively to hierarchical leadership and moved toward a flat approach. But a flat approach often falls flat. Instead of controlling leadership, there is an *absence* of leadership. This typically produces an anti-institutional approach to spiritual formation and being the church, and often leads to instability and a confused and unfocused approach to mission. It tends to be stagnant; there is little movement. In the name of flat leadership we operate as if all voices have equal weight on all concerns. This creates a church

with individuals talking a lot but going nowhere together, or passive-aggressive bullying attempting to steer people's votes in a certain direction. This is why flat leadership is no leadership.

So, what is your ultimate aim? Do you want to create a culture that helps develop mature missional disciples who live in the world for the sake of the neighborhood?

In the words of Stanley Hauerwas, we're trying to cultivate people who

> can risk being peaceful in a violent world, risk being kind in a competitive society, risk being faithful in an age of cynicism, risk being gentle among those who admire the tough, risk love when it may not be returned, because we have the confidence that in Christ we have been reborn into a new reality.[3]

Which approach to leadership will help cultivate those kinds of people? A hierarchical approach or a flat approach?

Polycentric leadership. Before looking at the benefits of polycentric leadership, it might be helpful to define it. Suzanne Morse helps us understand polycentric leadership:

> Successful communities, even those with long traditions of organized community leadership, will continue to broaden the circles of leadership to create a system for the community that is neither centralized nor decentralized, but rather polycentric. The polycentric view of community leadership assumes that there are many centers of leadership that interrelate.[4]

Instead of a solo approach to leadership, leadership is shared. It revolves among many leaders, and at times it even includes those who are not a part of the formal leadership of the congregation. The beauty of polycentric leadership is that it includes a relational group of people who learn to share responsibility, engaging in both leading and following, giving time for each leader to be on mission. Polycentric leadership models the interrelations of the Trinity, an interdependent, communal, relational, participatory, self-surrendering and self-giving approach to leadership.

Polycentric leadership lends itself to a relational approach to leadership, a communal approach to spiritual formation and being the church, an incarnational and distributive approach to mission, and a multiplication approach to movement. What kind of people do you think that approach to leadership might form?

Approach to leadership. No matter what kind of leadership approach we take, there will be problems—because we are human. But the polycentric approach has potential, and difficulties are worth working through to get to its benefits. I (JR) talked with someone working through a polycentric approach to leadership with other leaders, and he mentioned how tough it was at times. It was tough because the leaders were in tight community, and as a result ego issues in his life would surface, which he had to deal with. I would say that is a good kind of problem to have.

Of course polycentric leadership brings other challenges. There is a financial challenge. (Developing a financial framework

> Polycentric leadership models the interrelation of the Trinity, where there is an interdependent, communal, relational, participatory, self-surrendering and self-giving approach to leadership.

helps to mitigate this becoming a large issue.[5]) Decision making tends to be slower on the front side, but implementing decisions in shared leadership flows smoother because direction is discerned in community. And because more people are involved in decision making, they grow in wisdom. In hierarchical leadership decision making tends to be faster up front but slower on the back end because of the need to convince others of the wisdom of the decision. This approach also takes away a meaningful way for other leaders to grow in discernment.

Polycentric leadership requires mature people who live and minister together over a period of time, because a strong mutual trust is needed to practice this well. This is why the apostle Paul places character front and center when he sends Timothy and Titus to appoint elders in the various churches. Table 2.1 summarizes the different forms of leadership and how it shapes us for mission.

How do we approach polycentric leadership? What does it look like? This leadership approach can be worked out in many ways. Instead of prescribing one way, we will provide some analogies to cultivate your imagination and encourage you to apply it to your unique situation.

Think about a jazz band with four or five skilled players who trust one another. When they get into the groove, they rotate the lead instrument. Of course this takes mature players who understand, trust and know how

Table 2.1. Comparing hierarchical, flat and polycentric leadership

Form of Leadership	Leadership Style	Spiritual Formation	Mission
hierarchical	controlling	programmatic and individualistic	extractional
flat	absent	fuzzy and unfocused	stagnant
polycentric	shared	communal	multiplication

to play with each other. In the same way, polycentric leadership requires people who have developed the character and skills of leadership and have a proven track record of working with a team.

Geese fly long distances in a V formation. There is always a lead goose, but the leadership rotates because one goose cannot bear the physical load of continually being in front. They can fly long distances because they share the job of being on the point. In the same way, if we want the church we serve to make it in the long run, it would serve us well to rotate the point of leadership.

When we combine a polycentric approach to leadership with an understanding of the fivefold typology, we will be a step closer to realizing the church as movement.

A three-dimensional reading of Ephesians 4. Paul says, "To each one of us grace has been given as Christ apportioned it" (Eph 4:7). Every believer fits into the fivefold typology, not just leaders. These are God-given theogenetic codes—types of intelligences. Calling, ministry and leadership are only different by a matter of degree and capacity.[6] As you can see in figure 2.1, the outer circle represents the first dimension, showing how all have a fivefold *calling*.[7] Moving inward the second circle represents the second dimension, speaking to five kinds of *ministries* in the church. The inner circle represents the third dimension; that is, some will be *leaders*.

We like to think about the player-coach continuum. Everyone is a player, but not everyone has been given the grace to be a coach. Everyone has a calling and a ministry that flows from that calling, but only some are given the grace to devote more time to equipping others.

A = Apostle, P = Prophet, E = Evangelist, S = Shepherd, T = Teacher

Figure 2.1. Ephesians 4 in three dimensions

One of my (JR) vocational intelligences is an evangelist. By the end of the first five years of my first church plant, when we had one hundred people, I noticed that I was with half of them when they came to Christ. I realized if we were going to move forward in mission, I needed to move from a player to a coach. So as I continued to live as a player, I started coaching more and more. We have to discern whether God has called us to be players who help others or player-coaches who equip others more.

Why do some push against a nonhierarchical approach to leadership? One of the chief reasons might be that humans find too much value in our roles or titles instead of who we are and whose we are. When we read the first thirteen verses of John 13, we see how Jesus helps us move into a more submissive, polycentric approach to leadership by reminding us that when we know who we are and whose we are, we never have to prove anything and never need to lose face. We can do the job of the servant and wash others' feet because we know who we are.

FORMATIONAL LEARNING

 Meta-Learning

• How does our approach to leadership form us in positive and negative ways?

 Reflective Learning

• What are the strengths and weaknesses of hierarchical, flat and polycentric leadership?

• Have you ever experienced polycentric leadership? If so, what was your experience like? If not, why not?

• What makes you uncertain or passionate about polycentric leadership?

 Experiential Learning

• Where can you begin to live into polycentric leadership? What is the first step?

2.2 Living into Polycentric Leadership

It's good to understand polycentric leadership and the beneficial way it shapes us and the missional community we serve, but beginning to live into it takes much wisdom and a good sense of timing. Unless you are starting a church or a missional-incarnational community with another person or persons who are mature in character, competent in shared leadership, mutually compatible (see section 4.5 on the five Cs of building a team) and trustworthy, polycentric leadership is something to live into, not start with.

Change requires wisdom. For most people, introducing polycentric leadership will be a change from what they have experienced. Moving into polycentric leadership is good, but it can be dangerous. Change can build momentum or take the wind out of our sails. If we seek change in the wrong way, it can have unintended negative consequences. It all depends on how we approach it.

Leading through any kind of change takes wisdom. When approaching change, we first need to determine whether it is minor, medium or major change. This is discerned by how many people are affected by the change. A change in leadership style is a major change. Part of what it means to be a leader is to cultivate an environment where change is normal. The only constant in starting and sustaining missional-incarnational communities is change. Managing change requires prayer, preparation and planning.

At this point, we will be assuming that you are a solo leader looking to move into polycentric leadership. Not only is the following learning tool helpful for moving toward polycentric leadership, it's helpful for training people in any unfamiliar task. We will first examine how this tool can help people learn different competencies, including moving into polycentric leadership. The beautiful thing about learning new things and engaging in new experiences is that it reveals our character. And in discipleship, character is prime.

Stages of learning. If you want to prepare others for polycentric leadership, then it is important to understand the different stages of learning.[8] The four stages we move through when we train people in new skills, including shared leadership, are illustrated in figure 2.2.

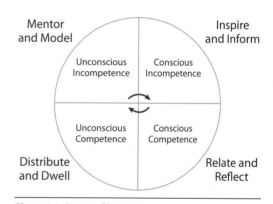

Figure 2.2. Stages of learning

Unconscious incompetence: Mentor and model. In new endeavors like starting a church or starting a missional-incarnational community, we are totally unaware of some competencies that we desperately need. We all have blind spots. The unconscious incompetent stage is when we are not aware that we don't know. At this stage of learning we need mentors and models. We need guides, people to make us aware of what we don't know, people who will lead us into an experience or challenge that reveals what we don't know. This stage is the "I do, you watch" stage of learning. The goal is to move from blissful ignorance to acute awareness, from blindness to sight.

When we study the Gospel of Mark we see the relationship between those who see and those who are blind and the impact sight or lack of it has. Literary critics have identified three types of characters in Mark—the disciples, the religious leaders and the minor characters or what Hollywood calls "extras." The amazing thing about Mark is that the disciples are the only characters who remain blind throughout the story. They don't seem to get what Jesus was about. Jesus says to them, "Do you still not see or understand? Are your hearts hardened? Do you have eyes but fail to see, and ears but fail to hear?" (Mk 8:17-18).

This part of Mark's story is intentionally framed by two stories of blind men being healed, for the disciples didn't see what Jesus was all about. On the road to Jerusalem the disciples argue constantly about who is the greatest. Jesus tells them, "Whoever wants to be first must take last place and be the servant of everyone else" (Mk 9:35 NLT).

Jesus uses many different analogies and illustrations to help the disciples *see* what he was saying, but the actions of James and John and the arguments between all the disciples reveal that they are still blind to the heart of Jesus' mission, even though they think they see. What has blinded the disciples?

Is it possible that when our goal is to get to the top or stay on top for self-serving purposes, we become blind to the presence and work of God in our world? Is it possible that allegiance to power and self affect our ability to see?

Two businessmen were great rivals. When one got a computer, the other got two. When one got a smartphone, the other got two. When one bought a house, the other bought two. One day an angel appeared to one of them with this offer: "You can ask for anything you like and you will get it. However, your rival will get two of whatever you ask for."

"You mean, if I asked for a million dollars, I would get it?"

"Yes," the angel said, "You will get it, but your rival will get two million."

"How soon do I have to answer?" asked the businessman.

"I will be back tomorrow morning for your answer."

That night, the businessman tossed and turned, and when the angel came back the man had his answer: "I'll settle for one blind eye!"

How often do jealously and rivalry blind us? Solo leaders moving into polycentric leadership will require humility; it will require stooping down to wash people's feet and inviting others into a learning process so they can eventually share the leadership.

Conscious incompetence: Inspire and inform. The next stage of learning is knowing what we don't know. It is awareness that we lack something. A weakness is exposed. We realize we don't have the knowledge to do something and are uncomfortable. We have moved from being novices (unaware) to being apprentices, aware that we need to learn. We need someone to inspire and inform us. We need knowledge and understanding.

At this stage of learning, we need someone to consult with, to review what we are doing, to answer questions, give advice and get feedback. It is the "we do it together" stage.

If we want to make disciples and eventually have a polycentric leadership team representing the fivefold typology, we need to help people in our discipleship core start a mid-sized group that has a focused mission and knows who God has sent them to.

After we make them aware that discipleship will primarily occur through starting a missional-incarnational community, they will see and feel their need for knowledge and understanding. As we help them discover their persons of peace (see chap. 8) and move into incarnational ministry, we will help them move into the next stage of learning: conscious competence.

Conscious competence: Relate and reflect. At this stage, we know that we know how to do something, but it takes effort, concentration and focus to accomplish the task. We need practice. We need someone to relate to us, collaborate with us and reflect on ways to live into what we are doing with greater skill and confidence. With this help we become literate in an area where we were illiterate.

In this stage of development, as we disciple others to lead a missional-incarnational community, we start to involve them in decision making and in sharing leadership. This is the "They do, and you help" stage. One of the best ways to help them is building a close relationship with them and guiding them as they reflect on how they are doing.

Before moving others into fully sharing leadership in a polycentric way, we need to carefully observe their character and competency in practicing shared leadership and living on mission in the missional community. Be sure that the Holy Spirit has developed them enough to join the team. The final stage of learning is entrusting them to fully share leadership with you. This is the "They do, and you coach" stage.

Unconscious competence: Distribute and dwell. When we learn how to do something so well it becomes second nature, we have moved from conscious competence to unconscious competence. The competency we have learned becomes fluid and automatic. We can do the task without much thought. Though we have mastered a skill, it is still important to remain fully present and mindful.

This is the stage of learning where we pass on leadership to others. After three and a half years with the disciples, who were finally starting to *see*, Jesus tells them to "Go and make disciples . . . teaching them to obey everything I have commanded you. And surely I am with you always, to the very end of the age" (Mt 28:19-20). This is the church as movement.

After Jesus delegated his authority and distributed the work to the Twelve, he left them physically. But he stayed with them in heart and spirit. In the same way, as we entrust people to join us in polycentric leadership and distribute new responsibilities to them, we still take the time to dwell with each other, to hang out with them and live together as much as we are able. As they start to disciple others, leading them through the stages of learning, and their disciples do the same with their disciples, we begin to see movement because we are growing in discipleship depth.

Polycentric leadership is a skill, and it takes character to live into it. And like any other skill or competency, we must be willing to help bring people through the different stages of learning, not push them forward too fast or let them drag their feet too long. We need to find the balance between providing safety and time to stretch them to be who God is shaping them to be.

FORMATIONAL LEARNING

 Meta-Learning

- In your own words, articulate the four stages of learning.

 Reflective Learning

- When it comes to your discipleship core, why is it important to appreciate the stage of learning each person is in?

- In regard to polycentric leadership, which stage of learning are you in?

- Through which stage of learning do you most enjoy discipling people? The least? Why?

 Experiential Learning

- Consider who in your discipleship core is closest to living into polycentric leadership with you. What is the next step God would have you take with them?

2.3 Mutual Submission

Leadership is a million dollar industry within Christianity, and we understand why. It would be hard to find a person who does not want to become a better leader. In most people's imagination, leading means being in front of the pack, determining where people should go. In our modern imagination, to be a better leader is to focus on the skills and capacities of the lead dog and find ways to increase those skills.

We've attended numerous conferences over the years that offered self-helps to becoming a better communicator, better manager, better organizer, better vision caster and better recruiter of leaders. In our modern narrative, a leader is a hero. One of my (Dan's) favorite movies growing up was *Braveheart*, which encouraged me to do something significant, rally others around my charisma and receive affirmation for my great impact in the world. Those desires are primal and real, but underneath is a distorted ambition to sit at the top of the hierarchical organization chart. We need to interrogate our leadership ambitions to see how they sync with God's desire for us.

Interrogating leadership. What often goes unnoticed is the lens through which most leadership strategies are offered. The typical lens for framing successful leadership within the church as industrial complex is borrowed from CEO-style organizations rather than the story of the early church. The growth of most Fortune 500 companies is offered as a strategy for success. In 1995, for example, the book *Jesus, CEO* was published. We can easily cut and paste verses to fit our CEO mentality and use them out of context. For example, Deuteronomy 28:13 says, "The

LORD will make you the head, not the tail." This could easily be used in a triumphalist way on behalf of a leader.

There are serious problems with this model of church leadership. Primarily, it confuses the purpose of a corporation with the purpose of a church. Using the corporate model will inevitably distort our understanding of leadership. In order to increase effectiveness in the church as industrial complex, ever-increasing dominion is required by the leader. This is inevitable. But should dominion and authority be concentrated in church leadership?

Leadership in the New Testament. In the New Testament the word *leader* is generally avoided.[9] The apostle Paul avoided elevating himself over others and instead used terms like *colaborer, coworker* (1 Cor 3:9; Phil 2:25). Christian leadership is not intended to be a one-man band, with a solitary figure declaring from a pulpit or executive office, with everyone else as spectators. Instead the New Testament writers used the term *diakonia*, meaning "servant" or "service," to identify people in leadership.

The New Testament does not commend a relationship of rulers and the ruled among the first-century Christians. The writers of the New Testament epistles took Christ's words seriously: "Anyone who wants to be first must be the very last, and the servant of all" (Mk 9:35). Jesus was deconstructing cultural leadership for the church, flipping and subverting it.

The disciples were thinking in terms of hierarchical leadership, just as we are, which is why Jesus said,

> You know that those who are regarded as rulers of the Gentiles lord it over

them, and their high officials exercise authority over them. Not so with you. Instead, whoever wants to become great among you must be your servant, and whoever wants to be first must be slave of all. For even the Son of Man did not come to be served, but to serve. (Mk 10:42-45)

Jesus is instructing the church to resist the secular notion of leadership.[10]

The church, the living body of the Spirit, is called to submit to Christ as the singular head of the body and into mutual dependence on one another (1 Cor 12; Eph 4:1-16).

Mutual leadership. The pathway to upending the CEO-style, single-gifted, solo leadership platform is to transition toward mutual leadership. We must reimagine and reconstruct our leadership scaffolding to undo our over-individualized and over-professionalized leadership paradigms. Mutual leadership is an effort to share power among a trust-soaked, vision-distributed, emotionally mature, Christ-rooted team. For the sake of God's mission in the world, we need to distribute leadership.

This begins with a set of recognized equippers with certain gifts: apostles, prophets, evangelists, shepherds and teachers (Eph 4:11). These equippers are the first leaders, who then set into motion the rest of the gifted body. They are not only to equip but to affirm and call the rest of the body into its giftedness. These first leaders

and their gifts are recognized in order for them to build up and release the rest of the body for mission (Eph 4:12). Our leadership scaffolding should call us into a mutual submission out of *reverence for Christ* (Eph 5:21).

Submission is not an attractive word in the West. However, submission does not imply abuse, oppression, suppression or violation of dignity. Jesus modeled a submissional leadership. He was completely confident of his role and mission, but submitted to the Father. During his earthly ministry he was prepared to wash the feet of his disciples, a duty normally left to slaves, and he commanded us to do the same (Jn 13:15).

Mutual submission does not undermine authority but offers it accountability and character. The pattern in the New Testament church was a plurality of leaders, depending on one another, accountable to one another, submitting to one another and mutuality in ministry, which is why the leaders in Jerusalem could say, "It seemed good to the Holy Spirit and to *us*" (Acts 15:28).

The New Testament does not distinguish between elder, pastor and overseer (Acts 20:17; Tit 1:5-7; 1 Pet 5:1-3). The early church was tended by a collective of mature, spirit-filled leaders: "Be shepherds of God's flock that is under your care, watching over them [serving as overseers]" (1 Pet 5:2). The church today likewise needs a plurality of gifts and input in its leadership.

> Mutual leadership is an effort to share power among a trust-soaked, vision-distributed, emotionally-mature, Christ-rooted team. For the sake of God's mission in the world, we need to distribute leadership.

Certainly there are different roles, not identical, not superior or inferior, but all equally contributing to the movement. Mutual submission is a conscious choice, a decision to submit to the wisdom and counsel of one another.

When we speak of a more inclusive, participatory and mutually submitting leadership, some automatically see chaos and anarchy. My (Dan) experience has been the opposite. This kind of leadership is not without its struggles, but it is a framework that pushes to the surface the priesthood of all believers. The following are five principles that guide mutual leadership.

Community before clergy. The Scriptures contain a diversity of gifts in leadership (apostles, prophets, evangelists, pastors, teachers) and diverse voices (Barnabas, Peter, James, Timothy, Junia, Phoebe, Eudia, Lydia, Priscilla and Aquila). In the New Testament we observe mutuality, diversity, accountability, gifting and character. Before we apprehend our status as leaders, we must live into community that models a mosaic of voices, even if it slows our pace.

Great leadership pursues an emotionally healthy life together. We must work toward a shared rhythm of life that models mutual love, a servant posture and deep, forgiving friendship with each other. Too many organizations function more as task-oriented teams than they do as families. The leadership community is a covenantal space that becomes a prototypical spiritual family for the larger church body.

Submissional before sergeants. Together we have the wisdom of the Holy Spirit. There is no chain of command, no loudest voice among our leadership community.

Though our personal passions and gifts move us to emphasize certain things, we practice equality and mutual submission in valuing each other's opinions, experiences and perspectives. We must be trained in active listening. Listening refashions our individual knee-jerk reactions toward seeking understanding rather than winning arguments. Do we go on the offensive when someone shares an idea we don't like? Are we prone to judgment when someone operates differently than we do? Are we prone to anger, antagonism and passive-aggressive behavior when we are not getting our way?

Mutual submission invites us to grow up emotionally. We each lead out of our giftedness and then submit to the rest of the body. Each brings an emphasis, an issue or a proposal to the table, and the team discerns together their strengths and weaknesses. Each of us must submit their proposal to the rest of the leading community. Conversation opens us up to see other perspectives and look for slight adjustments and changes.

Together we make a joint decision and submit to the leadership of the person who offered the proposal. In the end we together discern the mind of Christ (1 Cor 2:16). Working in agreement is exhausting at times, but it cultivates shared responsibility. *Together* we use our gifts to bless and nourish our larger community. Trust is imperative as we decentralize our leadership. When we hear curious information about someone in our leadership community, we defer to trust, choosing to treat the person's reputation with honor and respect as we seek direct conversation for understanding.

Disciplers before deciders. Because we are all called to apprentice others as we apprentice under Jesus, the first role of our leadership community is to be disciple makers. Our team cannot make good decisions unless we are in the complicated but sacred space of being entrenched relationally with others on the journey of discipleship. This means actively sitting still with people one on one to navigate inner life, family, mission and community.

Leadership is not primarily about making decisions. Our first responsibility is to develop people, awakening their inherent priesthood and inviting them to submit all of life to King Jesus. Our ability to influence is built on our continued, transparent, relational proximity instead of structured programs with us at the helm. Incarnational discipleship must soften the hard edges of our decision making.

Consultative before concrete. Break bread with those in the larger community; dwell in unhurried conversation. Spend time meeting with people and discussing the movements of your church before forming a concrete position on an issue. Hold forums, dinners and coffee talks to receive consultation from your larger communities. It might feel threatening to receive ongoing honest feedback, but we must press into these spacious conversations. Let feedback weigh heavily on the leading community. Learn to compromise based on good insight from the church body you love. Believe that the Holy Spirit is in others just as much as he is in you.

Don't treat this like a hoop to jump through. Embrace it for what it is: listening to the voice of the Spirit through others. Leaders have the tendency to read a book or attend a conference and then place their learnings over the top of their church. A consultative posture must submerge us deep into contextualization, helping to remove our ignorance detached from incarnational complexities.

Accountability before autonomy. Our qualification for leadership comes not from our eloquence or skill set but because we've made vows of commitment and character. Skill is not the first thing that qualifies leaders in the missional church; character is. Leadership calls us to a way of life, not to a status. This accountability to the way we are human requires constant self-evaluation and a confessional posture.

Too many leaders entertain a private sentiment that *I don't need accountability because of the office I hold.* Leadership calls us to submit the details of our lives with appropriate vulnerability. Who we are is more important than what we are skilled at doing. This may take the form of public vows or covenants. It may also be a space for confession and transparency. In no way should we roast our leaders, but we should provide space for them to break through image management, entrusting themselves to the grace of the community, and in humility give them authority to say, "Follow me as I follow Christ."

FORMATIONAL LEARNING

 Meta-Learning

• What difference does it make to believe in the theology and act of mutual submission?

 Reflective Learning

• Which of the five principles are your weakest and strongest? Explain.

• How can you grow in your weakest area? What would help this growth?

 Experiential Learning

• In what two actions can you commit to grow in the theology and act of mutual submission?

• What might you need to stop and start to cultivate a more mutual environment?

Part 2

//DISCIPLING

3

Being Disciples

· ·

When so many are disillusioned by a manipulative church,
how refreshing will it be to find the church led by those
who know how to listen and don't need to control?

MANDY SMITH

Jesus' primary way of evaluating the local church is asking, are we fulfilling his command to make disciples? Simply put, do we look like Jesus? Does our church cultivate people who live on mission as Jesus did? This is the starting point, but before we invite anyone to be a disciple we must start with ourselves. This is the concept of *being* a disciple as we *make* disciples. Dis-cipleship does not start from the stage; nor do titles and diplomas grant us power to lead. Being a disciple others might follow begins with a fertile soul, one that presses into weakness rather than leveraging strengths. This section invites us into the work of cultivating a self-aware soul through the path of weakness.

Connecting to Movement

A movement of disciples who launch and care for missional-incarnational communities will not be sustained by dynamic personalities. Personality is great, but a sustainable movement is not built on it. Movements are built on character. As Jesus launched the movemental church, his who's who of disciples was not a team of great orators, organizers or even the most skilled. After the resurrection Jesus sent out disciples who understood weakness, humility and service as the basis for planting the church. As the apostle Paul said, "Follow my example, as I follow the example of Christ" (1 Cor 11:1), he also said "I came to you in weakness" (1 Cor 2:3). It's in weakness, in vulnerability, in our ongoing softness to God's Spirit, that a movement gains traction.

3.1 The Counterintuitive Disciple

In the summer of 2002 I (JR) moved into the New Hollywood Apartments. I'm not sure why they used *new* to describe the apartments. The building was constructed in the 1920s and renovated in 1963. There was nothing new about the building.

There are a couple of things I could always count on in the New Hollywood Apartments: walking up five flights of stairs with all my groceries (because the elevator was out of order) and doing my own maintenance work.

One day I was trying to fix something and got down to one last screw I had to loosen. I just couldn't seem to get it loose. A friend recognized that I needed some help, examined the situation and said, "Oh, this has a left-handed thread; it's a reverse screw. If you want to loosen it you need to go in the opposite direction." I'm thinking, *It took me ten years to find out how screws work, and now they change the rules on me?*[1]

Christian disciples and leaders often learn how to do something that seems to work well. We might *uncritically* adopt the latest business, marketing or leadership practices within the church, working tirelessly to tighten the screw. Yet all of the energy we're expending might be making us less like Jesus instead of more like him. As we engage in ministry, we must evaluate *who* we are becoming if we are going to ask people to follow us as we follow Christ.[2]

The upside down life. When we examine the teachings of Jesus, we soon recognize that he is calling us to live an upside-down kind of life. There is something counterintuitive about the life of Jesus. He teaches that if we really want to live, we must die, that the way to spiritual richness is to acknowledge our spiritual poverty, and that the way to rule is to become the servant of all. We must understand the reverse nature of the screw if we want to model a depth of *being* a disciple, for the emotional and spiritual health of the leader influences the health of the community.

The most significant thing about us isn't what we do or accomplish, but *who* we are. As we start and sustain missional-incarnational communities, our first order of business is to be a disciple. Disciples of Jesus need to develop an inner life that will be able to withstand the pressures encountered in our outer life.

As an extrovert I (JR) don't naturally take the time to examine what is happening inside me. I am naturally excited about what is happening around me and through me. But the longer I have lived, the more I have learned the importance of paying attention to my inner life, especially when I see how my actions have unintentionally hurt others.

If we hope to become more like Christ, it requires a truer and rawer self-knowledge and knowledge of God. Knowing God and knowing self are interdependent.[3] We may have a familiarity with our skills and gifts, but do we have intimate knowledge of what resides in our soul?

I am not talking about navel gazing but excavating what lies beneath the surface, allowing God to meet us there and bringing into the light those parts of ourselves we'd rather keep hidden. Conflict in relating with others in community often hints at things we haven't paid attention to in our own soul.

> The most significant thing about us isn't what we do or accomplish, but *who* we are.

Unhealthy actions on the surface are like the tip of an iceberg that leads us to much larger issues under the surface. To seek self-awareness, a measure of self-confrontation must occur. We must be intentional about unfolding our inner life in order to be a healthy disciple who can lead other disciples in holistic ways. As we allow God's Spirit to give us greater self-knowledge, and as we grow in the knowledge of God, transformation can take place.

A spirituality of imperfection. The counterintuitive disciple learns to embrace a spirituality of imperfection, a lifelong journey filled with struggle, wounds and weaknesses. When we learn to embrace our imperfection, we are able to appreciate God's grace more.

What does it mean to embrace a spirituality of imperfection?[4] It is understanding that our upward journey toward God, our inward journey to self-understanding and living in community, and outward journey of mission to love our neighbor, are filled with a sense of inadequacy and weakness. After honest self-evaluation, we realize, like the apostle Paul, that on this side of the new heavens and new earth, our wholeness is provisional (Phil 3:12).

Upward journey. While we are able to experience the power of the resurrection in our life in Christ (Phil. 3:10), our journey toward *holiness* and *union* with God often comes through *struggle* and *suffering*, which is why we need the psalmist to teach us to pray honestly.[5]

When we allow the psalmist to teach us to pray, we discover that there are broadly three kinds of psalms: psalms that articulate the joy of life going well, psalms that express anguish when life caves in on us, and psalms

of joy breaking through despair when we are overwhelmed by the goodness of God.[6]

We discover that through our struggles and suffering we find God in new ways. In my (JR) honeymoon stage with Christ, I sensed his presence frequently, and taking the time to gaze on his beauty came easily. He was my first love.

But as I stepped into ministry responsibilities, I found that ministry and its effects started to become my mistress. When God showed me this, I was in tears. I was reminded that nothing is more important than my relationship with God, nothing is more satisfying than being in his presence, nothing is more vital for fruitful ministry than our *communion* with him. And because these things are true, nothing is more challenging. Pursuing God is a struggle.

One of the things that has helped me in this struggle is learning to enjoy the journey toward God. The times he is silent somehow add to the times I hear him. It is important to enjoy the seeking as much as the finding.

A. W. Tozer said, "Come near to the holy men and women of the past and you will soon feel the heat of their desire after God. They mourned for him, they prayed and wrestled and sought for him day and night, in season and out, and when they had found him, the finding was all the sweeter *for the long seeking.*"[7]

Being a people-oriented person, I find that developing a relationship with an invisible being has its challenges. Not being able to see God with my eyes, hold him with my hands or hear him with my ears can be difficult. Being immersed in an audio-visual world makes this harder. But if we continue to seek, the triune God will meet us in mysterious ways.

Greater communion with God not only comes through struggle but through suffering. In fact, in my most intense moments of suffering I have found a greater experience of God's love in my life.

I have experienced some of my deepest wounds in starting and sustaining missional-incarnational communities when people I seek to love with all my heart hurt me deeply through some act of betrayal. As I reflect on how I have been hurt and bring this pain to Christ on the cross, I begin to better understand his undying love for me. I realize that Jesus experienced betrayal at an even deeper level than I have, by people he loved perfectly. As I take my suffering to Jesus, I am better able to understand the suffering he went through on my behalf and am overwhelmed by his sacrificial love.

Our spiritual experiences are like the seasons of the year. When we are experiencing winter and our relationship with God feels dead, we need to keep seeking. Spring is on its way.

The cross always precedes resurrection. Death gives way to new birth. The path to greater union with God and holiness comes through struggle and suffering. As you look at figure 3.1, reflect on how you are experiencing greater union with God through your struggle and suffering.

Figure 3.1. Upward journey

Inward journey. The inward journey is all about how the self is developed in the context of Christian community. The counterintuitive nature of this journey is that we experience a greater sense of *wholeness* and *community* as we understand our *brokenness* and *woundedness*.[8] We are broken people. We are clay pots. We have fractured souls that need ongoing healing. The good news is that as many times as we fall down, we can find forgiveness in Christ and the grace to get back up. The kindness of God in Christ is good news. We need to preach the good news to ourselves daily, lest we forget it.

I (JR) am often tempted not to be open about the areas where I am broken. But when I hide in shame, I never find healing. At one time in my ministry I had allowed my personal debt to climb to $30,000, due to a number of factors—primarily my own irresponsibility. Raising financial support, much like faith-based missionaries do, was a responsibility I had, since my first church plant was a majority of college students. It took a while for me to reveal my high personal debt, but I finally shared this with some trusted leaders. I was expecting correction. I thought they might ask me to step down from ministry, but I found grace. I have found that when I share my brokenness with trusted community, forgiveness and healing moves from being a theological reality to an experiential reality.

Not only are we broken but most of our brokenness comes from being wounded by our families and others in our communities. The wounds we have experienced, some very deep, have misshaped our souls. In our inability to process and unpack these wounds, we often revert to wounding other people in similar ways.

So how do we move forward? Disciples must confess regularly, or we will stockpile injuries that eventually fester and become infected. Healing and wholeness comes by confessing our sins both to God and one another (Jas 5:13-16). As we are aware of our brokenness and woundedness and share it with others, we cultivate an honest community in which true healing takes place. As you glance at figure 3.2, examine your inward journey and ponder how you are moving toward wholeness through understanding your brokenness and woundedness.

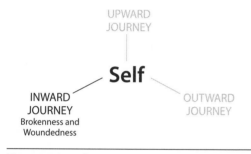

Figure 3.2. Inward journey

Outward journey. We discover much about ourselves as we move outward on mission. Our fears, our insecurities, our hypocrisies, our apathies and our chaos is revealed as we attempt to live a missional life. If we are going to flourish and sustain life on mission, we must not ignore what the act of mission brings out of us. Being sent into the world is a co-mission with the triune God. We do not go alone; we go with God and each other. We must ask God how to live on mission in our neighborhoods in a healthy, sustainable, rhythmic way. It is not enough to have zeal about doing missional stuff. As we seek to be God's hands and feet in the world, God's Spirit wants to take us on a journey of discovery and transformation.

How is the challenge to live a sent life changing you? What is it revealing about yourself?

One of the lessons Paul learned on his outward journey is that *powerful* and *fruitful* ministry is unlocked through *powerlessness* and *weakness*.[9] When Paul was facing the accusations of the superapostles (false apostles), he didn't appeal to his strengths but boasted about his weaknesses, saying, "When I am weak, then I am strong"(2 Cor 12:10). Paul understood that when his power comes to an end, Christ's power would rest on him and could work in and through him.

When Jesus sent out the Seventy to proclaim the good news of the kingdom, he didn't send them with tons of ministry machinery, as we often do. He sent them with empty pockets. They were like sheep sent to the wolves. They had to rely on the hospitality of those they were sent to. It seems that God loves to use the weak to shame the strong and the foolish to shame the wise (1 Cor 1:26-28).

Writing about the different metrics in ministry, Henri Nouwen says,

> There is a great difference between successfulness and fruitfulness. Success comes from power, control and respectability. A successful person has the energy to create something, to keep control over its development, and to make it available in large quantities. Success brings many rewards and often fame. Fruitfulness, however, comes from weakness, faithfulness and vulnerability. And fruits are unique. Community is the fruit born through shared *weakness*, meaningful presence in the

neighborhood comes through a long *faithfulness* and experiencing the surprise of the Spirit comes though our vulnerability. Let's remind one another what brings us true joy is not successfulness but fruitfulness.[10]

Look at figure 3.3 and think about your outward journey, taking some time to reflect on how your powerlessness and weakness allows God's power and strength to shine through you.

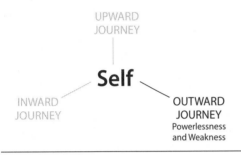

Figure 3.3. Outward journey

Being disciples of Jesus is both counterintuitive and countercultural. As you look at figure 3.4, consider how you can live as a counterintuitive disciple. If we seek to invite others on a discipleship path to start

Figure 3.4. Upward, inward, outward journey

new missional-incarnational communities, we must tend to our inner lives. As we make disciples we must be disciples. Paul says, "Though outwardly we are wasting away, yet inwardly we are being renewed day by day" (2 Cor 4:16). Are you developing an inner life that has a capacity to face the challenges of the common temptations we encounter in ministry?

FORMATIONAL LEARNING

 Meta-Learning

• In what ways is being a disciple of Jesus counterintuitive and countercultural?

 Reflective Learning

• *Upward Journey.* In what ways are you struggling and suffering, and how are you using this to draw closer to the Father, Son and Spirit?

- *Inward Journey.* What do you sense to be your unique areas of brokenness? What wounds are you currently nursing? In what ways are you trying to hide your weakness?

- *Outward Journey.* In what ways do you feel weak and powerless for the task of mission? Where do you feel inadequate to be present in the neighborhood or network of people you are sent to?

 Experiential Learning

- When you consider the upward, inward and outward journeys, which area needs the most attention in your life at this moment? Share in your discipleship group this week what that is and together move toward healing.

3.2 The Soul Under Pressure

I (Dan) have a seat in my backyard among a little garden of flowers and some crafted stone work. It's my little oasis in the urban noise. Sometimes when I sit down on that chair I forget that the cushion could be holding a week's worth of rain. It doesn't look like it at first glance so I plop down without a care in the world. Suddenly my backside is soaked and water gushes out of the cushion. I find myself frustrated, sitting in my oasis with wet pants.

I call ministry leadership "the great squeeze." Under great pressure stuff comes out of our soul that we'd like to ignore. Like that chair cushion, issues linger in us that we fail to explore. There is nothing like the close proximity of people and the unspoken expectations from within and without to put a vice grip on our character. My own soul has toxic matter sloshing around that, placed under the right weight, heat, demands and ambitions, starts to leak into the church I lead. Within us resides great beauty and the dynamic capacity to bless others. However, great brokenness also lies within us, holding equal capacity to use our leadership in hurtful ways.

We leaders need to be intentional and consistent about diagnosing our weakness and the ways it deforms our approach to leadership. It's at the exact point of our weakness that the pressures on our soul are most acute.

One way to understand the nature of our own temptations is to look at Jesus' wilderness temptation. In some ways this episode in Jesus' life is a prototype; it not only represents the kinds of temptations we face in the crucible of ministry, it also points us to healthy responses to those temptations. Let's take a look at how Jesus enters into this obstacle course of temptation.

> We leaders need to be intentional and consistent about diagnosing our weakness and the ways it deforms our approach to leadership. It's at the exact point of our weakness that the pressures on our soul are most acute.

The formation of identity. Before Jesus ever performs a miracle or dies on the cross, God the Father speaks audibly and affirms Jesus: "This is my Son, whom I love; with him I am well pleased" (Mt 3:17). In other words, "You are loved, acceptable and good. I am proud of you no matter what." These words of affirmation were not contingent on Jesus being successful. Remember, Jesus is just getting started in his public ministry and has not healed anyone, cast out any demons or taught anything.

These words from the Father were absolute words of identity formation. The Father is shaping Jesus' understanding of himself; his ultimate value was defined by how the Father saw him. This love from the Father is the self-understanding Jesus would root himself in over and over as he faced the fiery darts from the enemy and the expecta-

tions of the crowds. Soaking in God's infinite love for us has to go beyond an emotional experience in worship gatherings. It has to become a deep discipline of *communion* we exercise when facing the temptations because of our weakness. Only the love of God is capable of bearing the weight of our identity.

The following three soul pressures Jesus faced were real and powerful threats (see fig. 3.5). Notice that the temptations were primarily focused on Jesus' identity. Two times the devil led by saying, "If you are the Son of God . . ." As leaders, we should notice how the enemy operates here. The devil was seeking to pull Jesus into an approach to leadership that operated out of a distorted and broken sense of identity.

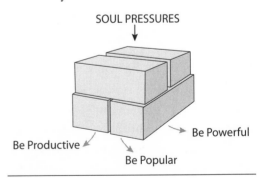

Figure 3.5. Soul pressures

Soul pressure 1: Be productive. Satan starts his assault by saying, "If you are the Son of God, tell these stones to become bread" (Mt 4:3). Can you hear the sense of entitlement in this proposition? "You are the Son of God! Use your power to meet your needs!" Satan was appealing to Christ's ability to produce what he needed when he wanted it. Jesus apparently had done nothing visibly significant for thirty years. *How could Jesus be satisfied with this?* Our church cultures ask the same question: What have you achieved? How have you demonstrated your usefulness? What have you produced?

When we listen to these voices we are tempted to move harder, push faster and press our will stronger. We may even go inward to depression when we don't get the results we want. Some leaders frustrated with lack of production in their ministries might even become passive-aggressive, blaming others for the lack of efficiency. Our ambition to make things happen in the face of resistant parishioners makes us vulnerable to the drug of production. When production is king, we demand that people respond to our leadership the way we want them to.

Jesus was tempted to skip over the long, painful route to achieve his goals, a route filled with rejection, including the cross. Instead, Jesus embraced his limitations. It is difficult for high-capacity leaders to show restraint in their ability to make things happen rather than embrace their limitations. The essence of this temptation is to bait Jesus to transgress the limits God had placed around him. This is a central issue for leaders to be aware of. Jesus replied to Satan by quoting a passage from Deuteronomy: "Man shall not live on bread alone, but on every word that comes from the mouth of God" (Mt 4:4). Jesus is saying that the satisfaction of our wants should not be the force directing our lives. As a son, he was confident that his Father would bring about production in a legitimate way.

Soul pressure 2: Be powerful. Next, Jesus was taken to see all the magnificence and power of the earth. Satan seemed to taunt him by saying, "Look at what everybody else has, and you don't have anything. Take control, apprehend what you deserve and command the angels concerning you" (Mt 4:5 The Kingdom New Testament). You might ask, where is the temptation in that? Essentially, Satan was telling Jesus to do something dramatic in order to trigger a powerful response from God. If Jesus threw himself off the temple, and God rescued him, Jesus and everyone else would know the power he held. Satan was essentially asking Jesus to manipulate God by forcing him to show his power in a public way.

When we envision what *can* be, we are tempted to control and possess success. So we speak boldly about our capacities and use spiritually charged lingo to declare how effective our church is going to be. We are impatient with growth, expecting return from our dynamic, well-oiled strategies. Power is the ability to possess success. Often our sense of self-worth is tied to the size of our impact. We are tempted to find ways to sensationalize, stimulate visibility and create buzzworthy results.

When God's Spirit seems to be moving sluggishly, we are enticed to manipulate the environment in our favor. I (Dan) am susceptible to this temptation. Early in my own church-planting story I felt the urgency to get people in the door of my church. I paced the floor every Sunday, desperate for more people to come. I felt great disappointment when there wasn't a crowd, instead of enjoying the people that were there. I carried nervous anxiety about my church's size or lack thereof. I feared the question other pastors asked me: "How big is your church?" It made me feel weak. On the inside I felt like I had something to prove.

When I'm ignorant of this subconscious impulse, I'm tempted to manufacture growth to make my church appear more powerful, which in turn makes me feel powerful. Yet Jesus has nothing to prove, and we can learn from this. Jesus will ultimately have to wait on God's timing to be vindicated for his ministry in the world. Jesus didn't heal every sick and demon-possessed person he encountered. He didn't build a great church in Capernaum when he was begged to remain in the city (see Mk 1:31-45). Our culture places a distorted emphasis on gathering a crowd as a sign of our personal power.

Soul pressure 3: Be popular. Satan invited Jesus to the highest point of the mountain and "showed him all the kingdoms of the world and their splendor. 'All this I will give you,' he said, 'if you will bow down and worship me'" (Mt 4:8-9). At this point people didn't think anything of Jesus. He was, in effect, invisible. Some of us are people pleasers and long for others to receive us, want us, affirm us, placing a high premium on what people think about us. We might lose sleep over someone's apparent disapproval of us. Our leadership self-image soars with a compliment and plummets with criticism. So maybe we avoid honest feedback because it hurts too much. We only want to hear the good. We are constantly seeking to impress with the cleverness of our communication, the brilliance of our insight and the confidence of our personality.

This impulse is growing wildly as a result of young adults' spiritual formation being heavily influenced by celebrity preachers. Listening weekly to a podcast of a preacher with a dynamic personality and a massive platform has the potential to wreak havoc on our desires. When we are spiritually influenced by popular communicators, we are tempted to imitate them as a means to success.

Vulnerability—being weak, flawed and inept in front of others—appropriately threatens our desire for popular success in ministry. Constant pressure to be "on" and lusting for more attention is popularity's dark side. We rationalize that it's good for the kingdom because we'll use our platform to save more souls. Leaders must beware the constant need of acknowledgment and adoration.

Seeking self-understanding. One of the greatest obstacles to leading people in a healthy way is our own lack of self-understanding. As we go through the stress and challenges of planting churches and starting and sustaining missional-incarnational communities, some things within us will be exposed. Whether we recognize it or not, our own brokenness will come to the surface. During these experiences we are tempted by *production*, *power* and *popularity*.

When this happens, we have to step back and explore the raw material of our leadership. Most leaders struggle with one of these temptations more than the others. Henri Nouwen says, "Befriend your brokenness," which means become well acquainted with how your brokenness resides in your leadership.[11] Come to grips with your Achilles' heel and bring it out into the open. Find ways to refresh your identity through these words, "This is my son (or daughter) whom I love and in whom I am well pleased."

FORMATIONAL LEARNING

 Meta-Learning

- Which of these soul pressures are you most susceptible to? Why?

 Reflective Learning

- What are some ways currently that you have been operating or behaving or responding out of pressure to be productive, powerful or popular?

- Can you identify a time when you hurt someone unintentionally because you were driven to be productive, powerful or popular? If so, explain.

- How do the words "You are my son (or daughter) whom I love and in whom I am well pleased" help you to recalibrate your identity? Write your response.

 Experiential Learning

- In the next couple of weeks, model weakness by sharing with someone in your community which of the three temptations (be productive, be powerful, be popular) you struggle with, and how and why. What steps can you take toward transformation?

3.3 Sacred Companions

Chuck Swindoll describes one of the most common hurts we experience as humans:

It is the most desolate word in all human language. It is capable of hurling the heaviest weights the heart can endure. It plays no favorites, ignores all rules of courtesy, knows neither border nor barrier, yields no mercy, refuses all bargains, and holds the clock in utter contempt. It cannot be bribed; it will not be left behind. Crowds only make it worse, activity simply drives it deeper. Silent and destructive as a flooding river in the night, it leaves its slimy banks, seeps into our dwelling, and rises to a crest of despair. Tears fall from our eyes as groans fall from our lips—but loneliness, that uninvited guest of the soul, arrives at dusk and stays for dinner.[12]

Tim Hansel shares the following from one of his journal entries: "Loneliness was so bad tonight that it sucked all the oxygen out of the room. It was so intense it felt like it could peel the paint off the walls. Lately, I have experienced loneliness so deep that I feel as though I need a second heart to contain all the pain."[13]

King David wrote in his journal, the Psalms:

Turn to me and be gracious to me,
    for I am lonely and afflicted.
The troubles of my heart are enlarged;
    bring me out of my distresses.
Consider my affliction and my trouble,
    and forgive all my sins.
        (Ps 25:16-18 ESV)

Loneliness may be one of the most difficult experiences any of us will have to face.

The inner ache of loneliness is part of reality on this side of the new heavens and the new earth. Paul put it this way: "Although we have the Holy Spirit within us as a foretaste of future glory, [we] groan to be released from the pain and suffering" (Rom 8:23 LB).

While we will experience the inner ache of loneliness till we die, God gives us his presence to live in and his people to be with to help with this pain. We were made to commune with God and enjoy community with each other. Leaders and disciplers need to learn how to go deep with people because of our relational needs and because it helps us to grow in self-understanding, which helps us grow in Christ.

Diving versus snorkeling. I (JR) enjoy snorkeling. But there is a big difference between snorkeling and diving. To go diving, a person needs to take a class. Snorkeling doesn't require much equipment or training; I just need a snorkel and fins.

It's no different when it comes to building deep, abiding friendships. We all have surface friendships. But if that is all we have, we're going to experience loneliness to a much greater degree. God desires that we have much deeper friendships. He wants us to have sacred companions. And when we go deeper, we'll see things that we can't see at the surface. We'll experience a whole new world.

Diving is not a natural skill, but it can be learned. Deep spiritual friendships don't come naturally, but there are tools that can help us to experience deeper community.

We need spirituals friends if we hope to start and sustain missional-incarnational communities well. Having sacred companions is not optional for disciplers; it's a necessity. Eugene Peterson says, "Friendship is a much underestimated aspect of spirituality. It's every bit as significant as prayer and fasting. Like the sacramental use of water and bread and wine, friendship takes what's common in human experience and turns it into something holy."[14]

We are told that before the fall, Adam and Eve were "naked and felt no shame." In other words, they were real with each other. They were open and transparent. They didn't have an image to live up to. After the fall, however, they tried to hide themselves, to cover themselves and blame each other. They felt the need to put on a mask. But the mask that protects is also the mask that isolates.

The irony is that I hide because I'm afraid that if the full truth about myself is known, I won't be loved. But whatever is hidden cannot be loved. I can only be loved to the extent that I make myself known. And I can only be fully loved if I'm fully known.[15]

It's not that we need to go deep with everyone in every place. John Ortberg identifies three stages of openness or disclosure: guarded communication, everyday authenticity and deep disclosure with close friends. What we are interested in is deep disclosure with our trusted friends, an intimate space.

Jesus demonstrated this; he chose to reveal more of himself to James, Peter and John. He opened up to them during his three and a half years with them. On the road to the cross, while in the Garden of Gethsemane, he said to his disciples, "'Sit here while I go over there and pray.' He took Peter and the two sons of Zebedee along with him, and he began to be sorrowful and troubled. Then he said to them, 'My soul is overwhelmed with sorrow to the point of death. Stay here and keep watch with me'" (Mt 26:36-38).

Jesus was experiencing the deepest struggle of his life, and he laid bare his soul with the three people he had developed an intimate bond with.

> Sharing our fears, our anxieties, our weaknesses and our wounds with people is risky. It's not easy, but it's necessary for companionship.

Sharing our fears, our anxieties, our weaknesses and our wounds with people is risky. It's not easy, but it's necessary for companionship. Many would prefer to snorkel at the surface instead of diving deeply into understanding and sharing themselves with others. Diving deeper takes more effort; we need to learn how to dive.

We need to ask God for help in diving deep, permitting us to get a better view of our own souls, to see ourselves as we truly are. The prophet Jeremiah says, "The heart is deceitful above all things, and desperately wicked: who can know it?" (Jer 17:9 KJV). After the fall, the part of ourselves that we are willing and able to share is like the tip of an iceberg. Below the surface, hidden underneath the thick layers of defense, are the memories of the deep hurts we have experienced and the things we are ashamed of, the stuff we have pushed down deep into our soul. And deeper yet, in the recesses of our soul are the unconscious parts of ourselves that unknowingly shape our behavior.

Johari Window. Imagine for a moment a four-paned window that represents everything there is to know about you. All your memories, fears, anxieties, hopes, dreams, thoughts and feelings, modes of operation, likes and dislikes, what you hate and what you love. This is called the Johari Window, which was developed by Dr. Joseph Luft and Dr. Harry Ingham.[16] We have found it to be a helpful tool to dive deep into our souls with others and gain the oxygen needed to enter into the part of us beyond our consciousness. Let's examine the window (see fig. 3.6).

	Known to Self	Unknown to Self
Known to Others	PUBLIC	BLIND
Unknown to Others	PRIVATE	BURIED

Figure 3.6. The Johari Window

Public: Known to self, known to others. The upper left quadrant of the Johari Window represents our public self, what I know about myself and what others know about me. This includes our physical appearance as well as aspects of our personality that people easily pick up on (e.g., introversion or extroversion). The public self is what others observe about us and what we are fully aware of as well.

Private: Known to self, unknown to others. The lower left quadrant represents our private self, what I know about myself but others don't know. This would include embarrassing memories that we don't like to share, our secrets, the things we do that we don't share with others. This quadrant represents the masks that we consciously wear. Both of the panes on the left side represent our conscious self.

Blind: Unknown to self, known to others. The upper right quadrant represents what others know about us but we don't know about ourselves, similar to blind spots drivers have while in their car. There are some things about us that most everyone else knows, but we don't have a clue.

Buried: Unknown to self, unknown to others. The final pane in the lower right corner represents the stuff buried so deep in our souls that we are unaware of it—information unknown to ourselves and to others. Deep, painful memories of the past are often stored here. While God knows every part of us, only he knows what is in the fourth pane. This is why the psalmist asked God to search him to see if there was any offensive way in him (Ps 139:23-24). He recognized his unconscious self.

Practicing a spirituality of weakness. The Johari Window can help us to grow in our self-understanding as well as deepen our relationships with trusted friends. Besides imitating the psalmist and praying that God would reveal to us those things hidden from us, this tool can help us practice confession, seek counsel and grow in self-understanding. Let's take a look at how we can use it.

Notice the four window panes in figure 3.7. In comparison with the first Johari Window, the public window pane has become larger and the other three panes smaller. If we hope to dive deeper into our buried self, we need relationships that help us expand the public self. This happens when we seek counsel from others and share our secrets with those we trust.

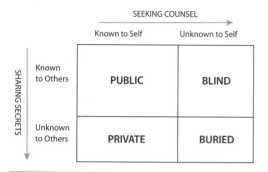

Figure 3.7. Using the Johari Window

Sharing secrets. In his book, *Telling Secrets*, Fredrick Buechner says, "I have come to believe that by and large the human family all has the same secrets, which are both very telling and very important to tell."[17] James tells us that if we want to find healing, we not only need to confess our sins to God but also to others (Jas 5:16). While I (JR) know this truth through experience, it has taken a while for me to engage in confession as a way of life. I still find confession a difficult discipline.

One thing that has been of some help to me is confessing to my trusted friends both the good and the bad of my life, both my dreams and my doubts, my victories and my failures. Sharing my secrets with trusted friends allows me to create deep bonds with them, as well as a new sense of freedom.

Here is a practical approach I have used in this area. I'm not saying it is foolproof; there are always risks in these endeavors, but it is worth the risk.

Take time to pray and then connect with your most trusted friend, asking if you can share something with them in confidence. Share what you might consider to be a small secret. Wait a while to see if your friend is able to hold that secret. If it seems this person takes confidentiality seriously, share another secret that goes a little deeper. Taking this step by step enables you to learn if you can trust your friend with your *deepest* secrets.

Seeking counsel. While I (JR) have difficulty sharing my secrets with some people, I often find myself seeking the counsel of others, asking people questions that help to reveal my blind spots. I might not always enjoy hearing the advice I get, especially if it is unsolicited. But proverbial wisdom tells us to "Get all the advice and instruction you can / so you will be wise the rest of your life" (Prov 19:20 NLT). It's good to learn from your mistakes, but it's even better to learn from the mistakes of others.

As leaders and pioneers we need to develop intimate friendships within our discipleship core. If we want to have churches where people find genuine community, it starts with us. People will imitate us. If our relationships are shallow, our community will be shallow. We need deep, spiritual friendships in our community. We will die on the vine without them.

FORMATIONAL LEARNING

 Meta-Learning

• Do you think Jesus craved friendship? If so, why?

 Reflective Learning

• What part of finding sacred companionship unsettles you or creates conflict within you?

• Do you have sacred companions who are a part of your missional community? If not, how will you go about finding them?

 Experiential Learning

• Consider who is in your intimate circle of friends, the one or two people *in your missional community* who you can be most vulnerable with. Decide the next step you can take to cultivate sacred companionship with them. What is it?

4

Making Disciples

· ·

You will know as much of God, and only as much
of God, as you are willing to put into practice.

ERIC LIDDELL

Don't be fooled by church attendance. Unless people are on an intentional discipleship path they will not be shaped for God's mission in the world. Jesus spoke to the crowds, but the engine of his ministry was his purposeful gathering and shaping of the Twelve. It seems like a small place to start, but it's vital. Discipleship doesn't occur in sterile classrooms or small group Bible studies. Discipleship is a move toward accountability and vulnerability to learn and practice the way of Jesus on mission. This requires rediscovery of face-to-face formation that creates safe space to be who we are but stretches us toward the narrow way of following Jesus.

Connecting to Movement

The beginning of movement isn't found in manufacturing buzz, putting up a billboard or creating a product everyone wants to consume. Movements are built on the smallest seeds; the apple seed carries the potent power of the whole apple tree. Discipleship is the work of shaping disciples to carry the seed of the entire mission. The seed is not the transfer of information through a sermon or a book. The first-century disciples heard Jesus' *teaching*, discussed its *implication* and observed his *embodied practice*. This is why Jesus could say, "go and do likewise." Like seeds, movements naturally scatter. Jesus scattered disciples all around the Mediterranean. Disciples are called to scatter and cultivate communities in cities and towns, which is why it's essential that the seed is cultivated in very tangible and hands-on ways.

4.1 Going Small in a Big World

It seems logical that if Jesus wanted to make an impact, he'd show up in all his glory at the largest venue possible, like the Roman Colosseum, and declare his divinity. These first-century arenas hosted spectacular public events such as gladiator fights and wild animal hunts. In terms of impact, captivating the attention of the largest crowd possible would make the most sense.

The first-century world was filled with spectacles that assaulted the senses and ratcheted up the emotions. Roman rulers knew this well, and so to increase their popularity and prestige they put on lavish shows across the empire.

Why didn't Jesus mimic the Romans? Why did he embrace smallness in his ministry? Instead of going for the crowds, he gathered a small handful of disciples to join him in bringing the good news to the world.

Isn't Jesus' method culturally unimpressive compared to the way modern leaders and rulers spread their messages? The God of the universe limited himself to a small band of ragamuffin disciples when he had all the resources of the world at his fingertips. Why do we focus on the crowds when Jesus focused on the Twelve?

Jesus the church planter. Here we learn from Jesus the most vital element of the church. Jesus founded the church: "He is the head of the body, the church; he is the beginning," or as *The Message* translates it, "When it comes to the church, he organizes

> The God of the Universe limited himself to a small band of ragamuffin disciples when he had all the resources of the world at his fingertips. Why do we focus on the crowds when Jesus focused on the Twelve?

and holds it together" (Col 1:18). Before we dig up best practices in the corporate world, we should take a look at Jesus and unpack the way he, the founder and head of the church, planted the church. We are invited to follow in the wake of Jesus, to imitate him.

One of the most significant elements of Jesus' ministry was that he was a disciple maker. Jesus formally invited twelve people to be his disciples (Mk 3:13-19). This was small numerically but atomic in significance.

At the heart of the revolution is a relational phenomena, a core committed to a dangerous journey together. A unique relationship is being shaped with the Twelve and Jesus. While Jesus invited others to join his kingdom movement, the Twelve had unique access to his life and message. The Twelve were invited into a separate (but not isolated) cluster where they were shaped for living and leading in the kingdom of God.

The Twelve knew what kind of relationship they were being invited into: an intentional relationship where they would learn what Jesus knew (competence) and discover who Jesus was (character). The engine of discipleship should be under the hood of starting new communities.

Cultivating a core. In the movie version of J. R. R. Tolkien's *The Fellowship of the Ring*, the Council of Elrond conceives a plan to cast the One Ring into the fires in Mordor, which will destroy the Ring and end Sauron's evil reign. When the question of what to do with the

Ring is brought before the Council by Gandalf the Great, fighting breaks out. Wills clash. Frodo the hobbit, with small stature and a quiet conviction, says amid the arguing, "I will take the Ring to Mordor." Silence settles in and the cost and courage required for what is next becomes clear to everyone.

Will they join Frodo? Will they do this together?

The Fellowship of the Ring is formed. Nine companions choose to take on the mission together. A community is formed around a daunting quest. Great exertion is required on the part of the Fellowship. They will face many unforeseen obstacles, their relational bonds will be taxed, and their resolve to be faithful will be challenged. That scene from The Lord of the Rings provokes tears from me (Dan) every time. I find the Fellowship of the Ring a helpful metaphor for cultivating a *discipleship core* to live on mission together. This is what Jesus did, calling others into a daring commitment to go on mission with him. Every disciple that joined Jesus could leave at anytime. But the center of the call was hot. It radiated significant heat in their lives.

Like Paul, we have to say, "Follow my example, as I follow the example of Christ" (1 Cor 11:1). This makes Jesus the exclusive focal point for the journey; at the same time it offers our own humble pursuit as a model for what it looks like to follow Jesus in a particular place and time.

Formational learning. When starting a missional-incarnational community, it is vital to cultivate a fertile learning environment for discipleship. Discipleship involves *heart*, *mind* and *body* learning, not just the transfer of information and beliefs. Merely transferring

spiritual information can inoculate us to on-the-ground practice. Practice is being formed and informed by the bumps, bruises and baptism of application. To embody our beliefs and work them out in real-time practice is at the soul of being a Jesus follower. But more than that, it is the material for credibility as the people of God. "Be people who live out the truth, not people who merely receive it and fool themselves. When you do this you are like a person who looks in the mirror, walks away, and then forget what they look like" (Jas 1:22 The Kingdom New Testament).

The methods we implement for maturing as Jesus followers either leads to increasing integrity in our lives or an increasing lack of authenticity. Within the church we have the tendency to take our cues from the halls of academia or training seminars in the business world. We launch a program or start a sermon series in order to "master" a spiritual topic. While this approach may be quicker and easier, these types of programs often shield us from direct contact with each other and with material of the real world.

Resist the urge to remove the clunky channels of relationship and the slow work of forming trust with one another. Jesus wasn't looking to fast track or graduate disciples with a fill-in-the-blank eight-week class. Jesus addressed the *heart*, the *mind* and the *body* by using three different learning approaches with his discipleship core (see fig. 4.1).

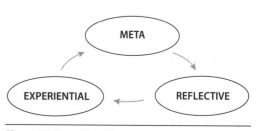

Figure 4.1. Formational learning

Meta-learning. Meta-learning is the effort to expose a learner's *mind* to a new reality through information that brings sudden awakening. We stumble across something that captures us and gets the *gears* of our mind moving in new ways. The result is akin to the popular slogan, "you just blew my mind." Meta-teaching seeks to press toward the truth in a way that exposes assumptions, misconceptions and missed realities.

Creating meta-moments often happen when we contemplate stuff we've heard a thousand times before, but seek to deconstruct it in a way that reveals the *big meaning* hiding in plain sight. Meta-learning grapples with a beautifully unsettling idea.

Throughout the Gospels we see this type of learning. One time, Rabbi Jesus is teaching about the surprising and often misunderstood nature of God's love for all. He says, "People who are well don't need a doctor! It's those who are wounded who do! Learn the meaning of this, 'It isn't your sacrifices and your worship I want—I want you to be merciful.' For I have come to invite the hurting, not the self-righteous back to God" (Mt 9:12-13 The Kingdom New Testament).

Jesus is being explicit about his own nature, God's kingdom and what the heart of a disciple should be. He is telling a completely new story, renarrating life. Jesus is creating a shift in our understanding how God sees us and the mission we were designed for.

We long to live by story. I (Dan) see this in my little boy, who reenacts scenes in which he's a superhero. I may look at him and think, *stories are for kids*, but deep within me is a longing to live within a grand story, to sense significance in my life's unfolding plot. I am almost forty years old now, and that childhood whimsy is asking to be remembered and resurrected. It must not be ignored. More than ever, what I need—what we all need—is to know, feel, hear and be called into the truest story pulsing at the heart of God's world.

Discipleship is not merely concerned with blasting out more propositional truths in order to shore up belief. We cannot live by, be sustained by or be nourished by static propositional truth. Although I believe in orthodoxy and the historic doctrines of the church, they are not enough to sustain. The apostle Paul invites us to have a renewed mind, a renovated imagination about where we find ourselves:

> For the Messiah has been revealed, the one who is your life, who is revealing his glory in you. So lay to rest the Old World in your bodies and in your minds. See the New World coming about and put on the New Humanity. . . . From now on see everyone as defined by Christ, for all things are being renewed according to the image of the Creator. (Col 3:4-5, 9-10, my paraphrase)

Discipleship helps disciples see the world differently because it *is* becoming different. N. T. Wright explains, "Paul's mind and body know it's already daytime, while the rest of the world is still turning over in bed."[1] The apostle Paul understood the plutonium power of the *meta* because he understood the challenges that his churches faced. The victory of God in Christ might not have felt as though it was inaugurated for first-century Christians, given that they were running for their lives under pagan rulers. Their harsh circumstances challenged their imagination.

Paul's words poked, prodded and powerfully unsettled the church's mind's eye about what God was up to in the world through the body of Christ.

The same is true today. The only way to live on mission in God's world is to have a deep, pulsing, epic sense of this story. In the microspace of discipleship we should feel the boldness to follow Jesus' approach. In *meta-learning* we place the beauty and subversion of what God is up to in the world and funnel it into the center of our lives for our *minds* to encounter and grapple with it. When we seek *meta-learning*, we ask questions that get at the big meaning, the large shift that's taking place, the meaning behind the meaning in the story.

Reflective learning. Reflective learning is the effort to excavate deeper learning in the *soul* through good questions and conversation. It's using a *magnifying glass* to explore what's below the surface. God made us as relational beings, and he brings understanding through interaction and reflection. Contrary to some common assumptions, Jesus is not the ultimate Answer Man. He is more like the Great Questioner.

Jesus asks 307 questions in the Gospels. While he is asked 183 questions, he only answers three of them directly. He typically answers a question with a question. Inquiries pervade his ministry. Jesus was an expert at asking questions that challenged people's underlying assumptions. We would do good to model this in our discipleship spaces.

"'What about you?' [Jesus] asked. 'Who do you say I am?'" (Mt 16:15). Jesus was helping the disciples understand what was in their *hearts* by asking them questions and drawing them out. Good questions make space for God's disruptive Spirit to work. Sometimes the disciples are caught off-guard by Jesus' disarming questions, a technique he used to put them in a learning posture. Jesus wasn't seeking to create spectators but to make disciples, and making disciples involves reflective learning.

Jesus is guiding his disciples into reflection by pummeling them with excavating questions like,

- "Why do you notice the splinter in your brother's eye, but do not perceive the wooden beam in your own eye?" (Mt 7:3)
- "Who is my mother, and who are my brothers?" (Mt 12:48)
- "Who do people say the Son of Man is?" (Mt 16:13)
- "Which of these three, in your opinion, was neighbor to the robbers' victim?" (Lk 10:36 NABRE)

In discipleship we must cultivate open space for questions that seek not the regurgitation of information but the processing of meta-learning's implications.

Experiential learning. Experiential learning is the effort to create fresh learning in the *body* through real-time experiences, taking *active steps*. Imagine you're a first-century disciple dragged by Jesus into "table fellowship" with notorious sinners. There you are eating and drinking, reclining and conversing with people who could ruin your reputation. In this situation, you are forced to ask yourself some questions: *What is Jesus thinking? Why does he have me eating with these people? What is he trying to do?*

The first time he puts you in this situation, you find yourself sweating. You're anxious.

It's disorienting. After a few of these feasts, its starts to dawn on you, *Oh, this is what extending love and mercy is about. This is what it feels like to be with people different from me.*

You see, true learning doesn't take place until we learn experientially. And experiential learning often starts with someone modeling what we are to do. As you sit at the table, you start to be thankful that Jesus is *with* you, leading by example.

But then some religious inspectors crash your party and ask you a difficult theological question: "Why does your teacher eat with tax collectors and sinners?"

You are caught off-guard. You have no idea how to answer. You're being plunged into a living truth. This is a discipleship course that moves you deeper into the world rather than higher up in the synagogue. To learn from Jesus the Messiah we must participate. It's interactive learning, being on mission *together*, building relationships *with* others. Jesus didn't merely *preach* about "serving the least." He *served* the least. He taught by example. He invited his disciples to live with him on mission. It was an immersive experience. This *experiential learning* was neither haphazard nor accidental; it was the means for shaping disciples.

- How might you create pathways into experiential practice?

- How might you call disciples into hands-on experiments with what they are learning?

If you read through the Gospels and observe how Jesus made disciples, you will see that Jesus incorporated each of the three levels of learning: *meta-learning, reflective learning* and *experiential learning.* Essentially, Jesus led the Twelve through a formational journey that was the prototype of a church, and it shaped them in *mind, heart* and *body.*

Discipleship within community. While the Twelve had a unique discipling relationship with Jesus, they weren't the only ones who hung out with him. Mark tells us in his Gospel that "when he was alone, the Twelve *and the others around him* asked him about the parables" (Mk 4:10). Clearly, other people were with Jesus and the disciples (see fig. 4.2).

Figure 4.2. Discipleship core within missional community

The point is that *the Twelve* were a part of a clearly organized cluster that had a unique, formal discipling relationship with Jesus, but that discipling group did not operate in isolation.[2] It took place in the context of a larger group of people curious about Jesus.

At the end of those three and a half years of being discipled, Jesus turns to the Twelve and tells them, "Go and make disciples." If you were one of the Twelve, you would most likely be thinking, *Oh! You mean the thing you have been doing with us for the past three and a half years? You want us to find some other people and do that same thing with them?*

Essentially, they were being sent out by Jesus to disciple people in the way that Jesus had discipled them. Can you see how discipling the core is fundamental to church as movement? Each of these three learning modes should be joined together, *not* parceled out to different programs. Together they create a path we walk together.

Emotionally unhealthy disciple makers want others to follow them indefinitely, nurturing inappropriate levels of dependency. Good disciple makers will cultivate and release disciples to "go and do likewise." Without this process we stifle our movement's DNA. Sustainable movements must equip people to "go and do likewise."

FORMATIONAL LEARNING

 Meta-Learning

• Why did Jesus disciple like this?

• How does Jesus' approach to discipleship contrast with the way spiritual growth occurs today?

 Reflective Learning

• When it comes to the three areas of discipleship (meta-learning, reflective learning and experiential learning), where are your church's strengths and weaknesses?

• What part of this discipleship process creates conflict or confusion in you?

Experiential Learning

- Discern how to begin gathering a discipleship core.

- What is the one intentional step you can take this week to start and sustain a discipleship core, working through the process of meta, reflective and experiential learning?

4.2 The Discipleship Relationship

As you move toward an intentional discipleship core, you inevitably will need relational scaffolding. Scaffolding is a supporting structure to climb on that is used to help groups function well together. We will always be individuals, but discipleship will cause us to converge in purposeful ways. This orientation might feel unusual because some of us are fierce individualists raised with a scale-the-ladder-on-your-own mentality.

Discipleship is not a boot camp with a commander yelling instructions to see who can survive the challenge. Discipleship walks us on a relational trail from independence to interdependence. The relational component makes discipleship not only wildly human but extraordinary. So we begin to ask what we can expect on this discipleship journey. How do we orient who we are with each other?

These questions must be answered and revisited over and over. In our experience there are some specific but often unnamed social bearings that intersect, creating various chemistries within a discipleship core. These social bearings should not be hidden supports, but rather named, constructed and championed.

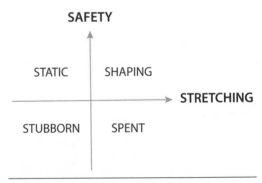

Figure 4.3. Safety and stretching in discipleship

A piece of the scaffolding: Safety. Safety is one piece of the discipleship scaffolding we must assemble. Safety with others is perhaps the most important and least recognized need of the human soul. Whether we admit it or not, at the nexus of our identity are these floating questions: Am I valuable? Am

I wanted? Am I loved? Am I welcome here? Am I understood?

These undercurrents cannot be ignored for the sake of getting to teaching time. Jesus said to his disciples "I have called you friends" for a reason (Jn 15:15). And at the Last Supper we also observe the disciple John warmly leaning on Jesus' chest. Safety was cultivated in the sacred space between Jesus and the disciples. Safety is established when the resources of emotional support and tangible presence begin to grow between individuals building a relational sense of belonging.

Safety is forged when we share ourselves, find out we're a little different and wait to see if we'll still be accepted. We rarely notice this ongoing social event happening between each other. Desiring acceptance might seem like an adolescent need, but we have yet to meet an adult who has outgrown it. Our cohesiveness comes from the disciplined work of extending belonging to each other even when we are dissimilar in some ways. The safer we feel, the less we are threatened by the instability of the discipleship relationship. Without safety in discipleship the basis of our group is more akin to a business contract rather than a bonded relationship.

The following are issues that undercut safety in discipleship relationships:

- *Distancing.* When we are together, we protect ourselves from being known by projecting a certain preferred image. Maybe we speak in generalities or say we are good when we aren't. Potentially we play hard to get, sending signals of distance. This can be communicated by averted eyes and a less-than-welcoming greeting. Some keep a distance because they want to keep up appearances, others because intimacy is unfamiliar and awkward.

- *Distrust.* Maybe we've been hurt in the past, or maybe we are a suspicious person, placing people at an automatic deficit. The response then might be to tell ourselves not to entrust ourselves to anyone. This can exhaust the discipling relationship. It becomes cyclical when in so many ways we communicate detachment, making others hesitate to trust us. Cultivating trust is not automatic, but it must be our ongoing intent.

Not only safety. Safety is essential, but over time it will slip into the static state (see fig. 4.3). *Static* is defined as lacking in movement, action or change. Though safety is essential for belonging, without being stretched we can drift into passivity where we fear face-to-face relationships that challenge us to step into our responsibility to change. We must not solely choose safety and stay there. Together we must understand that safety is just one aspect of a fruitful discipleship relationship. We cannot exclusively seek asylum with each other; we must also seek steps of action.

A piece of the scaffolding: Stretching. To be stretched with others is to embark on a journey toward transformation. Stretching acknowledges that parts of us need more exercise than others. The walk toward maturing in Christ can't be done in isolation; we can't understand ourselves outside of a localized discipleship space. In our commitment to being a discipleship core with a local mission, we exercise muscles we'd typically avoid using. We believe doing so will make us more nimble Jesus followers.

Years ago in a discipleship group, I (Dan) shared my own guilt in not connecting or knowing my neighbors. Rather than the core patting me on the back and merely saying it's okay (although they did extend God's grace to me), they invited me into accountable steps of introducing myself and extending hospitality to my neighbors. Even more, a participant in the discipleship core volunteered to go with me. This stretched me beyond idealism and guilt and moved me into new space for God's Spirit to work. This raw and real-time relating interrupted my tendency toward self-loathing and apathy. Sadly, many people have never experienced local, embodied discipleship; it's been replaced by disembodied connections: social media, books, podcasts and the like. We must seek to recover stretching in discipleship. To stretch is to "spur one another on toward love and good deeds" (Heb 10:24).

> We are shaped by experiencing deep, abiding safety, where we are loved as we are while simultaneously being loved enough to be invited into transformation, mission and doing some challenging things.

The following are issues that undercut stretching in discipleship relationships:

• *Deflect.* Stretching doesn't mean you set yourself up to be a verbal punching bag. Stretching really means holding your tongue, your emotions and your natural inclinations long enough to listen. Then you can give yourself the opportunity for self-reflection. Deflection finds ways to dodge this process and defray the blunt contact of constructive feedback or the honest assessment of something new.

• *Deny.* We are so sold on our interpretation of who we are and what we are that we cannot conceive that we may be viewed by others in a considerably different light. Denial sometimes occurs because we are more attuned to our own egos being injured than our desire for inner renewal.

Not only stretching. Stretching is essential, but over time, if unaccompanied by safety, it will drift into being *spent*. We can't simply choose to stretch, or we will experience exhaustion. Matthew 11:28-30 says, "Come to me, all you who are weary and burdened, and I will give you rest. Take my yoke upon you and learn from me, for I am gentle and humble in heart, and you will find rest for your souls. For my yoke is easy and my burden is light." To be spent is to burnout and potentially be bitter about the process. Stretching without safety becomes graceless and production-oriented.

With a combination of safety and stretching in our discipleship core we're guided into the space of *shaping*. This is an incremental but intentional move toward our missional, communal and incarnational capacities being expanded. To be shaped is to be formed into the image of Christ to do good works (Eph 2:10). We are shaped by experiencing deep, abiding safety, where we are loved as we are while simultaneously being loved enough to be invited into transformation, mission and doing some challenging things.

When we do not have a discipleship culture that offers both safety and stretching, we can slip into *stubbornness*. Stubbornness is resistance to others knowing us and telling us what to do. Stubbornness thrives in isolation, where no one has tangibly touched our character in an up close and personal way. Detachment from discipleship is easier in our technological age, which makes us prone to a hardened heart that is incapable of hearing God's Spirit speaking through another. A weird phenomenon is occurring: many of us eagerly receive information from and consider changing our opinions based on online avatars, but we are defensive and dismissive of feedback from local relationships.

We desperately need to recover the beautiful and full-bodied practice of discipleship. We're able to diagnose our discipleship core with this safety and stretching matrix. We should ask ourselves whether we are situated primarily in safety or in stretching. The flourishing of the church as movement must assemble these dynamic structures (relational qualities) for discipleship cores to climb on, offering support to help us thrive as followers of Jesus.

FORMATIONAL LEARNING

Meta-Learning

• What makes a discipling relationship so powerful for transformation?

Reflective Learning

• When it comes to your own wiring, what do you offer better: stretching or safety? Why?

• Why do you think you might be weak in one area?

Experiential Learning

- In light of the stretching and safety matrix, what is a specific step you can take together to bring this healthy tension into your group for the goal of healthier shaping?

4.3 The Phases of a Discipleship Core

I (Dan) remember the excitement my tenth-grade football team had the summer before our season started. During practice we looked around and saw talent. We had all the pieces for a winning season and maybe even a playoff run. We were confident about the prospects of the future. It was going to be a good year, in contrast to our past tough seasons. However, we were not prepared for the wakeup call we were headed for. The gears did not operate as smoothly as we had envisioned. We got whipped in our first two games. So we did what teenagers do best; we blamed each other. Our loyalty to each other was strained. I used to think that naiveté followed by conflict was an adolescent thing, but I've experienced this same dynamic with adults.

This is par for the course in the development of a discipleship core seeking to be the foundation of a church plant. Bruce Tuckman developed a helpful way of describing some of these bumpy challenges by outlining a predictable path of development: forming, storming, norming, performing.[3] Each stage brings certain challenges that have to be faced, worked through and resolved if the group is going to survive and thrive for future movement and multiplication.

The following is a brief sketch of Tuckman's stages, with one prevailing question that comes to the surface at each stage. It is vital to inform people of these stages so they are prepared and oriented when they begin to appear.

Forming: Connect or disconnect? The first stage is called "forming" because individuals join with others to *form* a group (fig. 4.4). At this stage the chief question of participants and observers is what it means to belong to the discipleship core. How to connect or disconnect is the pressing question. *Where is this group going? How do I fit in? What makes what they're doing different from what others are doing? Who are the primary shapers of this mission? How do others in the community see me and how do I want to be seen? Do I believe what these people believe?*

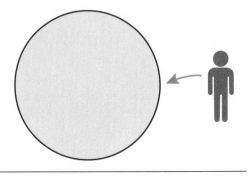

Figure 4.4. Forming

In essence, all of these questions point to the larger, overarching question related to belonging to this group or tribe. When the cultural behaviors of the discipleship core are visualized, it helps clarify the choice to connect or disconnect. This is why it is essential to mark out the scope, sequence, spirit and season of commitment to a discipleship core. We need to invite people into a long-term season of faithfulness, a rugged commitment to be with and for each other. Many of us are individualists with ADHD tendencies, quickly transitioning to the next shiny opportunity that distracts us. And we can't be fueled by inspiration, which comes and goes. We must be fueled by faithfulness, which reflects God's relentless faithfulness to us. We're not in a promise-keeping culture, so commitment sounds alien and potentially cultic, but missional church planting is made sturdy by commitment to a place and a people.

In the forming phase, people are looking for a certain amount of common ground. If they make it through this phase, they've most likely embraced the basics that create a good group, or at least they feel that some of the basics are not deal breakers. The desire for harmony and belonging are strong enough to continue forward.

The following are questions for a group member to ask at this stage:

1. What are the minimum essentials that this discipleship core rallies around?

2. What good could this discipleship core offer me if I fully immerse in the group?

3. What work is required of me to participate in the life of this discipleship core?

Storming: me or us. Eventually, people will begin to share with the group more of their personalities, and their own unique perspectives will be noticed by others. When this happens, it will create a subtle kind of *tension*. What once felt like a simple, unified group now starts to feel more complex. Participants notice some of the differences between them. They may also notice the work involved in participating in the discipleship core was not what they first expected. They begin to enter an internal *storming* phase (fig. 4.5).

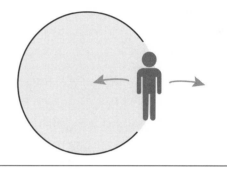

Figure 4.5. Storming

In the storming phase, people might feel at odds with some of the culture or at odds with an individual in the community. *Does this group have to fit like a glove for me to persevere?* Typical storming often centers around the desire for power and status. When we start with a group, we're happy just to belong, but eventually we want a greater voice. If we feel our voice isn't heard or is heard in the wrong way, storming begins. Discipleship cores storm around everything from nuances in theology to how our differing parenting styles should influence our missional community, to a lack of organization, to how money is used, to missional community growing too slowly, to a lack of communication, to an inability to forgive or to broken promises.

Sometimes people participating in a discipleship core are comfortable with the deconstructive stage, but when things begin to reconstruct they find themselves antagonistic about the formation of an actual church. In order for any group to bond, individuals must sacrifice some level of their autonomy and individuality for the sake of the discipleship core's mission. In other words, *we* must at times take precedence over *me*.

The following are questions for a group member to ask him- or herself at this stage:

1. Am I on board enough that I can make sacrifices for the whole?

2. Will I make my differences a point of contention?

3. Are people aware of our differences? Have we named them?

4. Am I willing to make some of the sacrifices (time, patience, initiating, etc.) to enjoy being *us*?

5. Am I observing my fit in the group through my own insecurities and preexisting antagonisms?

Norming: Settled and sharing. At the norming stage an individual moves past the conflict and begins to settle in. If the forming stage has to do with a level of differences, and the storming stage wrestles with those differences, then during the norming stage group members settle into who they are within the group (fig. 4.6). At this stage people feel free to contribute, not fearing too much rejection. People find unity despite their diversity. Therefore they begin to feel that *this is my tribe*.

In norming, some people become champions of discipleship, sharing with others what they are experiencing and helping them to understand the benefits of participating. They trust the group because they weathered some conflict and believe in the group even with its flaws. People at this stage want to see their discipleship core flourish and are less paranoid about their individuality. They begin to contribute their gifts, their time and their resources to the sustainability of the group. People at this stage may begin to wonder how they can make this available to others. This is a natural part of movement. Group members need to discern how to share what they are experiencing. Those who feel settled and secure in the group feel comfortable orienting portions of their life around its rhythms, culture and values. The mission becomes important to them, and they make the extra effort to actively share.

Figure 4.6. Norming

The following are questions for a group member to ask him- or herself at this stage:

1. How am I communicating to others that this is my tribe?

2. Am I orienting portions of my life around this core?

3. How am I contributing to the group?

4. How am I offering my gifts to the core?

Performing: Staying and stirring. Once members settle they can focus their energies and attention on the work at hand (fig. 4.7). Their suspicions about others in the group have changed to trust. They feel the group has learned to negotiate some of its flaws, realizing that some of the flaws are merely the reality of being in close proximity with others. At this stable stage the group is seeing some of the fruit of their labors. They have weathered some storms and are committed to staying.

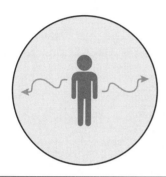

Figure 4.7. Performing

However, this stage is not without its challenges. Members who've made it to this stage may notice the trappings of routine. In the regularity of being together they might feel that the group has lost sight of something they previously felt compelling. Now they potentially see detrimental patterns. They are committed to staying but sense the need to question the group's complacency or vision drift. They feel challenged to initiate a small level of disruption to the group's good vibes. However, they might feel that stirring things up will cause suspicion about their loyalty.

When we communicate our commitment, we need to provide space for people to expose things along the way. In my own (Dan's) discipleship core we have people ask,

"Why haven't we multiplied already?" This questions whether we are getting so dependent on being together that we have no missional edge. Perhaps we should stir things up when our group gets so comfortable that we are no longer asking hard questions of each other, or when someone begins to dominate and it turns the group's focus inward. Our task is to discern how to communicate our commitment to staying yet stir things up for the betterment of the discipleship core.

The following are questions for a group member to ask him- or herself at this stage:

1. What needs to be reevaluated?

2. Is this a small thing or big thing?

3. Do I have the credibility to call something into question?

4. Have I communicated love and fidelity as I critique something?

These are healthy stages in the development of a discipleship core (see fig. 4.8). When we have unrealistic expectations, these stages can flip us over. Consumerism has trained us to demand a finished product that meets our highest standards. If we don't like the quality of something, we move on and purchase something else. Discipleship cannot be consumed; we must participate in it.

Evangelical discipleship has become intertwined with consumerist tendencies, and we are blind to this fusion. Beginning with the Twelve and moving into the early church, discipleship did not have embedded within it programs for felt needs, affinity groups and fill-in-the-blank accessibility.

When we view the church as an industrial complex we seek to eliminate personal messiness; we simply want to get people onboard as fast as possible. This creates discipleship programs that are not relational in nature but are heavy on the transfer of information. the different stages they are moving through is not pastoral; it feels more like a discipleship factory. If we aren't helping those being discipled to experience the four

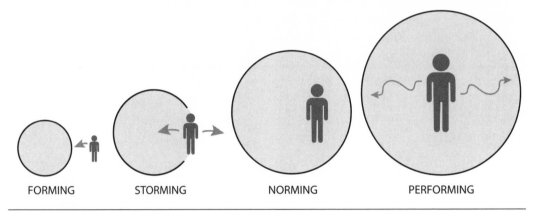

FORMING   STORMING   NORMING   PERFORMING

Figure 4.8. Stages of developing a discipleship core

mation. But discipleship within the church as a movement understands people are not products that need to be polished.

Discipleship cannot be microwaved, because people are fragile and each person has a unique story that makes the discipleship process difficult. A discipleship environment that doesn't help people identify stages, we might be tempted to use smoke and mirrors to generate the appearance of genuine engagement. This happens when discipleship is primarily a Bible study with fill-in-the-blank handouts. As much as it challenges our patience and efficiency, we must engage the relational work of cultivating disciples in community.

FORMATIONAL LEARNING

 Meta-Learning

• Why is discipleship such a dynamic process? Why can it be so volatile?

Reflective Learning

- From your vantage point, what phase is your current group in right now? Why?

- Share when you went through a storming phase. How did you navigate it?

 Experiential Learning

- What is a concrete step you can take to help each other work through the forming or storming stage?

4.4 The Spirit in Discipleship

Where is the Holy Spirit? Where is the space for God's surprising work in a disciple's heart? The Spirit gives us gifts that help us glimpse the world to come, yet we too often miss the ordinary ways the Spirit works among and in us. If we only have our eyes and ears accustomed to the most blatant signs that something dynamic is happening, we will miss the whisper of the Spirit.

How can we decipher the Holy Spirit's activity in the seemingly mundane parts of our lives? Too many have locked the Spirit in the church building for special events, but the New Testament makes it evident that the Spirit, like the wind, carries us into boundary-crossing mission. The Spirit guides us, disturbs us and provides unity for us to live into.

We need to learn to be present to the Spirit and hear his whisper in the ordinary: in intimate, everyday life. Jesus speaks of his real presence, through the Spirit, in his disciples:

> Truly I tell you, whatever you bind on earth will be bound in heaven, and whatever you loose on earth will be loosed in heaven. Again, truly I tell you that if two of you on earth agree about anything they ask for, it will be done for them by my Father in heaven. For

where two or three gather in my name, there am I with them. (Mt 18:18-20)

This text is about the sacred space cultivated when brothers and sisters in Christ enter into a deep, discerning, conversational, prayerful space that seeks understanding and agreement on what God is doing in their midst. God in Christ is installing belief in us to act in empowered ways, in his name, with each other. Jesus is connecting heaven to earth, and one key way they overlap is through interaction between disciples. Great authority is being given to disciples to be conduits of the Holy Spirit, discerning his movement in our lives in the seemingly mundane.

This discipleship space stirs up dialogical room for seeking wisdom and implementing what God is saying to us and through us. We can search the world looking for the Holy Spirit, but we'll find him in the temple of our active relationships within community. We need to recover this expectation that God will meet us in our discipleship clusters (three to four people). Can God really be this earthy, gritty and ordinary? Could this be one of the more essential aspects of the Holy Spirit's company?

Appreciating a fresh understanding of this truth is a critical issue for the mission of the church. The book of Acts records a number of powerful moves of the Spirit. Few of these happen in the context of religious services in a synagogue or a church. They happen on the byways, the streets, the neighborhood, places of work and homes.

At one point Jesus makes a bold claim to his disciples: "Jesus left the temple and was walking away when his disciples came up to him to call his attention to its buildings. 'Do you see all these things?' he asked. 'Truly I tell you, not one stone here will be left on another; every one will be thrown down'" (Mt 24:1-2).

Jesus declares that the temple, which symbolizes God's presence, will come down. So where is God's Spirit going? Where will the Spirit reside? The church as industrial complex still acts as if the Holy Spirit primarily shows up in a building at organized events; this is a brick-and-mortar temple mentality.

Yet Jesus clarifies what will happen: "It is for your good that I am going away. Unless I go away, the Advocate [Spirit] will not come to you; but if I go, I will send him to you" (Jn 16:7). The apostle Paul expands this picture of the new temple of the Holy Spirit when he says, "Do you not know that your bodies are temples of the Holy Spirit, who is in you, whom you have received from God?" (1 Cor 6:19). The church as movement eagerly seeks to return the Holy Spirit to the relational temple of average, ordinary disciples. Then they will be equipped and sustained with the presence of God.

We must embrace the truth that the Spirit is available and alive in the space of discipleship. Discipleship is a gift given to us to shape us for the purpose of mission. We cannot fully discern God's missional activity in our lives in isolation. While God can speak to us

> We cannot fully discern God's missional activity in our lives in isolation. While God can speak to us individually, we need community to discern his voice well.

individually, we need community to discern his voice well. And we can frame the way the Holy Spirit typically works as *disruption* and *direction*.

Disruption. Disruption is an interruption in our thought patterns and our safe emotional ruts. Disruption causes an unplanned deviation from our expected daily, weekly, monthly or yearly habits. Disruption is often considered a negative, but we're learning not to view it that way. The routines of our life train our inner character. God's Spirit wants to disrupt the unthinking ways of our life.

The apostle Paul speaks to this disruption when he says, "Do nothing out of selfish ambition or vain conceit. Rather, in humility value others above yourselves, not looking to your own interests but each of you to the interests of the others" (Phil 2:3-4). Our norm is self-centeredness, and the Spirit wants to disrupt this ingrained approach. If we want to hear the Holy Spirit's voice, we need to make ourselves ready for some disruption. We may be tempted to view disruption as a cruel joke from God, but it's a careful and kind testing of our false patterns in an attempt to make room for newness to spring forth in our life. Disruption is a tool of the Holy Spirit.

Direction. Direction is that timely help we need on the pathway forward. Direction is God hovering over the chaos of our life and calling forth steps on a different course. We see this when the Holy Spirit directs Paul away from Bithynia in Acts 16. How did God say no to him? It doesn't explicitly say. But Paul, by the Spirit, felt that some-

thing wasn't right about going to Asia. Then God guided Paul to Macedonia through a vision. The Holy Spirit directs us in many ways, sometimes clearly through a vision, other times lightly through a nudge.

The Holy Spirit offers us correction and calibration as we move outward and downward in mission. Mission is much more than a weekend project; it is an incarnational pursuit to be faithfully present to God's in-breaking kingdom in the ordinariness of life. There is no off-the-shelf blueprint we can buy. It's a tenuous journey of deciphering *who* and *how* and *when* and *what*. No wonder we need the Spirit's direction.

We need marked-out, rhythmic, relational discipleship space to listen to the disruption and direction of the Spirit's voice in each other. This is where *kairos* comes into the picture.

> A kairos moment is a disruption in time when the kingdom of God comes near to us and elicits a response.

Kairos moments. The word *kairos* is Greek for "opportunity" or "fitting time." The Bible uses the word *kairos* eighty-one times in the New Testament (e.g., Lk 19:44; Acts 24:25). A kairos moment is a disruption in time when the kingdom of God comes near to us and elicits a response. We see this disruption when Jesus called John and James to follow him; a window was flung open for them. Would they embrace disruption and follow Christ, or would they embrace the same-old and stay with their fishing nets?

Kairos is pregnant time, the time of possibility when God wants to birth something through us. It is a disruptive moment that calls us to respond to God's invitation. Kairos is the time when we sense God's

Spirit may be trying to get our attention, when we anticipate God's gracious meddling. The Holy Spirit is whispering, and we are challenged to listen.

Paying deeper attention is required to receive the gift of God's voice and then patience to unpack it. Cultivating a space with others to give room for discerning our kairos is essential. The world is pummeling us with pixels, noise, sound bites, images and news feeds. Our heads buzz with thoughts implanted from the voices of pop culture and political pundits. It requires a shared, rhythmic discipline with others to push back the noise and be still.

Practically speaking, what exactly does this look like? And how can we open up ourselves to a kairos moment that disrupts and directs?

Intimate space with two or three others is one of the more meaningful ways to engage in this practice. Valuing smallness is essential to the life of the missional church. Smallness can multiply, can be accessed by others and can be simplified for the ownership of the priesthood of all believers. Calling others into intimate space to regularly reflect on what God is saying is vital for making ourselves accessible to the still, small voice of the Spirit. It's tempting to think we can decipher God's Spirit on our own, but this is not the typical pattern of the first-century church. Jesus begins and the apostle Paul continues the theology of hearing God's Spirit in the community of disciples.

Our challenge is to create space for people where they can commit to intimacy with a couple other people and then believe in the work of the Spirit to open up organic possibilities. Paul understood the importance of this in his experience as a church planter. "Make a careful exploration of who you are and the work you have been given, and then sink yourself into that. Don't be impressed with yourself. Don't compare yourself with others. Each of you must take responsibility for doing the creative best you can with your own life" (Gal 6:4-5 *The Message*).

This verse inspired the Jesuit practice of the examen of consciousness founded five hundred years ago. It was an inner examination done with each other to move past the myths we believe about ourselves and into the exploration of God's voice in our lives. There is mutuality in this space as we together acknowledge our brokenness and need for grace. We also access the powerful and beautiful things God is massaging into our lives, asking good questions matched with good listening to sharpen our openness to the Spirit.

The following tool helps us pay attention to the disruption and direction the Spirit is offering (see fig. 4.9). We encourage you to meet regularly with two or three others to journey through these reflective questions, seeking agreement in the Spirit toward steps to practice.

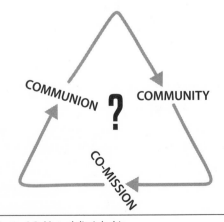

Figure 4.9. Mutual discipleship

1. *Communion. What is God's Spirit doing in me?* This question calls us to pay attention to what is clanking around in our heart. We seek knowledge about the careful surgery taking place within us. This is a question of communion. Is there static on the line between God and me? Is there insecurity, anger or uncertainty in my connection with the Father? The question *What is God doing in me?* fosters deeper self-awareness about our personalities, our histories, our choices and what God is saying through them. Our vertical relationship with God needs more than clichés to enhance it; we need to peel back the grace, love, pain, beauty, doubt and hope hidden beneath the layers of our life. It is essential to regularly audit our communion with Christ. The Spirit speaks to us as we ask this question of each other in the safety of other trusted disciples.

2. *Community. What is God's Spirit doing around me?* We realize our relationships need careful attention, and God uses them as instruments for speaking to us and exposing the hurt feelings we've been nursing. God also uses community to expose our judgment, hatred, bitterness and callousness toward people. Who am I challenged to love? Where am I experiencing conflict? Who do I need to forgive? We learn how to mature in love within our spiritual family. It is essential to regularly audit the temperature of our community with the local body of Christ.

3. *Co-mission. What is God's Spirit doing through me?* God is sending us into the brokenness of the world, not alone but with others. What is the unique missional ministry God is inviting us to? Who is God calling us to be present with and to sacrifice for? How do we love our neighbors? Where are we experiencing fear and frustration? As we are seeking to live into sentness, parts of ourselves will be exposed to the light. Without reflection we may miss how God's Spirit is instructing us and giving us insight into our own character. We are not heroes but beggars who are seeking to tell other beggars where to find food. The Spirit speaks to us as we reveal our intention to live missionally.

4. *Next step. What is our response to the Spirit?* As we examine what God's Spirit is doing, we reflect, record and then respond. Our response is a vital part of this intimate discipleship cluster, which is not mere catharsis (although that may take place). We seek to be present to kairos rising to the surface. This is a yearning and a searching for the next step in order to move from revelation to practice. We don't seek to light the entire path with stadium lights; we need only a flashlight to see our next step. The question mark in the center of the triangle (see fig. 4.9) symbolizes asking, *What will I do?* as a next step. Together in vulnerability, we foster accountability to the Spirit's disruption or direction. This is likely what Paul meant when he said "work out your salvation with fear and trembling" (Phil 2:12).

FORMATIONAL LEARNING

 Meta-Learning

• Why is Paul's reference to the temple relocating so significant for mission?[4]

 Reflective Learning

• Why do we need the Holy Spirit in our discipleship approach?

• Where do you detect fear, uncertainty or nervousness about listening to the Spirit with others?

• Have you ever experienced a kairos moment? Please share when it happened and what it was like.

 Experiential Learning

• What steps can you take toward gathering others in intimate space to discern the Spirit's activity in your life?

4.5 Gathering Your Discipleship Core

Starting and sustaining a missional-incarnational community is not a solo venture; it requires a team of disciples. While you will have a myriad of decisions to make as a leader, one of the first and most far-reaching is who to invite to become a part of the discipleship core of the missional community you are starting. This choice can make or break your community. It can either help you accomplish the mission God has called you to or haunt you for a long time.

No wonder Jesus spent an entire night in prayer before inviting the Twelve to follow him (Lk 6:12). He understood the weight of that decision. He needed wisdom, discernment and confirmation from the Father before making these critical choices.

The right team will have its weaknesses and flaws, but history reveals some fundamental factors to consider when discerning who should serve with you (see fig. 4.10). Obviously, you will have higher criteria for those who will have greater leadership responsibilities. If you are simply bringing someone into your discipleship core, he or she won't be strong in every area but should desire growth in character and competency, and show a level of compatibility with the vision God has given those starting the group.

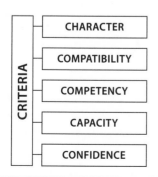

Figure 4.10. The five Cs of discerning a discipleship core

Character. The first criterion is character.[5] When you are forming a team, you want to find people who are maturing and have a strong desire to develop the virtues of the Spirit in their life. If you choose people to be a part of your discipleship core who don't have strong character, you are in for a rough ride. To gain an understanding of what character looks like, we can look at the life and teachings of Jesus, especially the Sermon on the Mount (Mt 5–7), his parables and the narrative of Scripture as a whole. Scripture paints this picture of a maturing disciple: a person who is able to equip others through example, teaching and ministry. This includes the virtues we find in the Pastoral Epistles (1 Tim 3:2-7; 2 Tim 3:1-11; Tit 1:6-9), the fruit of the Spirit (Gal 5:22-23), the fundamentals of faith, hope and love (1 Cor 13:13), and Peter's description of maturity (1 Pet 5; 2 Pet 1).

The following is a list of virtues to consider in assessing people's character:

- *Faithful.* A faithful person fulfills promises and obligations and demonstrates consistency in values, skills and actions. He or she has learned to trust others as well.

- *Servant.* A servant does not lord it over others but serves from the heart. He or she is willing to do lowly jobs and connect with those of no reputation. This person is not willful or controlling but is others-centered. A servant builds God's kingdom, not his or her own.

- *Lover.* A lover has experienced the love of God and thus loves God fervently from the heart. He or she loves the unlovely, friends as well as enemies.

- *Peacemaker.* A peacemaker does not gossip or slander. He or she realizes that conflict is natural, but unresolved conflict is not. This person actively seeks to resolve conflict in healthy ways and experientially knows that forgiven people forgive people.

- *Faith-filled.* A faith-filled person maintains spiritual vitality through a rhythm of life involving spiritual practices. He or she is a risk taker and demonstrates courage to actively move past fears. This person trusts God to move mountains.

- *Humble.* A humble person demonstrates a healthy sense of self-forgetfulness. He or she rejoices with other people's success, is cooperative, a team player, seeks advice and responds well to authorities. This person displays healthy interdependence.

- *Hospitable.* A hospitable person is a friend to strangers and welcomes others into their home. They go out of the way to meet people they don't know.

- *Generous.* A generous person demonstrates a mindset of abundance, not scarcity. He or she encourages a gift-oriented culture.

- *Devout.* The devout person lives a morally pure life and seeks to please God in everything.

- *Joyful.* A joyful person rejoices always and is thankful in everything. He or she radiates contagious joy and has joy that provides strength to persevere through all things.

- *Patient.* A patient person waits on God in the midst of a driven society that applauds productivity over faithfulness and fruitfulness.

- *Self-Aware.* A self-aware person has a good sense of his or her own strengths, weaknesses, gifts and calling. He or she is emotionally intelligent and reads social dynamics well.[6]

Of course, none of us can develop this kind of character on our own. Becoming more like Jesus is not a self-help program. It is not a matter of trying harder but of yielding to God by setting the sail of our lives to catch the wind of the Spirit. This is why we encourage a discipleship core to develop a communal rule and rhythm of life—practices that engage our senses, grab our hearts, form our identities and reshape our desires toward God and his kingdom (see chap. 6).

Compatibility. The second criterion to look for is compatibility, which is second in importance. We look for compatibility with the *team*, with *theology* and with *tactics*.

Compatibility with the *team* can be determined in part by asking, is there mutual enjoyment when we hang out? Compatibility is distinct from sameness. We can be compatible with people from diverse backgrounds. We can also ask, is this a life-giving person for the team (and me)? Are they for us? Do they desire to see the team be faithful and fruitful in mission? Does he or she believe in the work of the Spirit in our team? No one will always agree with everything others think. You're not looking for yes-men and women but for people who know how to disagree in an agreeable way.

When it comes to *theology*, some questions to ask are, How does this person understand the nature of the gospel? What is his or her understanding of the kingdom of God, the narrative of Scripture and the renewal of all things? To help in discerning theological compatibility, we encourage planters to develop a *rule of faith* that describes the core story and theological truths that shape the community.[7]

Other good questions to ask are, Does the person have a high or low view of Scripture? What is their interpretive lens? Do they have a generous orthodoxy or a rigid interpretation of Scripture? Do they seek to interpret the Scripture alone or in the context of community with the help of the Holy Spirit, taking into account theological history, the current context and reason and experience? Of course, more questions exploring theological compatibility can be asked. Remember that a lack of compatibility here can lead to much frustration and can even split the community before it has a chance to start.

Regarding *tactics*, ask whether this person is compatible with the team's basic strategy and approach to accomplishing its mission? Two things are needed for a missional-incarnational community to be fruitful: faith and unity. If the team trusts God to work and has common underlying assumptions, practices and strategy, nothing will be impossible. On the other hand, a team divided against itself will not stand.

Competency. The third criterion in selecting people for the discipleship core is competency. Has this person demonstrated the ability or desire to disciple other people? Does he or she have the potential to help a mid-sized group grow as a team? How about the desire to learn to live on mission? What is his or her experience in this? The initial discipleship core does not need all the competencies, just a desire to learn. But as we multiply missional communities, we need leaders who can equip others. And these leaders need to be competent.

The titles of the eight chapters of this book highlight the skills needed to help start and sustain missional-incarnational communities. We need *movement intelligence*, where we look at the church through the lens of the church as movement. We also need to learn how to live into *polycentric leadership*. At the center of church as movement is learning how to *be disciples* and *make disciples*. We need to go deep as we go wide.

We should be able to take a bird's-eye view of things, learning what it means to have a *missional theology*, as well as understanding *ecclesial architecture*, designing systems and structures for mission. Finally there are the much-needed competencies of *community formation* and *incarnational practices*.

At the beginning of their journey in starting a missional-incarnational community, a discipleship core should assess their competencies and the other Cs. We've developed a form to help them do this, which can be found at the church as movement website (churchasmovement.com). This can also be used for self and group assessment along the way.

> If the team trusts God to work and has common underlying assumptions, practices and strategy, nothing will be impossible. On the other hand, a team divided against itself will not stand.

Knowing one's primary and secondary vocational intelligence (apostle, prophet, evangelist, pastor and teacher) is helpful in building a discipleship core. It's not only good to have each of these people gifts represented on the team, but it also clarifies how each person will add value to the team. (It might be good to review the fivefold list in section 1.3 of this book.)

Potential leaders can learn how to do these things as they implement discipleship groups (personal space) and build missional-incarnational communities (social space). Anyone with growing character and good compatibility can always grow in competencies.

Capacity. In building a discipleship core, we also want to ask, Does this person have the capacity to be part of the group in this season of life? This deals with *schedule* and *stress*.

While a typical person may dedicate two to four hours a week to being a part of a missional community, those who take part in the discipleship core will likely need to serve four to six hours a week (including the gatherings). Someone might be a great match for the discipleship core but is overwhelmed with other responsibilities (e.g., working full-time, starting school part-time with a baby on the way). In these cases it may not be the best season for such a person to serve in this capacity.

In addition to examining their schedules, we should help people consider the stress factors of being a part of a discipleship core. A person will have to endure emotional and spiritual hits related to helping to start and sustain a missional-incarnational community. Does this person have the capacity to withstand these pressures? John Mark

bailed on Paul because the trip got too rough (Acts 15:36-41). Capacity is an important factor to consider.

Confidence. The last criterion is confidence. Does this person feel compelled by God to be a part of this particular discipleship core? It is possible to persuade people that aren't called to be a part of the team, especially if we are good recruiters. If they become part of the team simply due to our persuasion, when we hit some bumps on the road and they start to suffer, they will quickly find someone to blame. Guess who? However, if we first ask potential members to seek God about joining a discipleship core, they are more likely to handle bumps without seeking to find a scapegoat.

How did Paul know that Timothy was supposed to join him on his second missionary journey? Timothy demonstrated his level of confidence in joining Paul's team by being circumcised as an adult. That's commitment! How will *you* discern someone's sense of call to be part of the leading community?

Conclusion. Who you invite to become part of the discipleship core is one of the first and most far-reaching decisions you will have to make as you start a missional-incarnational community. It is not enough to simply look at the person's competency and experience. This participant should also be compatible, be growing in character and be confident. Gathering your initial discipleship core is one of the most important factors in being faithful and fruitful in mission. There is hardly a more important work you can give yourself to.

FORMATIONAL LEARNING

 Meta-Learning

• Why are the five Cs important to consider when forming a discipleship core?

 Reflective Learning

• Which of the five Cs are your strongest?

• Which of the five Cs are your weakest?

 Experiential Learning

• Go to churchesasmovement.com and download the 5 Cs assessment. Take some time this week to use the assessment to determine whether you are bringing the right team together.

Part 3

//DESIGNING

5

Missional Theology

· ·

*Too often we choose a few verses here and few verses there and
from there build a simplistic theology rather than look at the profound
theological motifs that flow through the whole story of Scripture.*

ERIC LIDDELL

Starting and sustaining new communities can be reduced to techniques and pragmatism, a mentality of "add this, tweak that, and—poof—you have a movement." Being the church should be informed deeply by theological reflection, not by new techniques. Theology is not only for academics but also for practitioners. We must each understand in our bones the story we are called to *and* the story God is writing in the world. Despite all our familiarization with Bible verses, very few of us have a vision for the story of God's mission, incarnation and formation of community in the world. This is what stirs us, compels us and anchors every technique we consider.

Connecting to Movement

The basic tools for starting new communities are varied, but we should never be without praxis. Praxis is the process by which theology is enacted or applied in a real time. We must equip disciples and the communities we form in a full, rich theology that can be practiced. Dead orthodoxy cannot fuel a movement. We need a living theology that captures us and compels us to dive deep into the world with news of Jesus' arrival. As we shape disciples we must ask *why*. As we form welcoming communities we must ask *why*. As we build rhythms of presence in the neighborhood we must ask *why. How* is important, but *why* is the driving force behind our activism.

5.1 The Social and Sending Nature of God

The first church I (JR) joined after becoming a Christian was movement oriented. The Great Commission was our drumbeat. Those who regularly shared their faith with others were honored. Discipleship was practiced. Leaders were developed from within. Our battle cry was to reach the world in our generation.

Most of what I learned was good, but not everything. There was a heavy emphasis on *us* accomplishing the Great Commission: "Go and make disciples." The focus was on what God called *us* to do. It was a job *we* had to accomplish. Sure, we were told that God would be with us. But Jesus called *us* to reach the world.

The almost exclusive emphasis on mission centered on the afterlife. The mission had an other-worldly focus. Now I recognize that the afterlife matters, but justice issues in this life matter as well. We should be praying for the reality of God's kingdom on earth. We are called to join God in the renewal of all things.

While I'm thankful for many of the good things I learned, a reductionistic gospel coupled with an undue emphasis on human agency led to many getting burned out and others abandoning the mission altogether.

When the gospel is reduced to a private affair between us and God, it not only seems self-serving but it becomes irrelevant to the world around us and the problems we face as humanity, whether it be poverty, senseless violence, ecological disasters or the breakup of families.

Over time I have discovered that people who hold a reductionistic version of the gospel eventually become ashamed of it, because it's not big enough to deal with the problems we face in the world. And when we put an undue emphasis on *us* accomplishing the mission, it lends itself to trying to accomplish mission with human strength in ways that don't reflect the nature of God.

The good news about God. The good news that we learn through the story of Scripture is that in the beginning is community. The Father, Son and Holy Spirit exist in an eternal dance of mutual enjoyment and love for one another.[1] "Community is the deepest and most foundational reality that exists."[2] This speaks to the social nature of God.

Not only is God relational, he is also a sending God. In other words, God is missional in his very essence. The Father sends the Son into the world to reveal and inaugurate the kingdom; the Father and Son send the Spirit into the world to continue their work, and the Son sends the church into the world, through the power of the Spirit, so that we can join our triune God in the renewal of all things (Rev 21:5).

We would do well to understand not just the God of history but also the history of God.[3] While the clear revelation of God as Trinity came through Christ and the Spirit's illumination, the reality of Three-in-One and One-in-Three has always been and will always be. "The triune God is the love behind all love, the life behind all life, the music behind all music, the beauty behind all beauty."[4]

Have you ever been to a Greek wedding? If not, maybe you have seen *My Big Fat Greek Wedding*, the indie movie that went viral. Jonathan Marlowe, a pastor and blogger, talks about how the Greeks have a distinct way of dancing. They don't just dance as couples; they dance in a group of at least three people. As they dance they weave in and out of these beautiful patterns of motion, going faster and faster while keeping in perfect sync with each other. Soon they are dancing so quickly that when you glance at them, it's all a blur. Their individual identities become a part of a larger dance. The Greek term used to describe this kind of dance is *perichōrēsis*. The early church fathers and mothers looked at that dance and said, "That's what the Trinity is like."[5]

Eastern Orthodox theologians coined the term *perichōrēsis* in the seventh century to describe the mutual indwelling of Father, Son and Spirit. It's related to our word *choreography*. The dance of God is about the togetherness, the joy, the self-giving, self-surrendering passion and life shared by the Father, Son and Spirit. Jesus described the closeness, saying he is in the Father and the Father is in him (Jn 17:21).

God is not a distant, divine, philosophical abstraction but a relational being who invites us into the dance of life—and not just us but the whole creation. And it is in our relationship with the triune God that we truly understand who we are and why we are here. Through the Spirit the great dance gets played out in our everyday lives, in our work and play, our laughter and romances.[6]

The Trinity in church history. The formulation of the doctrine of the Trinity was considered the crowning achievement of the first five centuries of the church and the central focus of theology.[7] Educated theologians weren't the only Christians who talked about the triune nature of God; the common people discussed it at the bakery and on the streets. But through the years the Trinity fell on hard times. It lost its center place in theology. It fell on especially hard times during the Enlightenment, when reason became the final arbiter of truth.[8]

It wasn't until the twentieth century that the Trinity became the centerpiece of theology once again. While Karl Barth and Karl Rahner are generally credited as the pioneers in restoring the trinitarian center, many other significant voices from Protestants, Catholics and the Orthodox added to the richness of our understanding of our triune God.[9] The recovery of the Trinity remains strong to this day.

Why take time to reflect on the Trinity? Because God is the center of reality, and our understanding of God shapes how we live. As we better understand the *social* nature of God, we learn what it means to live as a community *in* God. As we better understand the *sending* nature of God, we better learn what it means to live on mission. While the nature of God has many implications for the way we live, we'll consider just a few.

The social nature of God and community formation. How does our understanding of the communal, social and inner life of the Trinity shape how we approach community formation? Some theologians have asserted that when the church has emphasized the One over and above the Three, it has led to "(1) patriarchal and dominating patterns of

> As we better understand the *social* nature of God, we learn what it means to live as a community *in* God. As we better understand the *sending* nature of God, we better learn what it means to live on mission.

social and ecclesial life and leaders; (2) the problematic legacies of colonial missions; and (3) the rise of modern atheism."[10] If these are some of the negative realities that flow from losing sight of God as Trinity, how can our practices be reshaped when we envision God as communion?

First, as we live our life in the triune God, we learn what it means to be an inclusive community of loving people who want to share the joy of our community with others. Writing to the church at Ephesus, Paul says, "Imitate God, therefore, in everything you do, because you are his dear children. Live a life filled with love, following the example of Christ. He loved us and offered himself as a sacrifice for us, a pleasing aroma to God" (Eph 5:1-2 NLT). Paul not only speaks of Christ's love as a motivating factor of loving others in community, but he speaks of the Son's sacrificial offering of his life to the Father.

As we start to participate in the togetherness of God, we, like God, will desire to invite others to experience community *as a community*, not just as individuals. Too often we approach mission in an individualistic fashion, instead of communally. We get the impression that Jesus has sent us out alone, by ourselves. But typically he sent people in *at least* pairs. Why? Because there is something in our relationship with each other that not only brings the presence of Christ in a special way but draws others into what we experience with the Father, Son and Spirit. Maybe that is why Jesus says when there are two or three of us representing his name (i.e., relating to each other in the life-giving way of the Father, Son and Spirit), he can't just stand by idly, he has to join the party (Mt 18:20).

Theologian Miroslav Volf accents the connection between unity, community and mission:

> Because the Christian God is not a lonely God, but rather a communion of three persons, faith leads human beings into the divine communion. One cannot, however have a self-enclosed communion with the triune God—a "foursome," as it were—for the Christian God is not a private deity. *Communion with this God is at once also communion with those others who have entrusted themselves in faith to the same God. Hence once and the same act of faith places a person into a new relationship both with God and with all others who stand in communion with God.*[11]

This speaks to how vital unity is to genuine mission, and why the unity of the church is a consistent theme throughout the New Testament. Without unity as the people who live in God, others will not believe that the Father sent Jesus (Jn 17:20-23). The Celtic symbol of the Trinity illustrates the interrelatedness of the Father, Son and Spirit (see fig. 5.1).

Figure 5.1. The Celtic symbol of the Trinity

Second, as we participate in the mutual care, intimate sharing and mutual self-giving of Father, Son and Spirit, we will approach mission in the spirit of reciprocity instead of unidirectionally, and we will connect with people as fellow humans, not mission projects.

When Jesus sent the Seventy out to

proclaim the kingdom, he sent them out with bare feet and only the clothes on their backs. No wallets or purses. No big budgets (Lk 10:1-24). Why? Jesus engaged in a form of asset-based community development (ABCD) before it was in fashion.[12] That is, he didn't send his disciples on mission with all the resources they needed, but worked with the people that already existed in the community. He understood that poverty is not simply being without, it is without being. In other words, when we approach mission unidirectionally, coming to meet needs and to share the good news, we can unintentionally exacerbate the already marred image of God in those we have been sent to. When we have them participate in mission, bringing their gifts to the table, they wake up to the fact they are made in God's image.

Jesus sent the Seventy in such a way that they had to receive from those they were being sent to. Why? Because at the core of the web of lies people believe about themselves is that they are without value, without a contribution to make, without a valued sense of calling.[13]

When we do unidirectional mission, we contradict the very message we want people to hear and accept. And that is, people are valuable enough to the Father that he sent his only Son, valuable enough to the Son that he endured the shame of the cross, and valuable enough to the Spirit that he desires to live in them and help them live out their calling.

Finally, as we live into the dance of the Trinity, it will lead us to move from a hierarchical approach to leadership to a more polycentric approach. Living into Trinity lends itself to the practice of interdependent

participatory forms of leadership, where leaders enable their fellow priests to live to their sacred potential.[14]

We need to remember that we all are born into the family of God through a response in faith, and that all of us are to be students of Christ and to make disciples.

Starting with the social nature of the Trinity reframes our imagination as disciplers. Rather than beginning with a product to deliver to our city, we begin with community. This is a significant shift. The Father, Son and Spirit gifted their community to us; we were welcomed into their self-giving relationship. This is the beginning of mission. Before we think about concrete ways that God might have us be a blessing to the neighborhood, we must see that our greatest gift is our life together, our interdependent, love-filled community.

Just as the Trinity is community, the church is community. When we begin to turn the church into more of a production or a franchise, we lose the beautiful relational witness of the Trinity. Community is the most potent, powerful witness we have as we live on mission in the world. Community becomes the blazing signpost that we have encountered the Father, the Son and the Holy Spirit.

The sending nature of God and mission. Having looked at how the social nature of the Trinity reshapes how we approach being a community on mission, let's look at how the sending nature of the Trinity prepares us to live missional-incarnational lives.

As we reflect on the sending nature of God we discover that God is missionary in his very being. In other words, mission doesn't originate with the church but is derived from the nature of God. As Jesus says, "As the Father has sent me, I am sending you" (Jn 20:21).

David Bosch says,

> *Missio Dei* has helped to articulate the conviction that neither the church nor any other human agent can ever be considered the author or bearer of mission. Mission is, primarily and ultimately, the work of the Triune God, Creator, Redeemer, and Sanctifier, for the sake of the world, a ministry in which the church is privileged to participate. Mission has its origin in the heart of God. God is a fountain of sending love. This is the deepest source of mission.[15]

Ever since the creation of the world, God has been at work. He blessed Abraham and called him to be a blessing to the world. He spoke through the prophets to share his intentions for the whole world. He took on flesh and bones and moved into the neighborhood to be and share the good news of God's kingdom. Jesus lived and died for the sins of the world. Then the Father raised him from the dead. On the basis of Christ's work, the Father and Son sent the Spirit to empower the church to be an ongoing sign, foretaste and instrument of God's kingdom.[16]

Getting caught up in God's mission shifts the center of attention to *God* instead of *us*. We are called to join God in the renewal of all things. Reflecting on the sending nature of God, we discover our own sentness; reflecting on the nature of the incarnation, we discover *how* we can live into our sentness. Reflecting on how the Father and Son sent the Spirit, we remember that in our weakness he becomes strong. Let's examine in more

detail how the sending nature of God shapes us for mission.

Initiating. First, God *initiates* mission. God is missionary in his very nature. Because our triune God is actively on mission in our world today, our work shifts from initiating missional plans to discerning the work and whisper of God among the people he has sent us to. We need to learn to notice again. We have become habituated to see what we see. Maybe that is why Jesus says that we must become like children to enter the kingdom of God. Children notice things we no longer notice. They ask questions we no longer ask. Jesus appreciated children. How can children help us notice the work and whisper of God around us?

Inviting. God *invites* us to live into our sentness as a community. We are sent to be disciples of Jesus in the way of love, peace, justice, compassion, forgiveness and reconciliation. We have been sent to bear witness to the risen Christ in public spaces, to speak with prophetic voices denouncing those who would dehumanize and exploit others. We have been sent to recognize the beauty and brokenness where we live, the hurt and the hopes of the people we meet, and then respond to the Spirit's call on our life.

Inhabiting. While mission sends us out, the incarnation calls us to go deep, to be rooted in our neighborhoods. Incarnation is about *inhabiting* the place where God has called us to live, to engage in grounded missional practices in the concrete realities of life. It's moving from Facebook to facing our neighbors in our neighborhoods and networks. It's about standing in solidarity with those who suffer and celebrating with those who are experiencing the goodness of life.

Inspiring. Starting and sustaining missional-incarnational communities is challenging. While the joy comes in the morning, nights can be long. I (JR) remember the first missional community I helped start. I couldn't believe it when some of the people I was giving my life to gossiped about me and slandered me behind my back. It was painful. Words hurt. I still feel the wounds at times. Sometimes I wanted to throw in the towel.

It was in those moments that I felt the breath of the Spirit. The Spirit brought to mind the promises of God. Promises like, "Let us not become weary in doing good, for at the proper time we will reap a harvest if we do not give up" (Gal 6:9). In those

moments when I felt useless and inadequate, the Spirit *inspired* me to persevere. He reminded me that "the one who is in you is greater than the one who is in the world" (1 Jn 4:4).

We have been called into mission by a social and sending God. As we learn to live in him and consider the relationship that the Father, Son and Spirit have, we are instructed in how to live in community. As we remember the sending nature of God, we can reimagine what it means to live on mission together, knowing that the Spirit is with us until we complete the mission Jesus gave us: to bring the good news to every nation.

FORMATIONAL LEARNING

Meta-Learning

- How does our understanding of the social and sending nature of the Trinity reshape how we approach community formation and mission?

Reflective Learning

- What did the church lose when the Trinity took a backseat in theology?

- Which of the four I's (initiating, inviting, inhabiting, inspiring) does your missional community live into well, and which is the most difficult for your community to live into?

Experiential Learning

- Understanding how the social and sending nature of God reshapes community, formation and mission requires that we develop new skills. With your discipleship core, write a couple of new skills needed to be able to join God in the renewal of all things.

5.2 The In-Breaking Kingdom

My (Dan's) junior high days were not my best years. Rather than being days of innocence, they turned into the days of fear when a handful of bullies started to rule the hallways. Smaller kids would inevitably find themselves pinned against a locker as one of the bullies shouted expletives in their face. The bullies' dominance extended into the lunch room, gym class and even the library. Eventually their reign of terror dissipated as some of us grew into our bodies and were able to stick up for ourselves. These bullies established a reign that cast a cloud of anxiety over my whole seventh-grade year.

The apostle Paul talks about Jesus setting us free from various kinds of powers. In Romans 5–8, Paul discusses being set free from the power of death, the power of law, the power of sin and the power of flesh. These powers exert their dominance over all of humanity. As a seventh grader I felt the powers on a microlevel, and now with adult eyes I can see them bullying all of humanity.

Victory over the bullies. God is at war with what has harassed and still harangues the world he created. Through the life, death and resurrection of Christ, these bullies have been defeated; a new reign is being established. When we are baptized into Jesus' death and resurrection we participate in this active victory over the powers of sin, law, death and flesh. This is part of what it means to be "in Christ." As N. T. Wright has said, "Creation and judgment meet in the resurrection. That's when the Creator says *yes* to his world, and *no* to all that damages, distorts or destroys it."[17] God loves what he makes: he made earth and has been faithfully, patiently and relentlessly inviting people into restorative labor in this world (Rom 8:21).

The narrative of Scripture portrays a God who is inviting people to participate in his reign, not by statically worshiping him but by worshipfully working with him in the here and now.

The prophets and poets of Israel spoke of

> The entire narrative of Scripture portrays a God who is inviting people to participate in his reign, not by statically worshiping him but by worshipfully working with him in the here and now.

a day when their kingdom would bring peace to the broken-hearted, justice to the oppressed and abundance to the hungry. God is renewing all things. We see this future vision in the song of praise to the Lion of Judah, the root of David, the Lamb who was slain and is able to open the scroll.

> You are worthy to take the scroll
>> and to open its seals,
> because you were slain,
>> and with your blood you purchased
>> for God
>> persons from every tribe and
>> language and people and nation.
> You have made them to be a kingdom
>> and priests to serve our God,
> and they will reign on the earth.
> (Rev 5:9-10)

This glorious vision is not suspended in a far-off galaxy; it is breaking into the now. The entire world—our cities, our neighborhoods, our communities and our own lives—are in the billow of God's in-breaking kingdom.

My (Dan's) own story of being present in the neighborhood has needed a theology of God's renewal. I live in a city where 30 percent of the population lives below the poverty line. The streets are filled with boarded-up houses, and fewer than half of the teenagers graduate from our city schools. As I look in the face of a depressed city, I need to know that God is near and has not abandoned us. It's easy to wander into hopelessness when our eyes are fixed on the blight, the inability of politicians to bring lasting change and the exploitation happening in the shadows. Is God here? Certainly we can turn on cable news and begin to doubt that God's kingdom is moving. If Jesus is truly reigning as Lord, how do we explain all the pain and suffering we see every day?

Already, but not yet. In *Christ and Time*, Oscar Cullman used an analogy from World War II to illustrate how Christ's victory over the powers is fleshed out, on the ground, in the here and now. Typically, a war's outcome is determined by a particular battle. In the Civil War it was Gettysburg. In World War II it was what we now call D-Day. The Allied forces stormed the beaches of Normandy on June 6, 1944, and established a beachhead, successfully sealing the fate of the war. Yet V-E Day, the final day of victory in Europe, did not come until May 8, 1945, almost a year later. Pain and terrible loss were still experienced between D-Day and V-E Day, but both sides knew it was only a matter of time before victory would be fully realized.

Living between the resurrection of Christ and that glorious picture of the kingdom in Revelation is a lot like living between D-Day and V-E Day. Jesus has established a beachhead and effected a decisive victory over the powers, but we still linger in the "already, but not yet" of the kingdom of God. During this time, wholeness and loss, healing and brokenness, injustice and liberation, life and death live in dynamic tension with one another.

This tension confused and frustrated John the Baptist, which is why he asked Jesus, "Are you the one who is to come, or should we expect someone else?" In his response Jesus claimed that the fulfillment was in fact present in his missional ministry. The fulfillment, however, wasn't taking place as expected. Hence John's confusion. The unexpected element was that fulfillment was taking place in Jesus, but without the eschatological finality.

The Jews of the first century, in keeping with what they saw in the Old Testament, expected the Messiah would fully usher in peace and prosperity in the land. Jesus, however, came with the message that before the kingdom would be consummated, it would come in his own presence and his burgeoning work in the world. Figure 5.2 sketches what this looks like.

writes, "God placed all things under [Jesus'] feet and appointed him to be head over everything for the church, which is his body, the fullness of him who fills everything in every way" (Eph 1:22-23).

The blazing beauty of Christ's kingdom is to be reflected in localized, gathered people who are surrendering themselves to his kingdom. The church is not perfect by any

THE IN-BREAKING KINGDOM

Figure 5.2. The in-breaking kingdom

This is the beautiful task of the church. The kingdom of God beckons us to have "eyes to see and ears to hear." In the midst of seeming decay, God's kingdom is sprouting new life in the most unlikely places. Jesus' entire life was the commencement of heaven's rule coming to earth. In his life, God's love in our places is revealed. Jesus' life was not an abstract principle; neither is the kingdom. The kingdom of God is saturated in the struggles of historical reality.

The work of starting and sustaining missional-incarnational communities is a key way God is applying his continued reign in the world. Through the gathered people of God, a new sphere of influence, one ruled by the agenda of Christ's kingdom, is leaking into the world. As Paul

stretch, which requires the patience of God as he partners with us. God *is* certainly working in the entire cosmos, but the clustered, covenanted and committed people of God are his primary plan for expressing Jesus' prayer, "may God's will be done on earth as it is in heaven."

> Jesus' life was not an abstract principle; neither is the kingdom. The kingdom of God is saturated in the struggles of historical reality.

The church as a sign, foretaste and instrument. The kingdom of God drives us deep into the church, and the church drives us deep into the world. In fact, the church in a provisional way is to be a *sign, foretaste* and *instrument* of God's kingdom.[18]

- *Sign.* The purpose of a *sign* is to point to something not yet fully visible. Our way of life together ought to point people to God's future.

- *Foretaste.* The church serves as a *foretaste* when people get a taste of God's future in the present. When people encounter the church in the world—a place where people are learning to embody forgiveness and live in harmony—they ought to experience a greater sense of love. The church ought to be a tangible appetizer of God's future.

- *Instrument.* In the light of God's future, the church is an *instrument* bringing a sense of joy, beauty and justice to the neighborhood. Followers of Jesus have no greater calling than to cultivate a way of life together in light of this truth.

Kingdom smallness. Thoughts of *kingdom* often conjure up images of mighty armies and noble families. Kingdom language can lead to the acquisition of power, popularity and capital. This is the cultural current running through the church as industrial complex.

Yet the in-breaking kingdom appears as a mustard seed, which encourages us to embrace smallness as God's style. Much of our kingdom work follows the lead of acclaimed celebrities, awarded philanthropists or the fastest-growing companies. But the kingdom of God calls us into solidarity with the poor, cultivating belonging for the lonely, fighting for the oppressed, sharing the good news with the lost, welcoming refugees and reconciling ethnic divisions. A discipler's task is to call a community to join the work of the in-breaking kingdom, but this work is not for the mighty and the mega.

FORMATIONAL LEARNING

 Meta-Learning

- How does the already, but not yet impact our understanding of justice, mission, evangelism and community?

 Reflective Learning

- What aspects of God's in-breaking kingdom bring you clarity, conflict or confusion?

Experiential Learning

- What one way can your discipleship core be a sign, foretaste or instrument of God's kingdom in the next two weeks? How will you take that step?

5.3 Sharing a Holistic Gospel

Novelist Ursula K. Le Guin said, "There have been great societies that did not use the wheel, but there have been no societies that did not tell stories."[19] When we are listening to a lecture or sermon and the speaker starts to share a story, our interest is piqued. Why? What is it about stories that capture our imagination and command our attention?

Stories touch us deeply because stories shape our story. Stories speak to our identities, our desires, our emotions, our spirituality. We are a story-formed people. We are born into stories, and stories shape our destination. In fact, scientists tell us that storytelling evokes a strong neurological response.[20]

God is the author of stories, and his chosen method of revelation is story. From eternity past all the way to the new heavens and the new earth, God uses narrative and stories to reshape us. From the story of creation to the fall in the garden, from the story of Israel to the story of Jesus and the church, we learn the power of story.

Conversion is changing stories. One of the chief ways to share our faith today is sharing the story of God revealed to us in Scripture and *how* that story has shaped *history, our community* and *our personal story.* Ultimately, conversion is not about mentally assenting to some truths, it's about trusting God and "switching stories."[21] As we repent from trusting in the "American story," the "Hollywood story" or other stories that clamor for our trust, and instead trust in the gospel story, we start to live by a different script.

Evidence of the work of the Father, Son and Spirit in our lives is living our lives in Christ, in the inaugurated kingdom of God. It's trusting both the *work* and *way* of Christ. For Jesus is the *way*, the *truth* and the *life* (Jn 14:6). Jesus was willing to die for all of us, but he was never willing to kill. His is the way of peace, not war: "Blessed are the peacemakers, for they will be called children of God" (Mt 5:9).

Jesus cried out, "Father, forgive them, for they do not know what they are doing" (Lk 23:34). His is the way of forgiveness, not revenge. His is the way of encouragement, not gossip; of serving, not dominating; of humility, not arrogance. His is the way of devotion, not distraction; generosity, not greed. He was faithful till the end. If his *way* isn't our way, we need to ask whether we trust him and have fully applied his *work* to our lives. Salvation is not about leaving this world but leaving the *ways* of this world and entering into God's world, which arrived through the life, death and resurrection of Jesus Christ. It's trusting that in the end heaven and earth kiss.

Do we have the story right? In our current context some are rightly skeptical of hearing the Christian story. Jonathan Wilson-Hartgrove notes,

> Salvation is not about leaving this world but leaving the *ways* of this world and entering into God's world, which arrived through the life, death and resurrection of Jesus Christ. It's trusting that in the end heaven and earth kiss.

> It is not uncommon in our post-Christian culture to hear Christianity derided as bad news. Its Crusades were violent, its Inquisitions inhumane, its gender norms oppressive, its truth claims intolerant, its political imagination undemocratic. . . . The good news that the church has proclaimed for 2,000 years isn't any less true for our failing to live it. Christ had died. Christ is risen. Christ will come again. This is the news we proclaim. But given the signs of the times, most people aren't interested in hearing our careful reflections on the work of Christ until they see some difference that it makes in our lives and in the world. The good news we most need is a good news the world can see.[22]

Wilson-Hartgrove is not calling for some "heroic Christianity—holier-than-thou asceticism or utopian communitarianism," but he is calling us to authentic living, being a people who learn to forgive and ask forgiveness as we struggle to abide in Christ so we can be a sign, foretaste and instrument of God's coming kingdom.

Graham Tomlin, after studying the New Testament pattern of evangelism, makes the case that evangelism works best in the context where it's an answer to a question. In other words, when we live out our calling as the people of God, under the reign of God—when we become the church in which the poor find riches, the lonely find community, the sick find healing, the broken find wholeness—then our words about the person and work of Christ become meaningful.[23]

Everybody lives inside some narrative. We are all a part of some story, and the story we live in shapes the script we write day to day. So we must first ask what story we are living in. And how does that story shape our relationships and calling? Does it enable us to experience constructive transformation in our lives and the lives of others? Does it lead us to seek the transformation of our neighborhood for the common good? Does it give us a sense of hope or despair?

The beauty of the story of God is that our hope is not dependent on our faithfulness. Our hope is in the triune God's ability to bring about new creation—the redemption of our bodies and the redemption of the world. And one thing people need today is hope. We can be a people of hope because our confidence that the new creation will be fully realized someday resides in the fact that Jesus lived, died and rose again. Therefore it is not a matter of optimism or pessimism, but faith.

Stanley Hauerwas suggests that "just as scientific theories are partially judged by the fruitfulness of the activities they generate, so narratives can and should be judged by the richness of moral character and activity they generate."[24]

Living faithfully in God's story. Thus our first task is to live in the story of God and have God's story living in us, for on that basis others will desire to hear the good news. As we do acts of beauty and justice in our neighborhoods and cities, people will ask us why we do it. This leads us to share how God's story has shaped the story of our community, and how this story is able to shape them as well. Let's look at the six primary acts of God's story: *creation, fall, Israel, Jesus, church and new creation.*

Creation and fall are distinct. We must know the story inside and out. Each part of it is important if we want to truly understand, live in and share the good news. For example, the ancient Gnostics, and those influenced by them, conflated creation and fall. Thus they deemed the material world the problem. So the solution becomes escaping this world. But in Scripture the world was created "good." In Hebrew language the story of creation is poetic, and like the chorus of a song, the author ends with the refrain, "And God saw that it was good."

Figure 5.3. Creation and fall distinction

The first three days involve separation. On day one God separates light from darkness. On day two he separates the sky from the ground, and on day three the dry ground is separated from water. Each day ends with "And God saw that it was good."

Then on days four, five and six God fills each of the three spaces (light, sky, ground). The creation of the sun and stars in day four correlate with light in day one. On day five God fills the sky with birds and the water with fish, which correlates with day two. Then God fills the dry ground with animals and humans on the sixth day, which correlates with day three.

Why take the time to work through this? Because, as Michael Wittmer writes, "Contrary to popular opinion, the Christian hope is not that someday all believers get to die and go to heaven. *Indeed, the only reason anyone ever goes to heaven is sin.* If Adam and Eve had never sinned, they would have continued to live on this planet, enjoying the beauty of creation as they walked in close fellowship with their Creator."[25] If creation is the problem, then escaping creation and going to heaven is the solution. But creation is *not* the problem; the material world was created as good. The reason we experience hunger, war, injustice and death is because of *sin* (see fig. 5.3).

Sin is taking a stand against God and his loving reign, against life and against well-being. Seeking autonomy from God, we alienated ourselves from him, each other and the created order. Our fractured selves experience shame, guilt and condemnation. We are fallen, broken and depraved, often making gods in our own image rather than accepting that we are made in God's image.

Because of the fall our relationship with God, with each other and with all creation is broken. The fall was not just personal (between us and God). It was relational and systemic as well. It was personal, communal and cosmic in nature.

Israel. In a surprising response to the human rebellion, God chose to redeem the world by forming a nation as a sign pointing to God's shalom. God chose Abraham, blessed him and through him blessed all the nations. God gave Abraham his promised son, Isaac, and Isaac gave a special blessing to his son, Jacob, whose son Joseph, saved the whole family in Egypt. But when a new Pharaoh arose, the people of God were enslaved for four hundred years, until God sent Moses to deliver them. God rescued them from their enemies, took them through the Red Sea and after forty years of wandering, the next generation entered the Promise Land.

God used judges and prophets to help Israel live out its calling to be a blessing to the nations (see fig. 5.4). The Hebrew prophets pointed to a time when God would intervene and bring restoration to his people in Israel and to all of creation.

Figure 5.4. Israel icon

The word *shalom* best captures this idea of complete restoration. The prophets used *shalom* to speak of a day when all things would be made right again. Those things that were corrupt and polluted would be remade. Through imagery and story, the prophets painted a picture of how life is supposed to be. People would no longer be tools and property in the hands of the powerful; they would live fully as people made in the image of God. People would not try to build their own kingdom but would gladly be a part of the kingdom of God, letting God be God so that peace would prevail in the world. The prophets picture a world in which the environment, which was originally created good, would be free from the curse. They speak of a place where people would genuinely love each other.[26]

Then Jesus arrived and proclaimed, "The kingdom of God is at hand." In other words, shalom is at hand.

New creation. Before looking at Jesus, the center of the story, let's first look at how our story ends, for knowing the beginning and the end helps us to better understand the middle of the story. How does our story end? And how does the end of our story inform us of the nature of the gospel? John the apostle says,

> Then I saw "*a new heaven and a new earth*," for the first heaven and the first earth had passed away, and there was no longer any sea. [The sea represented evil in John's time.] I saw the Holy City, the new Jerusalem, *coming down* out of heaven from God, prepared as a bride beautifully dressed for her husband. And I heard a loud voice from the throne saying, "Look! God's dwelling place is now *among the people*, and he will dwell with them. They will be his people, and God himself will *be with them* and be their God. 'He will wipe every tear from their eyes. There will be no more death' or mourning or crying or pain, for the old order of things has passed away."
>
> He who was seated on the throne said, "I am making *everything new!*" (Rev 21:1-5, italics added)

Notice God doesn't say, "I am making all *new things.*" He says, "I am making everything new." That is an important distinction. That is John's picture of our future, and when we understand the end of the story we are given a glimpse of the nature of the gospel. We learn that everything lost at the fall is redeemed in Christ (see fig. 5.5).

Peter's first sermon speaks of the restoration of all things (Acts 3:19-21). And Wittmer writes, "Just as sin began with individuals and

Figure 5.5. New creation icon

rippled out to contaminate the entire world, so grace begins with individuals and ripples out to redeem the rest of creation."[27]

Living into new creation. As we reflect on God's future new creation and let it shape our sense of calling, we can join God in writing a new story for our neighborhoods and our cities. In other words, if God's future is the elimination of hunger and thirst, how are our economic practices at this moment anticipating the reality of abundance? If God's future is the elimination of weapons and war—people living peacefully with each other—how should we treat our enemies at this moment? If God's future includes a renewed creation with clean air, fresh water and beauty, how do we approach living sustainable lives in the present?

In the churches I (JR) have been a part of, we have sought to join God in acts of beauty and justice, anticipating the new heavens and the new earth. In Hollywood we hosted a bimonthly "Artist at the Fountain," where we brought in local bands to play music, sold tickets for ten to twenty

dollars and gave the proceeds to help local and global justice causes. In this way we sought to help sustain our justice endeavors locally and globally as well as bring more beauty and music to the neighborhood. We started a foundation where we learned to walk with the poor in the Turkana region of Kenya, giving microgrants to help people start small businesses. Did we do this because we thought we were able to change the world? No. We do it because we know that these are signs of what God is going to do in the future. And as we seek to live into God's story, people ask us questions. And then, over a period of time, we were able to share with them the story of God.

The center of the story: Jesus. By examining the beginning, end and center of the story —the life, death and resurrection of Christ— we learn that the gospel is the work of God

Figure 5.6. Jesus icon

in Christ through the Spirit to restore humans to communion with himself and one another, to restore wholeness to all of creation and within ourselves so we might live for the good of others and the good of all God has made.

When we embrace God's grace through faith in the life, death and resurrection of Christ, he forgives our sins, makes us right with him, cleanses us of our guilt, takes our shame, purifies us, redeems us, justifies us and delivers us from the grip of death and evil (see fig. 5.6). He places us into his body, unites us, heals us, seals us and empowers us to carry out his mission in the world, for the good of the world and the glory of God. That, my friend, is the good news.

The church. The church is the body of Christ, which is composed of those who believe in God and who confess and follow Jesus through the power of the Spirit. The church is to be a sign, foretaste and instrument of God's coming kingdom (see fig. 5.7). Proclaiming God's kingdom demands the denunciation of all injustice, oppression and exploitation, personally, socially and in relation to nature. The church is not an aggregate of individuals in pursuit of a personal experience of God but a communal way of being that enables us to be and make disciples of Jesus Christ.

Figure 5.7. Church icon

Table 5.1 is a summary of, and an aid to memorize, the six acts of God's story.[28] Each part is important, and knowing the whole story is vital, because too often our story has been co-opted and corrupted through the powers that be.

Be the story, tell the story. Jesus told the early church, "You will be my witnesses." In *Be My Witnesses*, Darrell Guder reminds us that *being* always proceeds *doing* and *saying*. Being witnesses is living out the *missio Dei*; it speaks to our identity as a sent people. God is a sending God, and we are a sent people— sent to testify to the hope we have by our deeds and words, the hope of new creation.

Our hope isn't about positive thinking; it's a hope we embody as a community, based on the love of the Father, the faithfulness of the Son and the power of the Holy Spirit. And as we bear witness by our deeds, we will be ready to share the story. For the message we have been given to deliver is not just good advice, it is the good news that "the one true God has now taken charge of the world, in and through Jesus and his death and resurrection."[29]

Table 5.1. The story of God in six acts

Acts	Icon	Summary of the Six Acts of God's Story
Creation		God creates the heavens and the earth and charges people made in his image to tend to creation and create culture.
Fall		People turn against God and the rebellion rips through all creation—personally, socially and cosmically—creating a world of brokenness, sickness, decay and death.
Israel		In a surprising response to the rebellion, God chooses to redeem the world by forming a nation to be a sign pointing to shalom, a foretaste embodying his presence, and an instrument bringing his justice and peace, seeking to bless all nations.
Jesus		Amid the rise and fall of Israel, God becomes flesh as Jesus of Nazareth, the ultimate sign, foretaste and instrument of God's kingdom, displayed through his life, death and resurrection.
Church		After Jesus' ascension into heaven, his followers are commissioned to carry on his work of being a sign, foretaste and instrument through the indwelling of his Spirit as they continue to look ahead to his glorious return.
New Creation		At his appointed time, God makes his permanent home on earth and Jesus' reign is consummated. The long-awaited renewal of creation takes place, bringing total justice, peace and life.

FORMATIONAL LEARNING

 Meta-Learning

- What is the good news, and what does it mean to share the good news as story?

 Reflective Learning

- Why does it matter how we share the good news?

- What methods of sharing the good news lead to a reductionistic gospel?

- Is it necessary to have six acts? Why or why not?

 Experiential Learning

- Take some time in your community to practice sharing basic acts of the story in creative ways, thinking how God's story has shaped your story, the story of your faith community and the story of the world.

5.4 Sacramental Markers for Mission

I (Dan) do not dig birthday parties. I don't care for all the fanfare and over-the-top celebration—I'd rather be somewhere else. It probably doesn't help that I'm an extreme introvert and a little bit cheap. Early in our marriage I purposely asked my wife not to throw parties for me; I'd rather have a quiet dinner in a quiet house on my birthday. You're probably thinking I'm a curmudgeon; in some ways I am. My bad attitude about birthday parties came to a head when my wife and I had a child. I remember the first time my delightful wife said, "We're throwing a birthday party for Daniel."

My irritable stance came to the surface, and we had a long argument. I lost. I'm glad I lost now that I look back on it. The case for my argument was, "I tell my son I love him every day. I kiss him. I hug him. Why does he need a party when he's already secure in my love?" My wife's response swept the day: "A birthday party is a public way for others to hear how grateful we are that God brought our son into the world."

She was right. This public party wasn't about me. It was a visible witness to our gratefulness and love. I'm still a little cheap about birthday parties, but I've learned to have a better imagination for them.

In the fifth century Saint Augustine described a sacrament as "an outward and visible sign of an inward and invisible grace." A sacrament is a public witness of an interior and sometimes hidden reality. As much as I didn't think birthday parties

were important, they are important for the formation of my son and our public love. They symbolize what already existed in our home. A sacrament is similar. It acts as a marker on the public horizon, making visible the convergence of our own inner life with God, the life of our faith community and the observing world. These three aspects of humanity overlap in the practice of a sacrament.

Sacraments as rebellion. Historically our idea of *sacrament* developed from the Greek word *mysterion* and the Latin word *sacramentum*. Like our word *mystery*, *mysterion* means "something hidden or secret." The exact language surrounding sacraments did not develop in the church for some time. We hear of the ritual of baptism in the Christian community in the book of Acts. We also see the "breaking of bread"—the Lord's Table—in Acts (Acts 2:38, 41-42). These celebrations were called by their name; there was no general label for these practices.

The word *mysterion* began to be used in the third century to describe these Christian acts. In order to avoid any confusion with pagan thinking, Western church father Tertullian began to use the Latin word *sacramentum* for *mysterion*, particularly in explaining baptism. The problem was that when Roman citizens took a political oath of allegiance to the emperor, it was referred to as the *mysterion*. Tertullian suggested that just as the soldier's oath was a sign of a way of life under the empire, so too the

> A sacrament acts as a marker on the public horizon, making visible the convergence of our own inner life with God, the life of our faith community and the observing world.

Christian community ought to see baptism and the Lord's Table as signs of a new life under the reign of King Jesus. Early on the word *sacrament* stood for the countercultural allegiance to Jesus' alternative kingdom. Sacraments symbolized belonging to a higher king whose name was Jesus. Today some might see sacraments as mere religiosity. But sacraments are *not* mere religion.

Signs and symbols. Human beings need signs and symbols to express what cannot be expressed in words. Daily we see symbols that simplify communication—road signs, badges and logos. These signs point to an important reality. A heart, for instance, is a symbol of love. It is a human organ that keeps us alive, but we imbue it with elements of life, energy, commitment and passion.

A symbol has many meanings, which vary for different people. Its depth is inexhaustible and is able to communicate meaning beyond words. The ways we interpret signs and symbols are shaped by the communities we belong to. Just as signs and symbols are necessary for human communication, so also—and perhaps more so—they are necessary in the communication between God, ourselves and our world.

The sacraments value *physicality* as a powerful tool to shape our understanding in ways that language cannot. We are spirits *and* bodies, minds *and* mouths, hearts *and* hands fused together and inseparable. What we do with our bodies informs our souls, which shapes the neurons in our minds. We are what we do with our bodies. This is why

> Human beings need signs and symbols to express what cannot be expressed in words.

the incarnation says so much to us. God has unveiled himself by participating in an embodied life. Jesus is the manifestation of God in a way we can touch and feel and see (Jn 1:14; 1 Jn 1:1). Jesus is the perceptible, outward sign of God. God in his essence is beyond propositions, but he became visible in Christ. Christ is visible in the church, and the church becomes visible in the sacraments. The mystery within our bones becomes a mystery we publicly bear witness to.

Missional marks. We want to briefly examine two core sacraments as acts of missional witness. Many faith traditions have more than two sacraments, but all include these two: baptism and the Lord's Supper. As you cultivate your faith community it will be helpful to consider the nature of the sacraments and what other core sacraments might be meaningful rhythmic markers to guide you toward mission.[30]

Baptism: Water that flows into the world. Baptism has its origins in the symbolism of Moses leading the Hebrews out of Egypt through the Red Sea.[31] The parting of the Red Sea was a miraculous event that jumpstarted Israel's freedom and enabled them to enter into God's mission for them. The water powerfully symbolizes a *pathway* provided by God into a new identity, a new calling.

The pathway through the Red Sea signified a transition from the old world into the new world. God spoke to Moses: "Speak to the Israelites and say to them: 'I am the LORD your God. You must not do as they do in Egypt, where you used to live. . . . Do not follow their practices. You must obey my laws and be careful to follow my decrees. I am the Lord your God. Keep my decrees and laws, for the person who obeys them will live by them'" (Lev 18:2-5). The Israelites previously inhabited a destructive and dehumanizing land for four hundred years. Their models for living as a community were ruinous. God does not want them to imitate what they had learned there. Their new missional identity was to be as a light, a city on hill, a refuge for strangers, a home for the homeless, a new humanity. Passing through the water was a marker of leaving behind the old to enter the new. The Red Sea was their baptism.

> Baptism is a marker for mission; joining us to God's mission. Jesus demonstrated this important sacrament in his own life, as his baptism marked the start of his missional ministry.

This reminds us of Paul's words: "If anyone is in Christ, the new creation has come: The old has gone, the new is here!" (2 Cor 5:17). Baptism is like the Red Sea, the water through which a person is initiated into a new community, a new mission in the world. It is a physical, visible, social, symbolic act of being submerged into God's waters and becoming the fruit of God's new creation.

This is why Jesus commanded his disciples to baptize all new disciples (Mt 28:19-20). Baptism is a marker for mission, joining us to God's mission. Jesus demonstrated this important sacrament in his own life, as his baptism marked the start of his missional ministry (see fig. 5.8). So now Jesus invites us to be immersed in his "living water," continuing the mission of Christ, sent by the Father and empowered by the Spirit (Jn 4:1-42).

We like to call baptism "the waters that flow into the world." These waters of baptism should continue to flow in us as we spend time with our neighbors, our friends, our coworkers, helping them to explore the pathway God has provided for them. A missional-incarnational community should not shy away from sacraments that mark their life together and in God's mission. The Old Testament is filled with sacraments that commemorate God's intervention in the life of his people, and Jesus is continuing and fulfilling that tradition for his disciples in the act of baptism.

Lord's Table: Food that flows into the world. Jesus said, "Whenever

Figure 5.8. *The Baptism of Christ* by Martin Erspamer

you do this, do it in memory of me" (see 1 Cor 11:25). What is "this"? Many Christians don't realize that Jesus and his disciples were celebrating the Seder dinner. Passover Seder is performed by a community retelling the liberation of the Jewish people from Egypt. This story is unpacked in the book of Exodus. Seder itself is based on the biblical verse commanding the Hebrews to retell the story of the exodus: "On that day tell your son, 'I do this because of what the LORD did for me when I came out of Egypt'" (Ex 13:8).

Traditionally, Jewish families and friends gather on the evening of the Passover to read the text of the Haggadah, the book with the story of the exodus and the Seder ritual. It's the narrative of God's mercy and the freedom he offered to the Hebrews. The Seder is not a solemn event but a joyous one; drinks flow and there is good food for all to share. It is a fun, dynamic, interactive communal story told through food that gives participants a glimpse into God's grace-filled ways. Seder reminds them that despite appearances, God is present, coming, moving and making beautiful things out of seemingly stalled things.

Even sojourners and strangers who had been given refuge in the city could observe and participate in the Seder. The meal reminds the people of God that they are a part of something much bigger. So it is a bit paradoxical that God in Christ says,

> "I have eagerly desired to eat this Passover with you before I suffer. . . ."
>
> After taking the cup, he gave thanks and said, "Take this and divide it among you. . . ."
>
> And he took bread, gave thanks and broke it, and gave it to them, saying, "This is my body given for you; do this in remembrance of me." In the same way, after the supper he took the cup, saying, "This cup is the new covenant

in my blood, which is poured out for you." (Lk 22:15, 17, 19-20)

The Passover Seder is a meal celebrating God's joyous work, but Jesus sounds like a killjoy. He's talking about death, but the Seder testifies to life (see fig. 5.9).

Figure 5.9. *The Last Supper* by Martin Erspamer

The sacrament of the Lord's Table offers us as a weekly reminder that God's work in the world brings together the scandal that *death* brings new *life*. Our abundance comes from God giving up so much for us. God dwelt in our ugliness so that beauty could be birthed in the world. This is the double meaning of the Lord's Table: (1) God laid down his life. We should never forget this, and we should do the same. (2) God is joyously welcoming the world to his Table, and we should do the same.

As we start a missional-incarnational community, we might be tempted to adopt pragmatism as a means to success. Yet gathering around the Table is a mystery that refreshes and reconstitutes us for mission. There is nothing idealistic about being sent on mission in the world; we encounter distracting idols, difficult seasons, financial hardships, sudden tragedies and personal struggles. Rather than using a pep talk to recenter a community for mission, the Lord's Table is the most powerful and historically rich tool offered to us. The Lord's Table reminds us of and launches us back into the world with a purpose.

The Lord's Table is the Seder 2.0. Grasp the emotional and mental power of this sacrament as it is practiced on a weekly basis in community. Let the Lord's Table carry more weight, more meaning. The Lord's Table is not an isolated act. It catalyzes us to create tables of missional hospitality in our homes, at the local diner and at places in our neighborhood. When we encourage and disciple others to cultivate tables for the sake of community and mission, it should not be driven by mere strategy but should be fueled by the way of Jesus.

FORMATIONAL LEARNING

 Meta-Learning

- Why do you think that Jesus instituted the sacraments of baptism and the Lord's Table?

 Reflective Learning

- Have you been baptized? What does it mean to you?

- How can the Lord's Table be connected and used for God's mission?

Experiential Learning

- We are told in the New Testament that the breaking of bread was something the early church was devoted to. How can we make the Lord's Table even more central in our gathering? How can you follow through with this?

6

Ecclesial Architecture

· ·

> *Christians cannot exist without a community, as they require,*
> *like all of us, nurturance by a people who, while often unfaithful,*
> *preserves the habits necessary to learn the story of God.*
>
> **STANLEY HAUERWAS**

Many church structures revolve around a dynamic preacher, a great band and a decent budget, with a few good programs thrown in for good measure. This is a very American way of imagining church. Americans are fierce individualists, and so much of our ecclesiology has been shaped by this way of engaging God and his body. We need to recover the simple, timeless and relational ways the first-century church. From a distance it might seem archaic, but when we look closer we'll discover something innovative, true to being human and necessary for the future. We want to belong to a community. We want to be close enough to be known. And we want to do something meaningful with others.

Connecting to Movement

How people gather is essential for understanding movement. Movements must be accessible and relational for people to access the pulse of the movement. As we look at the first-century church, we see that social space (groups of twenty to fifty) became central to the way Christians expressed themselves in a city. Rather than being known for their big events, they were know for their communal way of life. A social distance between Jews and Gentiles collided in the construct called *oikos*. *Oikos* is the Greek word for household. Twenty to fifty people gathered for worship, community and mission. Today we might think that movements are generated from a stage, but authentic movements are catalyzed by highly relational architecture.

6.1 The Essence of the Church

What comes to mind when you hear the word *church*? Take a minute to write down three words that describe the essence and function of the church.

Have you ever been in a conversation with someone when the other person said, "Oh, I believe in God and Jesus; I just don't like the church"? A growing number of people today have no interest in the church, let alone going to a weekly service. I (JR) once attended a movie preview in Hollywood. As I was waiting in line to enter the theater, I talked with a guy next to me. He was warm, friendly and conversational. We talked about a number of things in our long wait.

And then the question came: "So what do you do?" he asked.

I replied, "I'm the pastor of a church."

As the words left my mouth, I wished I could take them back, because when I told him I was a pastor it was like a brick wall went up between us. The air got cold. He no longer wanted to converse.

Some people are like that when they hear the word *church*. They don't want to have anything to do with it. When they hear the word *church*, many people think of inquisitions, crusades, racial discrimination, homophobes, scandals, the abuse of wealth and power. No wonder they want nothing to do with the church.

Who is the church? But *who* is the church? This question is fundamental because when we understand its nature and essential functions, we are free to reimagine what it means to be the church for the people God has sent us to.

So, what three words did you come up with?

Let's see if we can discover the essence of the church and the critical functions that flow from it. First, it's helpful to examine the New Testament word used most often for church— *ekklesia*. This term comes from the Greek verb *kaleō*, "to call," and the preposition *ek*, "out of." Thus the church comprises the "called out ones."[1] In other words, the church is not a building, a weekly gathering or a program, but a people God has called out of the world and sent back into the world to redeem and renew the world. Paul says, "He has rescued us from the dominion of darkness and brought us into the kingdom of the Son he loves" (Col 1:13).

> The church is not a building, a weekly gathering or a program, but a people that God has called out of the world and sent back into the world to redeem and renew the world.

Think about the images Peter and Paul used to refer to the church: "the people of God," "the family of God," "fellowship," "a chosen people," "a royal priesthood," "a holy nation," "living stones," "holy temple," "bride of Christ," "pilgrims," "sojourners," "sent ones," "household of God." The list goes on. The New Testament makes no attempt to standardize these images. They are meant to give us a multifaceted picture of this new creation designed by our triune God.[2]

For the church to be a movement, the way we express *being* the church should flow out of our theology; this is praxis. According to Craig Van Gelder, if church is merely a combination of different activities like a Sunday service or a Bible study, or if it is simply a combination of different functions like evangelism and discipleship, "we can be seduced into placing too much confidence in our own managerial skills or use of organizational techniques" instead of being who God has made us to be and doing what he has called us to do.[3]

> Functional and organizational approaches to understanding the church rely heavily on the social sciences. While insights from the social sciences can be helpful, these perspectives tend to emphasize the human capacity to create outcomes. The church is not just another human organization. Therefore it's critical that we consider the nature of the church before proceeding to define its ministry and organization.[4]

In other words, we must start with theology before sociology, for the church is both holy and human.

The nature and function of the church. A number of New Testament images can be combined to help us understand the church's nature and function. Throughout church history different branches of the church have favored different images. Eastern Orthodox ecclesiology sees the church as an icon of the Trinity. Roman Catholic ecclesiology (after Vatican II) sees the church as "pilgrim people on the way to the heavenly city."[5] Lutheran ecclesiology sees the church as people of the Word and sacraments. Reformed ecclesiology sees the church as a graced covenant community. Free church ecclesiology (Anabaptist, Baptist, Methodist, Quakers) sees the church as the fellowship of those who believe in Christ. Pentecostal-charismatic ecclesiology sees the church as a charismatic fellowship empowered by the Holy Spirit, and the ecumenical movement is trying to live out what the Nicene Creed means when it refers to "one, holy, catholic and apostolic church."

Three memorable words we (JR and Dan) use to help us grasp the essence of the church are *communion*, *community* and *co-mission* (see fig. 6.1). These three words create a holistic picture and also naturally flow into embodied practices.

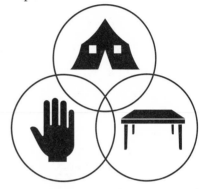

Figure 6.1. The essence of the church

Communion. God wants to dwell with us. The plan all along was to dwell in the world, to reside with us that we might enjoy communion with him. As we see in the Pentateuch, God dwelled in a tent—"the House of God" or the tabernacle—which was pitched in the middle of the camp of Israel (see fig. 6.2). Whenever Israelites looked at this tent they would say to themselves (and teach their children), "That is the house where God lives among us."

Figure 6.2. Communion

John 1:14 says, "The Word became flesh and made his dwelling among us. We have seen his glory, the glory of the one and only Son, who came from the Father, full of grace and truth." The word *dwell* in this text is actually *skēnoō*, "to tabernacle." Through Jesus,

God came to dwell with us and places his Holy Spirit in our lives. We have been invited into a life of *communion* with the Father, Son and Spirit. We are the bride of Christ and the people of God. We are a holy priesthood who, in light of what Christ has done for us, offer ourselves as living sacrifices to God through a life of worship in the Spirit.

Communion is not merely a meeting. It's learning to live in the life and dance of God throughout our ordinary life. Gathering to commune with and worship God certainly helps us live in God throughout the day and week, but communion and worship go beyond a mere meeting. It's a way of life; a rhythm of life.

Community. We are God's family. The early church had everything in common—the Greek word *koinōnia* (fellowship) refers to a common life together. Those who had much shared with those who didn't have enough. They prayed together, broke bread together, laughed together and labored together. They were not *like* family; they *were* family. They called each other "brothers and sisters." Acts 2:46 reveals the common life forming around the table: "Every day they continued to meet together. . . . They broke bread in their homes and ate together with glad and sincere hearts." The table symbolized that God's Spirit was shaping a new social existence, rallied in mutuality, under the lordship of Christ (see fig. 6.3).

Figure 6.3. Community

For most of history a child's family determined what he or she would do in life. It shaped what they could become. Someone born to indentured ser-

vants was likely going to be an indentured servant. A child born to a king was destined for royalty. When we are born again, we are born into the royal family of God. We are part of the household of faith, children of the Most High. God has placed us into a family that crosses every human boundary. We are a people from every tribe, tongue and nation.

Co-mission. We are the body of Christ. We have been gifted and empowered by the Spirit to live as gift-shaped interdependent communities *co-missioned* by Christ to make disciples who seek the renewal of all things. We are the hands and feet of Christ in our world today, sent out to continue his ministry until he returns (see fig. 6.4). We have

Figure 6.4. Co-mission

been co-missioned to proclaim good news to the poor and to release the captives. We are called to be peacemakers, reconcilers, activists, stewards of creation, people who care about the environment. Jesus' mission was robust, and he sent his Spirit to live in us so we might be a sign, foretaste and instrument of his coming kingdom. A friend of ours once said that the church is called to be the welcoming committee to the kingdom, not the managers of the guest list.[6]

This is the essence of the church: a people who find their identity in the arms of God (communion), rallied around tables welcoming each other (community) and sent out into the world with serving hands (co-mission). In the Gospels this is the pattern of Jesus' life. We get a snapshot of this pattern in Luke 6:12-19. Jesus goes up on a mountain to pray. He then selects twelve people to devote the next three years of his life to. Then he comes down from the mountain and pours his life into broken and hurting people. Jesus models something quite simple, which we should imitate. We need to cut away all the excess and clean out the clutter to help people wrap their arms around and live into the essence of the church in communion, community and co-mission.

How can we do this?

Rule and rhythm of life. Our bodies are formed by the shapes we press them into. I (Dan) discovered this truth in a painful fashion. For months now I've been writing, hunched over a desk for up to twelve hours a day. This is not typical for me; my days normally include more mobility. At the three-month mark of pressing my body into this pattern I started to feel an unbearable pain in my right leg and up the left side of my back. I decided to visit my chiropractor.

The doctor took a few x-rays and gave me the news. He first asked a question: "What do you do for work? Are you sitting in a hunched state all day?" The last three months of writing was deforming my vertebrae from my skull to the middle of my back. The doctor's advice was clear: "We can't fix this overnight, but we can incrementally put your spine back in place with purposeful actions."

The rhythms that shape us. The routines we engage in shape the curvature of our lives. I was a bit naive about the impact that a subtle, repetitive posture would have on my body. Many Jesus followers are similarly naive about how certain rhythms shape

their spiritual lives as disciples. Rhythms shape us for good or bad. Rhythms affect our mindset, our opinions and our sense of identity. Much of life is sustained by rhythmic patterns. In nature bees form their honeycombs methodically, robins put together their nests piece by piece, and planets loop around the sun in strict cycles. None of these expressions of nature is spontaneous or random. They are exuberant, but they are organized around a rhythm.

A rule and rhythm of life. A *rule* is a routine, regular and repeated, communal spiritual practice we engage in. "The Latin term for 'rule' is *regula*, from which our words regular or regulate derive."[7] A rule speaks of the tangible spirit-forming practices we participate in, practices like prayer, silence and solitude. *Rhythm* refers to how often we engage a particular practice (rule). The church needs to reevaluate its patterns of *togetherness*. Lesslie Newbigin observed, "We are shaped by what we attend to." An intentional rule and rhythm of life exercises our communal muscles. As we do this, we grow to be the kind of people God wants us to become.

Most people should be able to participate in a healthy rule and rhythm of life for a *community on mission*. Be sure to solicit feedback from the community before you invite people to participate in it. Let's take a moment to look at some of the practicalities of communion, community and co-mission as a gathered people (see fig. 6.5).

Communion is a rhythm that guides us to abide in the love of God. First Corinthians 11–14 illustrates this communion

> A *rule* is a routine, regular and repeated, communal spiritual practice we engage in.

space where God's people share in thanks-
giving for what he is doing: breaking bread
around the table, opening Scripture and
welcoming the Holy Spirit's presence in
their midst.

There are many ways to engage in communion with God as a gathered people. For
example, engaging in different kinds of
prayer: intercession, supplication, praise, lis-

Figure 6.5. Rule and rhythm for a gathered people

tening prayer and prayers for healing, to
name a few. The same kind of creativity can
be used for engaging Scripture: lectio divina,
responsive readings and even reenacting a
short story of the Bible. Singing, praying,
prophesying, confessing, sharing stories of
God's recent work and partaking in the
Lord's Table are ways to draw each other
into the presence of God.

At times, it is appropriate for the leader(s)
of a missional community to be front and
center, directing the group in specific topics
or tasks. But social space is meant to be
social! In order to take advantage of the
unique dynamics of social space, it's crucial
to find ways to be interactive. Developing a
consistent rhythm of communion as an extended family helps us decenter ourselves
and recenter our desires on God.

Community is a rhythm that encourages
us to share life together in the midst of a
fiercely individualistic world. People long for
community and belonging. One simple way
to cultivate togetherness as a gathered group
is through *availability* and *spontaneity*. Let's
take a quick look these.

The centripetal pull for belonging in community is the table. We see the appearance
of the table in many places throughout
Scripture. Meals are a pivotal part of the biblical narrative. And the table represents the
way God in Christ came near to us, the way
he made himself available to humanity. Jesus
dining with humanity symbolizes that we
will ultimately sit at the table and dine with
Christ in the new creation.

The table beckons people to sit a little
closer to each other than they normally do.
The flat surface of a table (or sitting in a
circle with a plate of food) symbolizes
equality and togetherness. The table brings
us together in the midst of frenzied activity
and isolation. We should cook food together,
bring dishes to pass around, welcome the
kids' noise, engage in Lenten practices, experiment with meals from other countries,
share about our week. Similarly, we might
make a big brunch, invite people of peace
and host it on the front lawn of a missional
community's house. Keep it low cost, make
space for others to participate and share the
burden of meal preparation.

The weekly rhythmic pattern of gathering
around the table molds our stubborn bodies
and stuffed schedules into a circle of community, fashioning something new as we
linger with others. The table stands for a
place of deep, divine belonging in the wilderness of fragmenting American life.

We also need to be together for the sole purpose of having a good time. Game nights, picnics in the park, karaoke, front-yard cookouts—any excuse can be used to get together and hang out. One way to do this is to attend public events together. If you can't have fun together, then don't be surprised when people have a hard time inviting others to hang out with the missional community. By making shared memories, we begin to feel a sense of safety and warmth. Over time, as we continue to participate in shared memories, individual memories begin to overlap and eventually form one large collective identity. The *I* starts to morph into a *we*, and a sense of belonging and identity is formed.

Co-mission is a rule and rhythm that guides our energies, bodies and resources toward being missionally present with the message of Jesus in a specific place. A missional context can be either a neighborhood (place) or network (people group). A neighborhood can be a subdivision, an apartment complex or even an arts district. A network can be any clearly defined people group, like a soccer league, single moms, skateboarders or gamers. Even a school can qualify as a network. A gathered community on mission creates spaces where people interact with the supernatural quality of Jesus followers. Here others can see and experience the life of an extended spiritual family who loves one another—and loves them.

Moving out on mission as spiritual family allows people to engage in mission without having to shoulder the weight of being a superstar evangelist. In a missional community people get to enjoy the safety of a group while being stretched toward others. This is an invitation to build meaningful moments outside the walls of a church worship service with those curious about Jesus and his followers. The following are some examples: hosting a monthly brunch, hosting a wine and cheese night, throwing a party (Halloween, Christmas, New Year's Eve), hosting a front-yard movie or concert night, spending consistent time at the local homeless shelter, helping people on moving days. We're not seeking to create *wow* experiences but *connecting* experiences.

It is nearly impossible to decide on our mission from a sterile classroom. In order to generate momentum, we need to learn the neighborhood or network we are sent to and experiment in co-mission activities regularly. Inviting people to hang out at social events is fine. However, we should also hold events that engage in social justice through serving in a tangible way. Or we could bring art and beauty to those we are sent to.

Organizing around communion, community and co-mission is kind of like building an exercise routine. Exercise is not about exhausting ourselves in one workout. Good exercise uses regular, incremental practices. Invite people into a rule and rhythm of life as the gathered people of God, which will shape them to dwell with God, dwell with each other and dwell in their neighborhood.

FORMATIONAL LEARNING

 Meta-Learning

- How are our thinking and actions reshaped when we start with who the church is rather than what the church does?

 Reflective Learning

- As you consider the nature and essence of the church as communion, community and co-mission, do you think any essential element is missing? If so, what?

- Which of the three essential elements of the church do you do well? Which is lacking? Which one intimidates you, and which excites you? Why?

 Experiential Learning

- What is one action your group can take to live into a rule and rhythm of life around communion, community and co-mission? How can you hold yourself accountable to this step? To help you develop a communal rule and rhythm of life, go to churchasmovement.com for a template.

6.2 Developing a Scattered Rule and Rhythm

What does the perfect person look like? In *Spiritual Fitness*, Allan Bloom says, "Students have powerful images of what a perfect body is, and pursue it incessantly. But . . . they no longer have any image of a perfect soul, and hence do not long to have one."[8] This is true not only for individuals but our society as a whole.

What does it mean to have a beautiful soul? Using the fruit of the Spirit from Galatians 5, Philip Kenneson provides a great picture. People with inner beauty cultivate a lifestyle of love in the midst of market-style exchanges; they cultivate a lifestyle of joy in the midst of manufactured desire; they cultivate peace in the midst of fragmentation; patience in the midst of productivity; kindness in the midst of self-sufficiency; goodness in the midst of self-help; faithfulness in the midst of impermanence; gentleness in the midst of aggression; and self-control in the midst of addiction.[9]

God desires to transform our lives so we reflect the character of Christ. But how does this happen?

Personal rule and rhythm of life. Not only do we need to be in a community with a rule and rhythm of life, but we need to develop a *scattered* rule and rhythm of life that we commit to in the context of our discipleship core.

While the communal, gathered rule and rhythm of life and the scattered rule and rhythm of life have much in common, the difference is that a communal rule and rhythm refers to the formal time of the entire missional community. So if the missional community meets once a week, it develops a rule of life for that once-a-week gathering. A scattered rule and rhythm of life is for personal use outside the weekly gathering (although, the scattered rule may involve other people in the missional community). Becoming like Jesus includes developing spiritual habits in our everyday lives as well as our collective lives (see fig. 6.6).

If you are new to living out a scattered rule and rhythm of life, as you develop it with your discipleship core don't try to start too many practices at once. Choose one key practice within the communion, community and co-mission framework. Feel free to improvise and approach your rule and rhythm in a grace-filled, flexible way. Keep a basic rhythm, but with sensitivity to the guidance of the Spirit—otherwise what was intended to be a gift may turn into a duty.

How does this work? Gather with your discipleship core and have each person share the scattered rule and rhythm of life they are committing to over the next season. Ideally

> A scattered rule and rhythm of life is for personal use outside the weekly gathering.

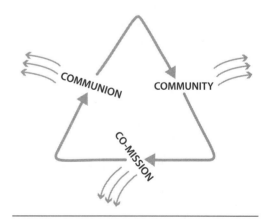

Figure 6.6. Rule and rhythm for a scattered people

each person will share the one concrete spiritual discipline they will practice. For example, I (JR) will share with my group the contents of table 6.1, saying, "This is going to be my scattered rule and rhythm of life for this coming year."

Table 6.1. Personal scattered rule and rhythm of life

Communion	Practice the presence of God daily and practice sabbath weekly.
Community	Meet with Joe and Matt weekly using the mutual discipleship tool.
Co-mission	Bless three people daily (at least one person outside of the church), and have a meal weekly with a non-Christian.

Note that the *rule* is a concrete practice, and the *rhythm* is how often you engage in that practice. *Sabbath* is the rule and *weekly* is the rhythm. Let's examine how I live into this particular rule and rhythm so you have a better idea on how to personalize your own scattered rule and rhythm of life. You can find additional resources for developing your scattered rule on the church as movement website.[10]

Communion. I like to practice communion in two broad ways. I seek to practice the presence of God daily, which is how I abide in Christ, and I also practice sabbath weekly. As a person who can easily live in my own strength, abiding in Christ is vital. Engaging in practices that help me *remain* in Christ is necessary. I get too much gratification from achieving; therefore sabbath helps me to *resist* the rat race. Abiding is about connecting. Sabbath is about disconnecting. Abiding is choosing to plug into the source of life. Sabbath is unplugging from everything that makes me restless and ragged and plugging into Christ.

Remaining in Christ. I choose to remain in Christ because Jesus says, "If you remain in me and I in you, you will bear much fruit" (Jn 15:5). If I don't abide, I realize that I will not be able to blossom as a person. A lack of abiding leads to a lack of flourishing and a lack of fruit. I cannot produce fruit on my own; it is produced only as I abide in Christ.

How do I abide? Jesus says, "If you remain in me and my words remain in you, ask whatever you wish, and it will be done for you" (Jn 15:7). Later in the same passage we are told, "Now remain in my love. If you keep my commands, you will remain in my love" (Jn 15:9-10). We *remain* in Christ through being nourished by his life-giving Word. We chew, eat and digest his Word. Through reading and meditating on his Word through Scripture and spiritual books, I practice his presence, knowing that what I eat and digest forms me.

The other way I like to practice God's presence daily is by being thankful throughout the day. I seek to be thankful in all things, knowing that even when God is pruning me, it is so I might flourish even more. So the moment I wake up, I thank God for the gift of a new day, for the fact I can see, taste, hear, smell, imagine and create. I take time to sit at the table with Christ and allow him to remind me that because of his sacrifice I am a child of God—I'm loved, forgiven, valued. The Counselor (Holy Spirit) lives within me. He's made me his ambassador to the world. He's given me a calling, gifts and purpose.

It's amazing how cultivating a thankful heart changes me. It changes how I see myself and how I see the world. Ingratitude makes my heart shrink and grow cold, but gratitude enlarges my heart. When we start the day by giving thanks and then find ways to thank and encourage others during the day, we see everything with new eyes.

Reading, singing and even writing psalms are ways I sometimes seek to abide in Christ. I read Scripture in order to hear God's voice and respond to the word he has for me. I sometimes pray in my room, on my roof, at the top of the mountain or in traffic jams. Of course, my prayers can be a little more raw in traffic, but at least they're honest.

I've also discovered some unconventional practices that help me commune with God. Hans Urs von Balthasar makes the case that the Spirit is able to guide us from art (beauty) to ethics (goodness) and then to theology (truth), since God first acts in creation, then in history and finally in Christ. So I've found ways to commune with God by appreciating beauty—through the fine arts (e.g., drawing, painting, sculpture, music and poetry), the visual arts (e.g., film, photography, performance and dance) or applied arts (e.g., architecture, design and fashion).

I have taken the six basic movements of lectio divina and developed what I call "cinema divina," which applies the six movements to film. As I explore how the six movements of the lectio work with film, I seek to apply them to the other forms of art. Spiritual practices can involve approaching some of our current, everyday practices with the intent of communing with God. The church as movement website will help you learn more about how I did this at the Sundance Film Festival.[11]

Resisting the rat race. We live in a hurried culture that encourages us to stay plugged in and busy. And too often this culture pulls me into the rat race. In *Working the Angles*, Eugene Peterson gives a beautiful description of unplugging from frantic noise by embracing sabbath. He says that sabbath is

> uncluttered time and space to distance ourselves from the frenzy of our own activities *so we can see what God has been and is doing.* If we do not regularly quit work for one day a week, we take ourselves far too seriously. The moral sweat pouring off our brows blinds us to the primal action of God in and around us.[12]

Ponder that for a while.

Marva Dawn provides four helpful concepts for a sabbath way of life. These have helped me to develop my sabbath in practical ways.

- *Ceasing*—ceasing work, ceasing productivity and accomplishment, ceasing anxiety, worry and tension, ceasing our trying to be God, ceasing our possessiveness, ceasing our enculturation and ceasing the humdrum and meaningless

- *Resting*—physical rest, spiritual rest, emotional rest, intellectual rest, social rest

- *Embracing*—intentionality, the values of Christian community, time instead of space, giving instead of requiring, our calling, shalom and our world

- *Feasting*—on the eternal, with music, with beauty, with a meal with others, with affection and with festival[13]

I have found that sabbath is a crucial life-giving practice, especially for pioneers and community leaders. Do you rest from work or work from a place of rest? The latter perspective is informed by a rich understanding of sabbath.

Community. The community part of my rule and rhythm is fairly simple. I meet with two trusted friends weekly and use the mutual discipleship tool that Dan took us through in section 4.4. Essentially it is sharing what God is doing in me, around me and through me. It's a place for me to practice confession, encouragement and reconciliation. For me, confession is not only sharing where I have fallen short but also where I walked with God. Confession involves sharing the good and the bad, my troubles and my dreams. It's practicing vulnerability. This is a life-giving space, where I'm able to practice giving and receiving acceptance. If we want to become more like Christ, there is no substitute for having spiritual friends in intimate space.

> Everyone has a rule and rhythm of life. Is yours forming you to be more like Christ?

Co-mission. The third part of my scattered rule and rhythm is in the area of co-mission. There are two parts of this rule for me: (1) Blessing three people each day, with at least one person being outside of the church, and (2) once a week having a meal with someone who does not self-identify as a Christian.

Finding ways to bless people daily has helped to cultivate a generous spirit in me. Sometimes I write a short, encouraging letter to someone. I often express a kind word to people I see at the coffee shop, my apartment complex or other places I travel. I especially seek to bless people who seem to be having a difficult day. I like taking the challenge of blessing those who are unkind to me, because I recognize that God can use me as the agent of transformation in their lives. Remember that as Christ-followers we are called to bless those who curse us.

Taking time to meet weekly with people who don't self-identify as Christians is a practical way to build strong relationships with agnostics, atheists and others who don't know Christ. Sometimes I like to bring one of my Christian friends along, which usually enriches the experience.

These are examples of what it means for one person to live into a scattered rule and rhythm of life. It's developing a personalized rule (spiritual habits) and rhythm (frequency) formed around communion, community and co-mission, which helps us to become more like Jesus. Everyone has a rule and rhythm of life. Is yours forming you to be more like Christ?

FORMATIONAL LEARNING

 Meta-Learning

- How would you describe a beautiful soul, or what it means to be fully human?

Reflective Learning

- Would you say your current life has an intentional rule and rhythm that shapes you toward communion, community and co-mission?

- Which of the three—communion, community and co-mission—do you find yourself gravitating toward? Which one do you find intimidating?

 Experiential Learning

- Develop a scattered rule and rhythm of life with at least one concrete practice within the framework of communion, community and co-mission. Share it with your discipleship core.

6.3 Four Spaces of Belonging

A new field called interpersonal neurobiology draws on one of the great discoveries of our era: the brain is constantly rewiring itself. What we pay the most attention to literally rewires our brains. The most dramatic rewiring is based on the quality of our relational bonds. As imaging studies by the UCLA neuroscientist Naomi Eisenberger show, for better or for worse we are social beings.[14]

Our brains' neurons *tether together* based on how much care we give and receive from a social structure. If there is minimal *giving* and *receiving*, then our brains change. Reciprocal loving relationships alter our brains significantly. As the brain registers communal relationships, it extends its notion of self to include others. Instead of the slender pronoun *I*, a plural self-image emerges. The brain rewires for a new self-understanding, a new identity that includes others, moving from *I* to *we*. Science attests to the fact that God has designed us for community. *Community* may be a buzzword, but when the church drifts from communal ways, we work against the way God designed our brains.

Being a disciple requires living in community. When Jesus delivers the Sermon on the Mount he does not individualize the kingdom of God but infuses it with intensely communal sensibilities. Dietrich Bonhoeffer stated that the Sermon on the Mount makes the invisible visible, clarifying what a community following Jesus should look like on earth. Something beautiful and countercultural is being brought into existence.

> Each space—intimate, personal, social and public— is designed to deliver something the other spaces can't deliver by themselves.

The church as movement does not find its power in individuality but in interdependence. Individualism offers the illusion that our choices, beliefs and actions happen best in the small space of our own will and desires. This is an illusion. For better or worse the New Testament charges us to live our beliefs *together*.

Moving from independence to interdependence is vital to starting and sustaining mis-sional-incarnational communities. Small group programs are not enough; community is at the center of what it means to be the church.

Since community is central to the witness of God in Christ, a discipler must be aware of how people gather and relationally orient themselves. We can't be haphazard about the architecture of community. Discipleship takes shape in the context of layers of community.

With the help of sociologist Edward T. Hall, Joseph Myers identifies four kinds of spaces in which we find a sense of belonging: intimate, personal, social and public.[15] Each space is designed to deliver something the other spaces can't deliver by themselves. Cultivating a movemental church includes recovering these spaces and prioritizing community as a way of being the missional church.

Let's examine how each space can help the church recover something essential for the future (see fig. 6.7).

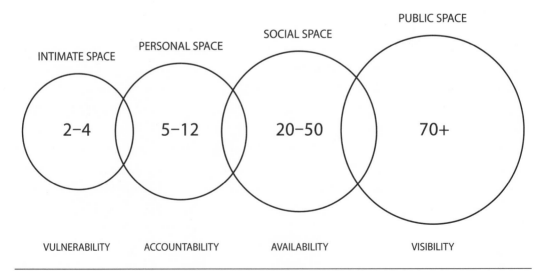

Figure 6.7. The four spaces

Public space: visibility. Public space begins to form in gatherings of seventy or more people. This space allows people to share a common experience in a larger setting. Public worship services are a good example of this. If a single church doesn't have these numbers, then a regional or citywide gathering can provide this same experience. We see this taking place when New Testament house churches occasionally gathered in larger places (e.g., the temple, a synagogue or a large house). In 1 Corinthians, for example, the apostle Paul speaks of an event in which "the whole church" came together (e.g., 1 Cor 14:23).

In public space, communication is often a one-way experience. One person communicates while the rest listen. Gathering in a group this size makes eye contact and genuine interaction difficult. These kinds of limitations determine the kind of experience public space can provide. We recommend people adjust their relational expectations for this space by using the term *visibility*. In a group this large we can expect to see and be seen. Much like going to a concert, we don't expect to have a conversation with the band or to be known by the rest of the audience.

Public space has benefits and limitations. Some of the benefits include public proclamation of the good news, which often brings encouragement for people in social space to be on mission, as well as help some come to faith. Public space helps the community to understand that God's truth is public truth. Jesus, as an itinerant preacher, drew large crowds as he shared the good news outside on a mountain or by the seashore. He typically didn't give a three-point sermon on how to live a better life. Instead

he spoke in riddles and parables about a kingdom that challenged current reigning kings and kingdoms. Parables are an indirect way to share a politically subversive message. When Jesus spoke in public, his message was received well by those who were left poor and abused by the system, but not too well by those who benefited from the corrupt system. Jesus spoke truth to power in parables, igniting a revolution. After Jesus spoke in his hometown, they were ready to throw him off a cliff. Paul also spoke about the kingdom of God with passion and incited riots. Too often we give talks that end in "Nice sermon, Pastor."

Public space is vital for movement, but we need to use it more like Jesus and Paul did. We think there is a need to reimagine public space so that it fulfills some of its original purposes instead of becoming a place that makes people into passive religious consumers.[16]

Public space is designed to deliver certain things; an experience of bonded community is not one of them. When people come to public space, they often want to maintain some distance to observe without being accountable. If we override this by trying to facilitate genuine interaction, it's often experienced as unnatural. As much as we might want people to experience genuine community, it's inappropriate to expect some emotional needs to be filled in this venue. If we expect intimate relationships to form in public space, we'll be disappointed. In modern expressions of the church, public space has typically received the most attention (for example, staffing and event preparation). This has created the attractional church, where the majority of resources are showcased in order to grow attendance at the public space. Churches typically spend 85 percent of their budget on this space. This is the typical "come and see" approach to mission, which can harvest some low-hanging fruit—that is, people who are attracted to what the church provides them. This space can be missional if it helps to reshape people's imagination and they consequently inhabit God's story and process their own life through that lens.

Public space often backfires when we try to reverse engineer it. We might try to attract people with dynamic preaching and worship in order to get them interested in community, mission and discipleship. This is a genuine challenge in a consumer society. Though public space is vitally important, it isn't wise to attempt to attract the curious through the worship gathering. As Neil Cole famously says, "What you win people with, you win them to."[17]

> Social space is small enough for people to experience authentic community, but big enough to mobilize people for missional movement.

Social space: availability. Social space is what the New Testament calls *oikos*, a Greek term typically translated "house" or "household." However, don't confuse the Greco-Roman household with our post–Industrial Revolution notions of household. In our culture a household is typically Dad, Mom and 2.5 kids. In Greco-Roman society the household was an extended family that included close and distant relatives, servants and employees of the family business, as well as friends of the family.

Oikos is the basic building block of society and its close network of relationships. It typically included twenty to fifty people. The average membership of a New Testament household church was this size. These communities gathered as the body of Christ in a variety of homes throughout the city. This social space provides the most fruitful environment for community formation and incarnational mission. This is a tangibly close relational space.

Social space is small enough for people to experience authentic community, but big enough to mobilize people for missional movement. Relationally, it is where people start moving toward a more genuine experience of community. Here, people are given the opportunity to experience the incarnation as they encounter the body of Christ. Contextually our society is riddled with isolation and individualism. Social space is where a community as mission is poised to become a signpost of the kingdom, making fresh space for diversity, faithful love and one anotherness.

The glue that holds the group together in social space is not a platform performance but gathering around a common missional context (neighborhood or network) and creating an environment where authentic relationship building can take place. We (JR and Dan) call this process "relational tethering" (see section 6.5).

The missional-incarnational community (social space) in the local context functions as the basic building blocks of a congregation. In this approach, public space (larger events) provides inspiration and momentum by gathering the stories of ministry and mission taking place through the network of scattered communities. Relationally, social space provides *availability*.

As people orient themselves in this mid-sized group (social space), they can expect to encounter people who are available for more relational interaction. Visibility is still present, but a new relational proximity has emerged. Availability means being within reach relationally, having access that is not available in the public space. In social space people explore closer connections and find affinities within the group. We long for this type of relational availability, one that remembers names, celebrates milestones, cares for illnesses, laughs over meals, allows kids to play, affirms each other's presence and makes room for each person to make a contribution. It creates an extended family people can tether to.

Even though social space is the optimal vehicle for communities to engage in mission, it too has inherent limitations. While most expectations for relational availability can be filled here, vulnerability and accountably are not genuinely accessible in this space. For example, the practice of confession (being vulnerable with others about our heart's deepest wounds or weaknesses) typically doesn't work well in public and social spaces. This inherent reality makes other essential practices, like accountability, equally challenging. It is nearly impossible to hold a group of twenty to fifty people accountable.

Some who have not inhabited a social space for a long period of time might expect everybody to be vulnerable and to be their best friend, which is not relationally possible. Without knowing this, expectations for this kind of relational interaction will be dashed.

Personal space: accountability. Pursuing deeper, more personal relationships happen best in a group of six to twelve people. Personal space is the primary setting for discipleship. Here, we invite others to join us in practicing a way of life where we embody (flesh out) Jesus in our neighborhoods and networks, taking a journey together to fulfill God's mission. This smaller space moves us beyond the intellectual assimilation of ideas and into a reflective and responsive space.

In personal space we invite people into a rule and rhythm of life, into wholeness, overcoming ruinous habits and building healthier ones together. With fewer people in this space, eye contact and physical proximity happen more readily. The opportunity to dive into deeper relational commitment starts to take shape. Certain interactions, conversations and languages start to form, which would make a spiritual seeker uncomfortable. Appropriate relational expectations in this space revolve around accountability and vulnerability. The smaller the group is, the more we expect from each other. We expect follow-through on our promises, consistency in our presence, accountability for our actions and vulnerability with our words.

Personal space functions best within the larger sphere of social space; in fact, it is important to structurally link discipleship with community formation and mission. So the discipleship core becomes the red-hot center of the missional-incarnational community. While we learn by instruction in personal space (discipleship core), we learn by imitation in social space (missional-incarnational community). This is vital to understand for movement. Experiencing a healthy sense of belonging happens best when we commit to a smaller cluster of people who also belong to a larger group and who share a common mission.

Intimate space: vulnerability. Intimate space is where we share experiences, feelings and thoughts in a group of two to four. Intimate relationships occur when another person knows the naked truth about us, without us feeling ashamed. This is similar to the space Jesus shared with Peter, James and John. This intimacy often grows out of relationships formed in social and personal space.

Intimate space might occur when a person gathers with a couple of people for coffee to continue a conversation and process experiences in other spaces. Ideally intimate space (mutual discipleship triads) are a part of the rule and rhythm of life in the discipleship core.

One size does not fit all. There is nothing more frustrating than trying to produce certain kinds of relational experiences from a group not designed to deliver them. When helping people navigate their journey into experiencing community, it's important for them to recognize the nature—the benefits and their inherent limitations—of these four spaces. This means helping people set appropriate relational expectations for each space.

The heart of multiplication. It's important for each church to ask, which space are we seeking to multiply?

While movement-oriented churches will eventually multiply all four spaces, it's important for the leaders to decide, and every active member of the congregation to know, how they will multiply disciples and missional communities. Multiplying discipleship cores in personal space is the primary way to cultivate leaders who in turn can lead new missional-incarnational communities. Multiplying missional-incarnational communities through social space allows disciples to reach new neighborhoods and networks. Future church plants potentially can emerge from these new missional communities. By recognizing the four spaces and their respective strengths and limitations, we can focus appropriate time and energy on the generative potential in each space.

FORMATIONAL LEARNING

 Meta-Learning

- How did Jesus use the four spaces in his ministry to people?

Reflective Learning

• Which of the four spaces is most comfortable for you? Why?

• Which of the four spaces do you find most difficult? Why?

• How can you use social space for mission?

• How can you directly link your discipleship core (personal space) to social space (missional community) for community and mission?

 Experiential Learning

• What is one step you can take to organize and gather people toward social space? What are the hurdles? Where are there possibilities?

6.4 Beyond Mission, Vision and Values

As we start, sustain and multiply missional-incarnational communities, we'll soon find that we have a church on our hands. And if we want to develop mission-shaped disciples who live in the world for the sake of their neighbors in the way of Christ, then we not only need to articulate our mission, vision and values, but we need to consider what it means to cultivate a missional culture.

Leaders create culture, and the culture recreates the congregation. In fact, the culture of a congregation is like gravity. It has the power to pull people down to their base instincts or help them live up to their redemptive potential. Every missional community has a culture, whether named or not. It is vital for the discipleship core to reflect on and record the kind of culture they want to live into and perpetuate. The more detailed, the better. The unspoken aspects of our culture often deform us without our knowing it.

The acronym LAAMMPS stands for the different elements that make up culture (see table 6.2). Let's start with an overview of where we are going and then double back on each of the components that make up the culture of our missional-incarnational community.

Jesus says, "You are the light of the world." And the apostle John writes,

> When I turned to see who was speaking to me, I saw seven gold lampstands. And standing in the middle of the lampstands was someone like the Son of Man. He was wearing a long robe with a gold sash across his chest. His head and hair were white like wool, as white as snow. And his eyes were like flames of fire. His feet were like polished bronze refined in a furnace, and his voice thundered like mighty ocean waves. He held seven stars in his right hand, and a sharp two-edged sword came from his mouth. And his face was like the sun in all its brilliance. . . . The seven stars are the angels of the seven churches, and the seven lampstands are the seven churches. (Rev 1:12-16, 20 NLT)

Table 6.2. The elements of missional culture: LAAMMPS

Language	What does the language of the congregation reveal?
Artifacts	What are the cultural goods that we have created to use, and how do they shape us as a congregation?
Assumptions	What are the faith assumptions and values that shape our decisions and actions?
Mission	What is God calling us to do?
Marks	What does it mean to be faithful and fruitful in God's mission?
Practices	What are the core practices we are engaging in?
Strategy	How will we fulfill God's calling together?

As we continue to read John's letter, we see how Jesus reveals the strengths and weaknesses of the seven different churches, which are called lampstands. He sheds light on the soul of these congregations, calling them to be faithful.

The ultimate goal in working through LAAMMPS is that our communities might be found faithful. For as Jesus said, "I'm putting you on a light stand. Now that I've put you there on a hilltop, on a light stand—shine! Keep open house; be generous with your lives. By opening up to others, you'll prompt people to open up with God, this generous Father in heaven" (Mt 5:15-16 *The Message*). Every new missional-incarnational community ought to be aware of these seven elements. In this section we will use the words *church* or *congregation* more often. These words refer to multiple missional communities that gather together weekly, monthly or every other week. It's a network of missional-incarnational communities.

Language: What does the language of the congregation you serve reveal? "'Let there be light,' and there was light" (Gen 1:3). Words create worlds. Words bring life and death. Words shape and form us. Words are at the heart of any culture. Lesslie Newbigin observes,

> Culture is the sum total ways of living developed by a group of human beings and handed on from generation to generation. *Central to culture is language. The language of a people provides the means by which they express their way of perceiving things and of coping with them.* Around that center one would have to group their visual and musical arts, their technologies, their law and their social and political organization. And one must also include in culture, as fundamental to any culture, a set of beliefs, experiences and practices that seek to grasp and express the ultimate nature of things, that which gives shape and meaning to life, that which claims final loyalty.[18]

When someone says, "Let's go to church," it reveals a lack of understanding of the nature of the church. The church is the *people* of God. Church is not something we

go to, it is something we are. We go to a weekly gathering, we attend a service, but *we* are the church.[19]

If we want to live into church as movement, we need to recapture ways to motivate the entire body of Christ to live out their calling. That means, in most contexts, that we ought to eliminate words like *volunteers* and use biblical words to describe the people of God, words like *sent ones, priests, saints, missionaries, ambassadors, ministers*. *Volunteer* implies that we can choose to be an active part of the body or not. But if we are believers, we *are* part of the body and we need to live according to God's design. Being a part of the body is not an option. In addition, our identities shape who we become.

The following are some questions to consider regarding language.

- What words are important in the culture of our missional community?

- What words do we want to leave behind?

- What words do we want to empty of meaning and fill with new meaning?

- What words are so familiar that they no longer have any power?

Artifacts: What are the cultural goods we have created or make use of, and how do they shape us as a congregation? Artifacts are the cultural goods we create. Newbigin mentioned musical arts, technology and law as different aspects of culture. Each of these are created cultural goods that shape us. Some of the artifacts integral to our community have been handed down to us, the Holy Scriptures for example. The narrative of this divine-human artifact shapes every aspect of our lives.

As you work through the following questions, you will analyze the cultural web that shapes who you are as a community and how you do ministry. Your website, your gathering space, the songs you sing and your liturgy are artifacts that shape you as a people. List some of the artifacts that you use or have created, and think about how they might shape you.

- What visual icons do we use to represent us?

- What pieces of literature do we use to help people understand us?

- What tools do we use that are synonymous with our values?

- What does our website reveal about us?

- Where do people find our mission statement, vision, values, practices, strategy and definition of success? Are they easily accessible?

Assumptions: What are the faith assumptions and values that shape our decisions and actions? Faith assumptions reveal what we believe about God, reality and ourselves. Values describe what is most important and distinct about our community of faith.[20] Our assumptions and values help guide us when we are discerning both small and large decisions. We have found that when a discipleship core doesn't take the time to articulate these, it can be a cause of unneeded tension and strife. We've seen churches split because leaders failed to identify early enough the underlying assumptions about ministry and reality. Typically our assumptions surface when we need to make decisions about what to do or how to do something. Taking the time to articulate these faith assumptions helps us maintain the unity of the Spirit as we live on mission.

Some churches take a "believe, behave and belong" approach to getting people involved in the life of the church. In other words, before people can belong, they need to believe certain doctrines and behave in certain ways.

Others hold to a "belong, behave and believe" approach, in which we give people a place to belong, guide them into a different way of living, which in time starts to shape what they believe. If these underlying assumptions are not understood and articulated, they have the potential to create unneeded conflict as we live on mission.

We reveal some of our faith assumptions throughout this book. Our faith assumptions shape how we see the church. We see the church as a movement, as opposed to a Christian industrial complex. We have assumptions about what movement is and how movement takes place. A number of our faith assumptions can be found in chapter five, where we discuss how our assumptions about God shape our approach to being community and how we do mission. The following are questions to ponder as a discipleship core:

- What are the six to eight core values of our community?

- What are our assumptions about God, and how do those assumptions shape our practices?

- What underlying assumptions do we have about discipleship and mission?

- What are our assumptions about who leads?

- What are our assumptions about how to relate to one another?

Mission: What is God calling us to do? We don't invent our mission; we receive it from God as we listen to his voice through the Spirit-breathed Scriptures. Our job is to find ways to articulate what God is calling us to in such a way that it shapes us well. A mission statement could be a few well-crafted words or a simple statement articulating the overarching purpose of our existence as a community of faith.

> If you don't define success, or what it means to be faithful and fruitful, others will.

I remember the first time I (JR) surfed across the church website of Theophilus, a church in Portland, Oregon. Their mission statement was communicated through three symbols: a tent, a table and a tear. That was a creative and memorable way to articulate mission. The *tent* (or tabernacle) represented worship, the *table* represented community and fellowship, and the tear represented compassion, the good they sought to do in the neighborhood.

The mission statement of Trinity Grace in New York captures a holistic gospel and articulates a missional theology: "Joining God in the renewal of all things." This mission statement demonstrates the understanding that a missionary God is at the center of the universe, and that we join him on mission, not the other way around. It also speaks to God's future, when he makes all things new (Rev 21:5). Thus, if we join God on his mission, we will seek to live the future in the present.

- Have we crafted a succinct statement about the specificity of our mission?
- Does our mission capture the imagination?
- Does our mission seem grounded?

- How do we help people remember and internalize our mission?

Marks: What does it mean to be faithful and fruitful in God's mission? If you don't define *success*, or what it means to be faithful and fruitful, others will. Defining the ends always shapes the means. We need to move beyond merely counting bodies, buildings and dollars if we want to be movemental.

Identifying the marks of the church ought to involve both stats and stories; the way we measure things is not neutral. As Joseph Myers says,

> We measure that which we perceive to be important. That which we measure will become important and will guide our process. That which we do not measure will become less important. So measurement has dynamic power over the journey and the results. It is not neutral. Our way of measuring is not a neutral tool that simply tells us what there is to see. No, our way of measuring influences the facts in a way that has a profound effect on our perception of reality.[21]

If we want to be movemental, we should not only count how many people come to a weekly gathering but consider how many missional-incarnational communities we are starting and how many churches we are planting. If we value discipleship and helping people become more like Christ, we might want to ask how many discipleship groups are happening in our congregation and how these disciples are displaying the fruit of the Spirit in their lives.

The first measurement is statistical, but how do you measure the fruit of the Spirit in people's lives? Is this important? It's difficult to measure this by statistics but easier to measure by stories. We need to value stories, stories about radical hospitality, stories of forgiveness and stories of how people have learned to love their enemies.

How would it shape us as leaders if instead of just asking how many people come to our church service, we ask each other, what are some stories of the way our congregation is helping to see personal transformation and transformation in the neighborhood?

Kevin and Christine Sweeny, who founded Imagine Church in Honolulu, went through the first V3 learning cohort. We love how they define the marks of their community. They identify what faithfulness and fruitfulness look like for the individuals who are a part of their community, for the community itself and for the mission God has called them to.

When it comes to *individuals*, they consider how many people understand and are on the route to radical transformation. They look at who is living risk-taking lives, who is living intentional and sacrificial lives as the result of trusting in God. They look at how many people are growing in self-awareness, who is learning to be present and experiencing conversion to Christ and his kingdom.

In regard to *community*, they look at how

intentional people are in building relationships, discipling others, embodying hospitality, carrying each other's burdens, and celebrating and enjoying life together.

Related to *mission*, they examine how many people have a sustained presence with the poor, how many are actively involved with the cultural-artistic life of the neighborhood, how present they are in their community, in what ways they are loving their neighbors concretely, including new people in community. They also look at the ways people are bearing witness to Christ interpersonally.

Both *what* we measure and *how* we measure are important. If we ignore statistics, it's likely we don't have systems in place to build capacity. If we ignore stories, it's likely we aren't measuring the heart of what we are doing. We need to measure both stories and stats.

- How do we assess our values?
- How do we regularly look at faithfulness and fruitfulness?

Practices: What core practices are we engaging in? While our values help us discern what we do, practices give teeth to our values. Practices describe the concrete spiritual disciplines we engage in so that as individuals and communities we move toward the marks we have defined. This requires writing down our gathered rule and rhythm as well as our scattered rule and rhythm of life. Solid practices reshape our hearts and lives toward God and his kingdom.

> Both *what* we measure and *how* we measure are important. If we ignore statistics, it's likely we don't have systems in place to build capacity. If we ignore stories, it's likely we aren't measuring the heart of what we are doing.

- What does the gathered rule and rhythm of our missional community look like?

- What is my scattered rule and rhythm of life, and have I shared it with my discipleship core?

- How is our gathered and scattered rule and rhythm of life helping people become more like Jesus in character and ministry?

- How do we let new people become aware of our practices?

Strategy: How will we fulfill God's calling together? A missional church that values movement will remove bottlenecks and create structures where good things can run wild. Movements occur with a well-defined strategy that is reproducible at every level. Structure must submit to the Spirit, who is consistently calling us to cross boundaries and include others. This means that we need to nuance our strategy based on our context.

When developing our strategy we need to ask, What is the core element we are reproducing? Is it easily reproducible? Will it lead toward movement? While every church is uniquely based on the gifts, passions and experiences of the team—the context in which we do ministry, theology and underlying assumptions—it is important to have a strategy that values communion, community and co-mission.

Jesus' strategy involved confiding in three, training twelve, mobilizing seventy and confounding the crowds through his parables and provocative stories. This is why, no matter what model of church we decide on, *multiplying missional communities (social space) through our discipleship core (personal space)* best enables movement.

- Can I draw out our strategy?

- Is our strategy too abstract?

- Who should know our strategy?

FORMATIONAL LEARNING

 Meta-Learning

- Why is it important to work through your cultural web?

 Reflective Learning

- Which of the different elements of the cultural web are you most clear about, and which one are you most confused about?

- What does it mean to be faithful and fruitful, and does your strategy help or hinder you from reaching those missional marks?

 Experiential Learning

- Go though each of the seven elements with your discipleship core team and record some thoughts to the questions dealing with language, artifacts, assumptions, mission, marks, practices and strategy. See churchasmovement.com for a worksheet.

Part 4

//DOING

7

Community Formation

It is possible to put together the semblance of community "a little of this and a little of that" and end up with a self-selected substitute community.

CHRISTINE POHL, *LIVING INTO COMMUNITY*

Community is the container that carries God's good news into the world, yet very few of us have experience with living into the shared life of community. So we have to learn about, experience and practice community. Disciples who covenant to a rule and rhythm of life cultivate a hospitable space for others to belong to and a platform for creating a missional-incarnational community. Community brings out of us new ways of relating to each other. Our beauty and brokenness converge as we seek to be the sent people of God together.

Connecting to Movement

The church as movement has three main components: a discipleship core, a dependable community space and a particular neighborhood or network to which God has called them. In this chapter we're focusing on the second component by diving into the mechanics of community. A community well-oiled with love, listening, hospitality and grace-filled friendships will multiply, birthing new communities. An unwelcoming, judgmental, boring and missionless community will fizzle out. A movement needs the energy that a vibrant community provides.

7.1 The Common Life

Are you a fan of *The Walking Dead*? I (Dan) find the show fascinating from a sociological perspective. The world is overrun by zombies, but community is on center stage. The biggest danger to the survivors is not necessarily the zombies but other people. One of our church elders recently said that the show is an illustration of how community affects mission. One of the wiser characters of the show says, "It's not the walkers out there that will kill us; *it's what's going on in here.*" The survivors' self-destructing relationships erode their ability to stay focused on the mission at hand. The mission suffers because their community is anemic. Community is the pod that carries mission.[1]

To understand community we must unpack the raw material of the early church's social existence. After the powerful kingdom interruption of Pentecost, the church became a movement scattered into small household clusters.[2] These communities gathered in pockets throughout the city, becoming the body of Christ in that place. The explosive quality of the gospel of Jesus was that Jews and Gentiles, women and men, slaves and free persons were being knit together to declare something with profound social implications.

A new temple was being constructed, but it wasn't made of stones. Rather it was a relational network of communities illuminating the centrality of love. It left its imprint on every facet of their social existence. The significance of this cannot be underestimated.

They did not have well-rehearsed worship bands, magnetic preachers and packaged Bible study material to buffer their church life. There was little to hide behind. This is why Paul was concerned that the churches quickly mature as unified communities of self-sacrificial love. To the church in Colosse he says, "Clothe yourselves with compassion, kindness, humility, gentleness and patience. Bear with each other and forgive one another. . . . And over all these virtues put on love, which binds them all together in perfect unity" (Col 3:12-14). He also tells the house church in Thessalonica to "make your love increase and overflow for each other" (1 Thess 3:12). To the church in Corinth he says the chief fruit of the Spirit is love (1 Cor 13:13). The story of God's intervening love cannot be communicated well without community.

God is gathering a people who, moving beyond their own self-oriented inclinations, are learning to love one another as Christ has loved us. The church cannot storm the gates of hell by gathering around consumer needs. A shared life and the shared story that Jesus is King are its rallying points. Christian community *is* the church. It's not a subset of the church or a program of the church but the concrete expression of God's body on the earth.

> The church cannot storm the gates of hell by gathering around consumer needs. A shared life and the shared story that Jesus is King are its rallying points.

Individualism. For many Christians faith is about "God and me." We are passionate about our own spirituality. Everything about God, Scripture, heaven, worship, happiness, missions and the like is seen through the perspective of our individual connection with God: "my hope," "my sin," "my walk," "my witness." Western Christianity has embraced individualism. Our hyperindividuality is taken for granted, and we assume it is blessed by God.

The sobering truth is that God doesn't primarily relate to us as individuals. When Jesus taught his disciples to pray, he used plural terms: "our Father," "give us," "forgive us," "lead us," "deliver us." However, we filter Scripture through individualistic lenses. When we come across the pronoun *you* in our Bibles we assume it means "me," individually. For example, look at 1 Corinthians 3:16: "Do you not know that you are God's temple and that God's Spirit dwells in you?" (ESV). In this passage Paul is *not* describing each believer as their own mini-temple; rather *you* is plural—you the "community." Together we are God's temple; God's Spirit dwells in us, *collectively*. This is not a small nuance. Everything changes when we grasp the power of *we* over *me*.

The church as industrial complex often leads by satisfying consumer needs. This inadvertently places the self at the center of a church's existence. The church as movement leads with the beacon of community, which echoes our deepest longings while simultaneously calling us out of self-centeredness.

The common life. The church as movement starts with a discipleship core, hospitality with others, presence in the neighborhood and an inviting spirit. This produces a life-giving social space. The common life of a community is most observable in this space. In community we can experience the privilege of being ourselves in the presence of others. Henri Nouwen says, "Community is the fruit of our capacity to make the interests of others more important than our own."[3]

The community stands as a protest against the tyranny of individualism and points to the renewed world under the reign of King Jesus.

> The community stands as a protest against the tyranny of individualism and points to the renewed world under the reign of King Jesus.

To be rooted in community is to understand that it is "not good for [us] to be alone" (Gen 2:18). We are floating, disembodied spirits when we are not tethered to an embodied spiritual family in a physical place. Because we are so conditioned to individualism, we need to labor against our inner conditioning in order to benefit from community. Choosing community means living with greater meaning.

We must create a pathway to community: the formation of a common life. Common life is the overlap between our individual existence and our collective experience. Jean Vanier defined common life as "a group of women or men who have been called together by the Holy Spirit to share their lives with one another in order to live a devoted life of service to Jesus Christ."[4] The biblical foundation of this definition comes from Acts: "They devoted themselves to the apostles' teaching and to fellowship, to the breaking of bread and to prayer. . . . All the believers were together and had everything in common. They sold property and possessions to give to anyone who had need" (Acts 2:42, 44-45).

For centuries women and men have turned to Acts to find what it means to live the common life of community. There is a close connection between the quality of our life in common and the quality of our Christian witness to the world. When we are living well in community, it shows in the integrity of our personal and communal testimony to Jesus. When we are not living community life well, it is obvious to all.

Common life isn't a given, it's a goal, a Christian task to be accomplished in mutual commitment, patience and love. In common life we learn that whatever we experience, we experience together in Christ. We are fragile vessels. In isolation our sufferings are intolerable, but in community we can taste the promise of the resurrection.

Recently, a missional-incarnational community I (Dan) visited in New York hosted a storyteller's night. Story after story highlighted people's journeys from isolation to community. One young woman's story stuck out to me. Monica, in her early thirties, thought of herself as well connected, but she still felt the sadness of isolation. Then she entered into the rhythms of this missional community and began to experience life differently.

At one point she found herself suddenly laid off from work and unable to pay her bills. She grew anxious and started to slip into depression. While her previous friends offered condolences, her missional community took her in when she couldn't pay her rent. They drove her to work when she couldn't make her car payments. She was welcomed to and included in everyone's dining rooms when she couldn't afford groceries. She wept, sharing that in the past when she was weak she would hide it and pretend she was strong, but something shifted while receiving love from this new community. She learned to be weak.

The common life of her community gave her space to get back on her feet while she was in a weak place. She was met concretely by the love of Christ in community life (see fig. 7.1). Many paths can be laid to create a common life, but the main walking trail is availability.

Availability for common life. Availability in community requires constancy, making space for each other to depend on each other. A

good parallel is that my (Dan's) ten-year-old son and I regularly go out for breakfast on Monday mornings. No matter how crazy the week is, we join for breakfast and laugh and talk about superheroes. This helps me stay faithful to my son and gives my son someone dependable to lean on. Patterns of availability

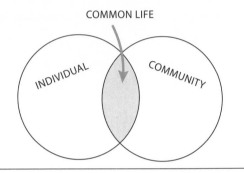

Figure 7.1. Common life

in community function the same way, allowing us to depend on each other. We can make new commitments to be available through regularly shared meals, babysitting each other's kids, working on each other's house projects, sharing tools, shopping, reading and playing together, enjoying holidays together, cooking together and even moving closer to one another. This, of course, takes time. We have to massage availability into our overly individualistic DNA.

Yet when we taste the beauty of being available, we renew imaginations. Sit down and talk about the patterns of availability you want reflected in your day, your week, your month, your year. Cultivating common life requires a pattern of availability. We often fear patterns because they hem us in and challenge our freedom. But with grace our patterns can be malleable. Our forgetfulness and failures need the grace of others in our community. However, if we desire a common life, patterns of availability are a necessity.

FORMATIONAL LEARNING

 Meta-Learning

- Why has God made community central to his mission?

- Why has the church drifted away from community as its primary way of organizing?

 Reflective Learning

- What has been your experience with community?

- What aspects of forming a common life make you nervous, uncertain or excited?

 Experiential Learning

- Sit down with your group to discern how you can cultivate availability. What concrete ways can you work toward forming a common life?

7.2 The Shared Table

Jesus reveals something important when he says, "The Son of Man came eating and drinking" (Lk 7:34). Robert Karris, a New Testament scholar, says, "In Luke's Gospel Jesus is either going to a meal, at a meal, or coming from a meal."[5] No wonder his enemies accused him of being "a glutton and a drunkard." This accusation echoes Deuteronomy 21:18-21: "If someone has a stubborn and rebellious son . . . his father and mother shall take hold of him and bring him to the elders at the gate of his town. They shall say to the elders, 'This son of ours is stubborn and rebellious. He will not obey us. He is a glutton and a drunkard.' Then all the men of his town are to stone him to death. You must purge the evil from among you." The Pharisees are implying that Jesus deserved to be punished because of his meal practices.

While Jesus' sermons certainly incited hostility, his wining and dining with "sinners" bothered the guardians of the law. Many expected Jesus to come with force, defeating God's enemies and vindicating his people. Instead he shared meals. We witness the radically different way Jesus sees people by who he chose to dine with.

Rewiring family. Jesus modeled the kingdom of God by the way he relaxed with others at table, circumventing the typical first-century use of table fellowship to communicate that God was coming near. Feasting at the table was primarily for members of one's family, which at that time meant the extended family. Yet Jesus was found feasting with others:

> While Jesus was having dinner at Levi's house, many tax collectors and sinners were eating with him and his disciples, for there were many who followed him. When the teachers of the law who were Pharisees saw him eating with the sinners and tax collectors, they asked his disciples: "Why does he eat with tax collectors and sinners?" (Mk 2:15-16)

Jesus is using the enfleshed practice at the table to immerse his disciples in a new social order of family, a kingdom family. In Greek culture, beyond the familial household, one might dine with the other members of one's district, class or social origins. Freeborn Romans, for example, did not dine with former slaves. Aristocrats invited other aristocrats to dine with them. Social rules of dining mirrored the sectarian structures of the first century in both Jewish and Greco-Roman life. Who one ate with was a serious matter.[6]

Yet Jesus uses the table to flip insider and outsider boundaries. For the Jews of Jesus' day meals were much more than nutrition; they bound participants to one another by covenants established between religion, persons and states. Jesus' meal practices contested, transformed and reinterpreted social mores.[7] Jesus cultivated community at the table, modeling other-worldly availability. Jesus reclined at table with doubters, cowards and betrayers, and called them friends.

Jesus used the table to express God's friendship with religious outliers. Eating

> Jesus' meal practices contested, transformed and reinterpreted social mores.

together, no matter how spiritual we feel, is a dynamic way to make ourselves available to God and to each other. Jesus' choice of table guests represents God's coming world, a foreshadowing of the feast at the kingdom of God (Rev 19:9).

The prophet Isaiah shares this beautiful and compelling picture:

> Here on this mountain, GOD-of-the-
> Angel-Armies
>   will throw a feast for all the people
>   of the world,
> A feast of the finest foods, a feast with
> vintage wines,
>   a feast of seven courses, a feast
>   lavish with gourmet desserts.
> And here on this mountain, GOD will
> banish
>   the pall of doom hanging over all
>   peoples,
> The shadow of doom darkening all
> nations.
> Yes, he'll banish death forever.
> And GOD will wipe the tears from
>   every face.
> He'll remove every sign of disgrace.
> (Is 25:6-8 *The Message*)

When we welcome others to our table, we practice God's future now. Sharing a meal is closely tied to the reality of God's in-breaking kingdom. It's a glimpse of the way things ought to be—and one day will be.

The disappearing table. Table fellowship has the same mysterious power today as it did in New Testament times. The modest kitchen table continues to be a center of activity. Even before electricity found its way into American homes, the kitchen table was used for numerous household tasks. Meals were prepared, children were taught and families grew and matured around the kitchen table. Considering how much time early American families spent around this basic structure, it's no wonder people continue to feel drawn to it. It doesn't take a psychology degree to see why—people are forced to relate with each other at the table. Today many forces—electronics, busy schedules, demanding jobs and fast food—are pulling us apart. But in the midst of our frenzied activity, the table brings us back together.

Nevertheless, growing numbers of people don't see meals as an important communal activity. Eating with others is losing its place in our lives. It's just one of several activities happening simultaneously, including checking on our favorite sports team, surfing the web and scrolling through Facebook. This doesn't mean we are any less social, but we're interacting less with people face to face.

The kitchen table should be the vortex of relational life. Tables create togetherness, encourage conversation and help prevent our relationships from withering and dying. The table is good for souls under the onslaught of twenty-first-century life.

Cultivating a shared table. As with the fading of the table practice in nuclear families, it has all but disintegrated in forming community beyond family. Yet Jesus piloted this practice. Something sacred occurs as we commit to coming together at the table. Meals are more than food; they are social occasions that represent friendship, community and forming a shared life.

Food is central to Christian identity: how we relate to God and to the story of God's love for us. Again and again in Scripture, relating with God in community is pictured as a feast. For example, when God leads the Israelites out of Egypt, the leaders are invited to climb Mount Sinai to eat and drink (Ex 24:9-11).

Food reminds us of our dependence on each other because we are finite beings. God is lavish in his generosity, and therefore we too should be with one another. Every meal is an opportunity to receive with thankfulness God's good gifts of food, family, friends and neighbors. Eating is an opportunity for a burgeoning community to delight in abundance instead of worrying about scarcity. A shared meal is a wonderful picture of what it means to be the church. "Every day they . . . broke bread in their homes and ate together with glad and sincere hearts, praising God and enjoying the favor of all the people" (Acts 2:46-47).

Jesus didn't command us to remember him with mere words but with a meal. A missional-incarnational community in Providence, Rhode Island, has sought to foster common life through weekly meals. It has become a powerful force in their lives, opening up space for refugees, sojourners, good friends and neighbors. As they eat, they share their lives' highs and lows, which naturally creates space for new exchanges. This table shared by formerly anonymous neighbors is changing the climate of their neighborhood.

At a shared table disciples hear each other's stories, which are filled with mem-

ories and meaning. Jesus-followers and Jesus seekers behold one another's pains and problems at the table.

I (Dan) invited a coworker to join our community's shared table after he'd mentioned he had nothing to do that night. He entered our full home, which was filled with laughter, kids running around and the smell of chili. He immediately asked, "Is this a family thing?" I replied it was simply a gathering of friends. We rallied around the table and feasted.

After the meal we shared our highs and lows around the table. My friend was fascinated, but I could tell he was nervous. When it was his turn to share, he sat silent for a moment and then told us that he was disappointed by how his life had turned out and how lonely he felt. He lifted his head to see wet eyes around the table.

A woman next to him turned and said gently, "It's okay. Nothing to be embarrassed of. We all have parts of our life we regret, but you're not alone tonight." At the end of the night when almost everyone had left, he lingered. I could tell he had something to say. As I walked with him to his car, he told me, "I've never experienced dinner like this before. Can I come again?" I said sure. He's come ever since.

This shared table becomes a place of conversations that overlap our lives. The rhythmic pattern of gathering around the table molds our stubborn individualism and stuffed schedules into a circle of togetherness. We

> The rhythmic pattern of gathering around the table molds our stubborn individualism and stuffed schedules into a circle of togetherness. We are fashioned into something new as we linger with others.

are fashioned into something new as we linger with others.

Personal space, which might include six to twelve people, is large enough to provide energy but small enough for conversation and connection. When it dips below six it starts to feel like an intimate dinner rather than a fun feast for a spiritual family. Cultivating a shared table in personal space creates availability in the wilderness of fragmented American life. The church is not formed around a stage but around a table. When starting a weekly shared table, those who attend should make a commitment to its function and to attend regularly. Church planters should start by opening their homes for a weekly community meal.

The great thing about using meals to foster a community on mission is that it doesn't add to busy schedules. There are twenty-one already-scheduled opportunities each week, and all that we need is love for people and for eating. It doesn't have to be elaborate or expensive.

We must be accessible to our neighbors, and a shared table creates space for listening and hospitality within the community. Invite members of your growing community for an evening meal. Everyone can bring some food or a beverage to share. On a larger scale, invite your neighbors to join your missional-incarnational community's table fellowship. They will be introduced to the body of Christ and observe the generous, hospitable, grace-filled way Christians relate. The shared table is an ordinary practice, but it might be the most extraordinary way we communicate God's love for us and between us.

FORMATIONAL LEARNING

 Meta-Learning

- How did Christ use food, a shared table, to cultivate community and provide space for mission?

 Reflective Learning

- What hindrances do you feel personally to cultivating a weekly shared table?

Experiential Learning

- Make a list of people to invite to join you for a shared table. What are specific actions you can take to invite and encourage those on your list to participate in a shared table?

- How will you invite those in your neighborhood?

7.3 The Five Environments

One of the most overlooked elements to making mission-shaped disciples is recognizing the environments that shape the culture of our missional community. We need to move from being programmers to environmentalists, learning to shape different environments in our missional communities, for those environments will in turn shape us.[8]

We need to nourish environments in our missional communities that will enable us to catch the wind of the Holy Spirit and move us into the neighborhood. Specific environments expose us to new realities and stretch us into new ways of being the body of Christ. Often when we think of church outside of a communal framework our knee-jerk reaction is to create a program to cover certain values. But when we have a communal framework, we work toward our missional community reflecting the whole of our values rather than compartmentalizing them

into a program on some extra night for those who opt in.

This is an orientation toward *oikos*, "household" or extended social network, believing that a holistic, vibrant community is more important than segregating people into separate spaces based on preferred values. This big shift takes place when we are convinced that a missional community is more than a glorified small group. Instead, it's an encounter with the body of Christ as illustrated in Ephesians 4, which includes the apostle, the prophet, the evangelist, the shepherd and the teacher. The *oikos* of the first-century church was a beautiful, messy, robust expression of Christ's body on the earth.

Let's examine the environments necessary for the cultivation of a missional community that shapes us to be more like Christ.

Learning environment. A learning environment allows people to inhabit the sacred text. A learning environment moves past monologue to dialogue and praxis. Learning is more than the transfer of information, although it does include that. Praxis takes place when thought, action and reflection operate in a cyclical fashion. We demonstrate we have learned when we are better able to live faithfully in God's story. A learning environment is cultivated as we allow God's future to reshape how we live in the present and as we avail ourselves of various sacred assemblies for mutual learning.

As you think about the missional community you serve, how would you rate it in regard to cultivating a learning environment? The following questions will guide your reflection:

- How do the Scriptures shape the community you serve?

- Is the community listening to God through the Scriptures and practicing what they are learning in their everyday lives? How?

- In what ways are people actively reflecting on what they are practicing?

- What percentage of the group is immersed in God's story and teaching the Scripture to others?

Healing environment. A healing environment allows people to work through their past hurts and move toward a sense of wholeness and holiness in the context of community. This happens when people sense an atmosphere of acceptance and understand that others are for them, no matter what they do. We are told to accept one another just as Christ has accepted us (Rom 15:7). Being for people means desiring God's best for their lives. A healing environment is cultivated when people find true friendships in which they can be open, raw, real and vulnerable.

How would you rate the healing environment in the missional community you serve? Think about these questions:

- Do the rhythms of the missional community make space for people to have down time and just hang out with each other?

- Are there regular times for people to be genuine with one another—with no masks?

- How well do people know each other and share life with one another?

- What percentage of people would consider this community their family?

- How many are experiencing healing from past hurts and moving toward wholeness spiritually, physically, mentally and emotionally?

Welcoming environment. A welcoming environment reflects our welcoming God. From the call of Abraham to John's vision of people from every tribe, tongue and nation gathering to worship the living God, we see God's welcoming heart. We cultivate a welcoming environment by following Christ in extending table fellowship and love to those society has marginalized. When we practice the art of hospitality, we give God room to work in people's hearts.

Is your missional-incarnational community cultivating a welcoming environment? Use these questions to attain a new vision for the culture of the group you serve:

- How many people genuinely welcome others into your community?

- How well does the group reflect the diversity of the neighborhood?

  - How willing are people to sacrifice their own cultural comfort to meet people where they are?

  - How many people are living into their *oikos* and connecting with people of peace?

  - How many people are willing to associate with people who are different than them?

Liberating environment. A liberating environment helps the missional community experience liberation from personal and social sins by forming Spirit-transforming communities. A liberating environment encourages people to overcome addictions, grow in personal holiness and speak truth to power by living in the power of the Spirit. A liberating environment is formed by connecting to our liberating God—the God of the exodus, the God of the cross, the God of the resurrection and the God of Pentecost—and by practicing the presence of God through the Spirit. For where the Spirit of God is, there is freedom.

How much of a liberating environment has been cultivated in the missional community you serve? Pray through the following questions:

- What percentage of the congregation is pursuing God's shalom in the power of the Spirit by listening to the Spirit?

- How many people are actively using their spiritual gifts to build the body and serve the neighborhood?

- In what ways is the group walking alongside the poor and oppressed?

- How is the community speaking to the powers and subverting systems that perpetuate injustice in the neighborhood and city?

- How much of the congregation seeks to be good stewards of all creation for the sake of the world?

Thriving environment. Finally, if we desire to create missional culture in our communities, we need to cultivate a thriving environment, where the group is encouraged to step into new territory for the sake of the gospel. Cultivating a thriving environment requires developing a strong discipleship ethos that contributes to people stepping out in new ways, seeking to multiply disciples in intimate and personal spaces. We also multiply social spaces through reaching people in the neighborhood. This happens as people understand their sense of calling and live it out. It takes place as people work out their mentoring matrix, finding experienced mentors—peer mentors inside and outside of their organization—and mentor others.

How is your missional community cultivating a thriving environment? Take some time to respond to these questions:

- How many people are stepping out into new territory, discovering their sense of call and living it out with great passion?

- To what degree is the multiplication of disciples taking place?

- What percentage of people are being mentored or are mentoring others?

- What percentage of the people have a sense of ownership for the group and demonstrate their sentness to the neighborhood?

- How many people see their work as a sacred vocation by which they are able to serve their neighbor and bring glory to God?

In Ephesians 4 Paul links the unity and spiritual maturity of the church to the five kinds of equippers operating in the church: apostles (thriving environment), prophets (liberating environment), evangelists (welcoming environment), pastors (healing environment) and teachers (learning environment). Table 7.1 summarizes the relationship of equippers to the environments.

live into these spiritual habits, each will have some challenging areas. For example, maybe someone has a scattered rule and rhythm of eating with a non-Christian once a week, but hasn't been able to do that well.

Those in the discipleship core who are vocationally gifted as evangelists are able to help this person live into this reality, especially if the person's difficulty involves fear or

Table 7.1. The five environments

People Gift	Environment	Description
apostle	thriving	helping the community step out into new territory, living out their "sentness" in their neighborhoods and networks by multiplying disciples, ministries and missional communities
prophet	liberating	helping the group pursue God, experience liberation from personal and social sins, and stand with the poor and oppressed in the power of the Spirit
evangelist	welcoming	helping the community extend the table of fellowship to all, especially those society has marginalized, by being witnesses of his great love
pastor	healing	helping people embody reconciliation as well as work through their past hurts and move toward a sense of wholeness in the context of community
teacher	learning	helping the community inhabit God's story in such a way that the community teaches one another what it means to live into God's future in an everyday way

As we discern our fivefold vocational intelligence within our discipleship core, we can each help to cultivate these environments in various ways. Two of the more significant ways are through the gathered rule and rhythm and the scattered rule and rhythm of life.

For example, everyone in a discipleship core participates in the gathered rule and rhythm of the missional community. But in addition to this, each person develops a personal scattered rule and rhythm that involves communion, community and co-mission. As each person in the discipleship core seeks to

inadequacy. On the other hand, if the reason is the issue of time, the pastor, prophet or apostle likely can help. The rule and rhythm of the discipleship core shapes the environment of the missional community.

The third way to cultivate these environments within the missional-incarnational community is for two or three leaders to assess their fivefold vocational intelligences and develop their roles to include ways to help cultivate these environments. A list of possible roles within missional communities oriented around the fivefold intelligence can be found at churchasmovement.com.

FORMATIONAL LEARNING

 Meta-Learning

• What kind of rule and rhythm will help you to cultivate these five environments within your community on mission?

 Reflective Learning

• Which two of the five environments are strongest within your missional community?

• Which of the five environments need the most development?

 Experiential Learning

• Take some time with your discipleship core to assign different people to focus on cultivating the five environments within the community.

7.4 The Relational Rope

Years ago I (Dan) joined a friend to do some rock climbing. I was a novice; he wasn't. He had invested quite a bit of money into good climbing and rappelling gear. Climbers' gear is highly valued. This investment keeps them safe as they are hanging from hundred-foot cliffs.

One Sunday afternoon we set out to explore a new place to climb in the mountains of southern Pennsylvania. We found the base of a cliff and opened the backpacks holding the gear—helmets, gloves, carabiners and ropes. My friend began inspecting everything and something caught his eye. He knelt down to examine one of the ropes. He lifted the rope to show me what he'd discovered. The rope had begun to fray. A rope is composed of individual strands tethered together to form a cord. The strongest and most durable ropes use three strands. When a rope frays, those strands start to pull apart. My disappointed friend said that the frayed rope was too weak to hold our weight.

Making a rope. A community also needs a *three-corded* rope, for there is strength when our lives are intertwined with one another. Solomon writes,

> Two are better than one, . . .
> If either of them falls down,
>   one can help the other up.
> But pity anyone who falls
>   and has no one to help them up. . . .
>   How can one keep warm alone?
> Though one may be overpowered,
>   two can defend themselves.

> A cord of three strands is not quickly broken. (Eccles 4:9-12)

A missional-incarnational community must practice healthier ways of relating, or community—our shared life—will pull apart. We need to learn how to diagnose frays in our relational rope of community. Through healthy relational habits we can form a rope, moving from thin (a single strand) to thick (a cord) community (see fig. 7.2). Our aim is a thicker community life. We must help people recognize and resolve what hinders community. If we don't, our missional-incarnational community may unravel.

The following tethering tool is a relational continuum for discussion, diagnosis and discipleship that, when taught and employed in community, can cast fresh light on complexities

> A missional-incarnational community must practice healthier ways of relating, or community—our shared life—will pull apart.

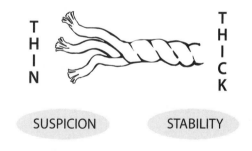

Figure 7.2. Trust building

and offer us opportunities for maturing. Relational tethering involves cords braided together to thicken and enrich our common life.

Trust building: From suspicion to stability. We build trust by developing habits that foster stability instead of suspicion.

The health of human bonds depends on the relational glue that holds them together. Our connectedness is constantly under stress. We must tend to our bonds, naming what contributes to stability. Often we enter into a community flush with ideals that will be humbled as we bond with others. Forming bonds is the work of trust building. There are gaps between what we expect people to do and what they actually do.[9] What we place in those gaps determines the strength and integrity of the relationships. We can fill them with suspicion, but this erodes our relational ties with each other. Our histories of failed relationships can torque us toward ongoing suspicion. The wounds we have experienced, some very deep, have shaped our souls. In our inability to cope with these wounds, we often revert to wounding other people in similar ways. Paul warns us, "If you bite and devour each other, watch out or you will be destroyed by each other" (Gal 5:15).

To overcome the cycle of suspicion that erodes relationships, we must defer to trust. A mature disciple has learned to be still instead of being defensive. When we see something disconcerting, we must approach the person in question to find out more. Obviously, it is difficult to immediately trust people we have just met. Instead, we must work toward building trust. The following points will help us to build thick community, cultivating strong bonds with each other.

- We deliver on what we say we are going to do.

- We say that we're sorry when we cannot follow through.

- We forgive and release someone who says they are sorry.

- We seek to cut others just as much slack in their motives as we do for ourselves.

- Communication related to unmet expectations is done face to face.

- We put effort into relationships when they begin to break down.

The next set of points creates suspicion, which leads to thin community.

- We often attribute negative motives to people before speaking with them.

- We speak passive-aggressively about people when we're disappointed with them.

- We abandon relationships that seem difficult to maintain.

- We hide big choices we're making (vocation, dating, moving, etc.).

- When someone does not show up, we do not call them.

- When someone is different in opinion or culture, we avoid them.

> Often we enter into a community flush with ideals that will be humbled as we bond with others.

Truth telling: From hiding to honesty. Truth telling involves habits that foster honesty instead of hiding (see fig. 7.3). For most of us, this is unnavigated social terrain. Paul says, "Each of you must put off falsehood and speak truthfully to your neighbor, for we are all members of one body" (Eph 4:25). What does truth-shaped living look like?

For many, speaking the truth conjures images of a preacher yelling absolute truths from a pulpit. Others confuse discontented grumbling with truth telling. Bluntness is not the same as truthfulness. Truth telling is first being honest about ourselves before pointing to the speck in someone else's eye.[10]

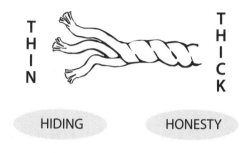

Figure 7.3. Truth telling

A truth-telling community will not necessarily be tidy; rough edges will be visible. Truth telling seeks to first understand before unloading an opinion. A truth-telling environment seeks to be honest and direct about who we are and what we're feeling. Direct speech brings clarity and keeps manipulation and hiding at bay.[11] Community cultures that don't permit honest speech often hide under the surface resentments, abuses and stifled feelings. Jesus shares the necessity of bringing truth to the surface:

> If you enter your place of worship and, about to make an offering, you suddenly remember a grudge a friend has against you, abandon your offering, leave immediately, go to this friend and make things right. Then and only then, come back and work things out with God. (Mt 5:23-24 *The Message*)

Too often we switch between passive silence and bitter tirades in the face of differences. We must work hard to practice a better way. Honest speech does not seek injury. Truth-telling communities must become wise to the way passive-aggressive communication festers. A passive-aggressive person grasps for power over others by judging their motives without direct, open communication. The relational strategy is indirect, so their anger cannot be identified but is still felt.

Pure passivity is not virtuous either. It assumes that when someone insults us it is virtuous to do nothing. A passive person tends not to say anything in the moment but later spews their bitterness or anger on someone unrelated. Genuine love does not delight in evil but rejoices with the truth. We must gently point out where we see untruthfulness, the nursing of wounds, angry inner tirades and postures that are less than genuine.[12] Truthfulness is a cord that holds us together in a world of dishonest relating.

The following points will help us build thick community through honesty, seeking sincerity with others:

- We speak honestly when we are offended.

- We speak well of others when they're not in our presence.

- We stop pretending and posing in our relationships.

- We model an open posture to hearing another speak the truth.

- We deal with the planks in our own eyes before picking at others' specks.

- We give people permission to offer feedback on our statements.

Thin community is fostered by masking or misrepresenting who we are (hiding). The following points will help us identify hiding behavior:

- When we are upset we avoid each other.

- We sit with and nurse our offenses until they separate us.

- We use antirelational mediums (email, Twitter, etc.) to communicate sensitive thoughts.

- We are immediately defensive when someone shares their opinion.

Peacemaking: From division to dialogue. Peacemakers engage in habits that foster dialogue instead of division (see fig. 7.4). Scripture calls us to be ministers of reconciliation (2 Cor 5:18). This has become more of a catchphrase than a serious pursuit in Christian circles. To be human is to have differences. In community we are faced with processing those differences. The temptation is to bail out or divide from community when conflict overtakes us. We must seek reconciling dialogue instead.

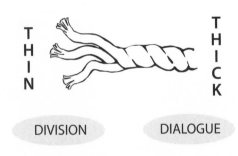

Figure 7.4. Peacemaking

The work of peacemaking is not sweeping hurts, disappointments and anger under the carpet. This only increases the potential for

carnage. We have been in too many churches where individuals or factions do not talk directly to each other, preferring to accumulate offenses, creating a mound that seems insurmountable.

Some seek to build a power base of support to gain ammunition against their offender(s). Others boil internally, eventually departing without ever having a face-to-face conversation. In an attempt to shed redemptive light on the situation, the path of peace opens up conversations about what is going on. "As far as it depends on you, live at peace with everyone" (Rom 12:18).

Reconciliation is not a mere human activity; it binds on earth what is bound in heaven (Mt 18:18). The Anabaptist tradition has historically called this "binding and loosing," seeing it as a sacrament distinguishing the church from the world.[13] We are to go to each other in a spirit of gentleness, aware of our own weakness.[14]

Conversing with others with reconciling intent is the most powerful way for a community to discover God's Spirit in its midst. It is striking that in the midst of the conflict in Corinth Paul never instructed readers to leave the community to find a healthier one. Instead, he instructed them to work it out (1 Cor 5–6). We are not a community if we can't move into conflict and move through it while maintaining our loyal love for one another. We must press into conflict with fidelity, not rigidity.[15] Peacemakers are the children of God.

Dialogue, seeking conversation in times of conflict, creates thick community. The following points can help us to move toward dialogue:

- We seek to create a "sit down and talk" culture.

- We are quick to listen and slow to speak.

- We seek solidarity with each other by asking open questions.

- We live patiently with differences not yet resolved.

- We seek reconciliation long before we seek separation.

Thin community is generated in part by division, collision that perpetuates separation. The following points help us to diagnose the spirit of division:

- We add toxicity to disagreements by slighting people's reputations.

- We build up a power base of support so we can win an argument.

- We shut out people who have a different take on a situation.

- When we are wrong we are unable to own our faults.

- When we are hurt we find ways to hurt back.

- When we let someone down we hope that no one notices.

FORMATIONAL LEARNING

 Meta-Learning

- Why is it essential to work on healthy relating in Christian community?

- Why are most of us not well equipped to identify thin ways of relating in community?

 Reflective Learning

- Which of the three ropes are *your* weakest and strongest? Why?

Experiential Learning

- What would it look like to teach these relational continuums? How can you disciple each other to live into thick community?

8

Incarnational Practices

· ·

The Come-To-Us stance developed over the Christendom period is unbiblical.

MICHAEL FROST

In *The Message* John 1:14 says, "The Word became flesh and blood, and moved into the neighborhood." God came close in Jesus, who moved into a neighborhood for thirty years. This is profound. How might we move deep into our neighborhoods? Disciples must see the neighborhood as a garden to till, and this of course takes toil. God is not bound up in our buildings; he is already moving along our streets. How do we call the church to care for the spaces we make home? How do we ignite disciples to move toward their actual neighbors? Make no mistake, this is a big shift. But it is essential.

Connecting to Movement

The church as movement is not a Platonic ideal. It's real people with dirt under their fingernails serving their neighborhoods. The movemental church must be grounded in concrete ways. God was place-based when Jesus moved into Nazareth. Therefore our churches too should be place-based, having a vision for the microspaces of a neighborhood, the places where marginalized people, forgotten people, people not interested in a slick worship service fall through the cracks. Movements do not stay bottled up in buildings; they move into the streets. The church as movement is an incarnational movement.

8.1 Coming NEAR Your Neighborhood

To meaningfully connect with the people where we are starting missional-incarnational communities, we need to interpret our cultural context. This is a basic task for every missionary. Exegeting a culture is an art and a science. It is understanding the people and place God has called us to inhabit, so that the power of the gospel might fully connect and be transformative. When we live with a missionary mindset, we will observe what is more important to our neighbors, what they worship, what they fear, what they believe and what they idolize.

Paul the contextualizer. Acts 17:16-33 is a classic text on exegeting a city. As you read this passage, note how Paul approached the people of Athens: what he saw, what he felt and how he engaged the people. When we exegete a particular context, we must know what to look for, allow time to honestly respond to what we see, and find ways to interact with people of peace in that context.

As we exegete the context we have been sent to, we will find the best way to make the gospel meaningful to a particular people. René Padilla observes,

> To contextualize the gospel is to translate it in such a way that the Lordship of Jesus Christ is not an abstract principle or mere doctrine, but the determining factor of life in all its dimensions and that basic criterion in

> Exegeting a culture is an art and a science. It is understanding the people and place God has called us to inhabit, so that the power of the gospel might fully connect and be transformative.

relation to which all cultural values that form the very substance of human life are evaluated. Without contextualization, the gospel will become tangential or even entirely irrelevant.[1]

The city as a context. We need to recognize our limits when we start a church or missional-incarnational community. When I (JR) moved to LA to plant churches, I moved into the second largest city in the United States. The population of the city is four million, and the city has 47,700 employees and an annual budget of $7.89 billion.

After I moved to LA, the San Fernando Valley and Hollywood tried to secede from the city: they felt they weren't being served well. However, neither got the votes to leave the city. If the city couldn't do a good job of serving four million people with 47,000 employees and billions of dollars, it would be proud to think that our church could somehow serve the entire city.

This is, in part, why we need a movemental approach to church planting. We can only spread ourselves so far. Eventually, we have to take ownership of a particular context as our *first step* in growing movement. Our group did this by starting missional communities in three distinct neighborhoods. We realized that we needed to accept our limitations and discern where God would have us lay the initial foundations for movement to take place. Theologian Gerhard Lohfink notes, "God does not act anywhere and everywhere, but in a concrete place. God does not act at any and every moment, but at a particular time. God does not act through anyone and everyone, but through the people of God."[2]

Exegeting your neighborhood. Of course, your city is the first context you will work in. But you don't reach a city by focusing on the whole. You reach a city by focusing your efforts on the more manageable contexts of particular neighborhoods and networks. A neighborhood is a clearly defined place where people live—for example, a subdivision or an even smaller pocket of the city that has multiple housing complexes. A network is any group of people who gather around a common vision or values—for example, people who meet regularly for recreation or sports.

How do we go about reading the context of a neighborhood? One way is by understanding its basic culture. While there are many good ways to do this, we suggest doing this by using a simplified cultural web. In seeking to come near to your neighborhood there are four basic questions you need to ask, based on the key elements of any culture. We use the acronym NEAR (see table 8.1).[3]

As a way to help you answer these four primary questions, we will dive a bit deeper into each element of culture and consider a number of other questions, with the goal of being able to answer these four primary questions with greater depth.

Narrative. *What story is our neighborhood calling us to embody?* When we seek to understand the narrative of a people, we need to consider their *theology*, what they believe about God (or if they believe in God); their *doctrines*, what they believe with confidence; and their *narratives*, the stories they tell each other based on their music and the media they are exposed to. The following are some questions to help us get to the heart of the overarching story of our neighborhood:

- What are the key slogans of this context?

- What are the prime landmarks, and how do they shape the narrative of this context?

- What kind of music do people listen to?

- What lyrics have they committed to memory, and what story do the lyrics call them into?

- What are people's favorite films, and what lines can they quote?

- What are people's dreams and hopes?

- What are their fears and stresses?

- What do people think about God, Jesus and the church?

- What places of worship are available, and what do they tell us about this context?

Table 8.1. Coming NEAR your neighborhood and network

N	narrative	What story is our neighborhood calling us to embody?
E	ethics	How do people in our context define success?
A	associations	What primary organizations and institutions are shaping people's identity and destiny in our context?
R	rituals	What core practices do people engage in that shape their identity and sense of mission in life?

- How do people think about money and power?

- What are the idols in this context?

- Who has "played God" in this context, and how has that shaped the story being told?

- What are important moments (or kairos moments) in the history of this context?

Ethics. How do people in our context define success? Ethics are the moral convictions that shape the life of community and speak to people's sense of *being*, which in turn shape what people *do*. To engage in ethics requires space and time for people to reflect on their lives and their contexts in order to examine whether they are promoting the common good.

- Does the pace of life in this context aid or hinder people's ability to engage in solitude, silence and reflection?

- Does the built environment (design of the city, neighborhood) help people to be fully human, or does it make it more difficult?

- Does the art scene help people in the neighborhood and city to consider the important questions they ought to address, or does it add to their stress?

- How do the primary modes of transportation shape people's sense of being?

- Who promotes and hinders justice in this context?

- How does the city shape people's conception of the good life?

- Does the city promote the American dream or God's vision for the future, and how does this shape people's imagination?

- Do the laws and law enforcement agencies

help each person of the city, no matter their class or ethnicity, feel like a person made in the image of God?

- Does this context's description of the "good life" cause people to consider others more important than themselves or to look out for number one?

- Which behaviors are rewarded and which are punished?

- How does the city government's budget reflect its understanding of success?

Associations. What primary organizations and institutions are shaping people's identity and destiny in our context? Institutions have certain *structures* that speak to the distribution of power and decision making, *systems* that either encourage the flourishing or demise of the city, and *symbols* of success and failure that shape people's sense of worth.

- What companies are the primary employers of the city?

- Do the primary employers look out for the common good of the city or their own good?

- Is the government centralized or decentralized, giving power to the local neighborhoods?

- Does the police force look out for the underprivileged or add to the divisiveness of the city?

- Do the lawmakers and judges treat the people with fairness or with favoritism?

- Do the various institutions deal with immigrants as people made in the image of God or a problem?

- Is the neighborhood being gentrified? Are the displaced treated as full human beings?

- Who founded the hospitals? How do they operate and do people have equal access to health care as people made in God's image?

- Is it easy or difficult for small businesses to flourish in the city?

- Which institutions are caring for the homeless in a God-honoring way?

- Are churches seeking to bring a greater sense of the kingdom to their neighborhood, or are they looking out for themselves?

- What is the reputation of the religious leaders' churches?

- Who are the most powerful people in the city, and do they promote justice or their own welfare?

- What are the most influential media institutions, and how does their reporting influence people?

- What are the primary educational institutions, and how are they shaping the life of the children and the city?

- Does everybody have equal opportunity when it comes to education?

- What are the significant universities in the city or neighborhood, and in what ways do they influence the people of the neighborhood?

Rituals. *What core practices do people engage in that shape their identity and sense of mission in life?* To understand the life-shaping rituals of a neighborhood or network in our city, we need to observe the formal ceremonies, or *rituals*, people engage in that are fused with meaning, the common *practices* of

people, and the everyday *liturgies* that shape their ultimate desires, identity and sense of the good life. The following are some questions that help us to understand the thick practices people routinely engage in:

- What activities do people engage in that give them a sense of worth?

- What holidays are celebrated with the most vigor?

- How are these holidays celebrated, and how do they shape people's ultimate desires?

- How do people approach their work? As a career or a calling?

- What do people do in their free time, and how much free time do they have?

- Other than work, what do people devote the most time to?

- What third spaces (such as cafés, clubs, parks) do people engage with the most?

- How do people spend their time, their money and their talents?

- In what ways do people seek to meet their need for beauty?

- Do people tend to work for the common good or their own good?

While this is not a comprehensive approach to exegeting a neighborhood, by answering these four primary questions, you will have a greater ability to understand how to be the good news in your context.

The more we understand the culture of our missional context, the better we can bear witness in word and deed to our context, bring the transforming power of the gospel, and make the invisible kingdom more visible.

FORMATIONAL LEARNING

 Meta-Learning

- Why is it important to exegete (interpret) the neighborhood or network God has sent you to?

 Reflective Learning

- When thinking through the narrative, ethics, associations and rituals of your context, which do you already have some familiarity with, and what areas do you need to spend more time with?

 Experiential Learning

- Plan a weekend when you can take your discipleship core on a journey in your neighborhood and city. Consider connecting with your mayor, council members or other people who serve the city, and then have everyone fill out a NEAR report.

8.2 The Missional-Incarnational Journey

I (JR) love the last lines of Robert Frost's poem *The Road Not Taken*, which is a helpful prelude to what it means to live on mission in today's context.

> Two roads diverged in a wood, and I—
> I took the one less traveled by,
> And that has made all the difference.[4]

Many churches today have a come-and-see approach to mission. This is known as an attractional approach to church planting. The road less traveled involves a go-and-be-with approach to mission, which is incarnational. While some like to pit these two against each other, the real danger is the extractional approach to being the church. This approach occurs when we elevate the weekly gathering to the point that we unintentionally extract people from everyday mission in everyday places. It's when we "teach people that church is something we 'go to' instead of something we are."[5]

For weekly gatherings to be missional, instead of merely consuming religious goods and services, they should combine worship and mission, reshaping people to inhabit God's story in their everyday lives. Public gatherings are best when they are subordinate to missional communities. When the weekly service becomes an end itself, the tail ends up wagging the dog.

The missional-incarnational journey. Missional is being *sent out*, and incarnational is *going deep*. Jesus says, "As the Father has sent me, I am sending you." Jesus left heaven to come to earth. We should be able to leave the sanctuary to go to the streets. Too often we expect people to come to us, but the Spirit is drawing us to go to them.

Every missional-incarnational community needs to ask, Who has God sent us to? To what neighborhood or network of people has he sent us? When we know this, then it is a matter of digging in roots. Living incarnationally is moving from going to a *space* (church building) once or twice a week to inhabiting a *place* (incarnation). Remember, "The Word became flesh and blood, and moved into the neighborhood" (Jn 1:14 *The Message*).[6]

When I (JR) was planting churches in LA, our team decided to break into three different congregations and *move into* three distinct neighborhoods. Each congregation sought to live, work and play in one of the neighborhoods. We understood what Simone Weil meant when she said, "To be rooted is perhaps the most important and least recognized need of the human soul."[7] We also agreed with Andy Crouch: "The twentieth-century American dream was to move out and move up; the twenty-first century dream seems to be put down deeper roots."[8] The congregation I was part of was located in East Hollywood. We understood that in order to live incarnationally we needed to go on the missional-incarnational journey as a community. We needed to move from being *for* the neighborhood and *with* the neighborhood to being *of* the neighborhood and *in* the neighborhood.[9]

For–with–of–in. Being *for* a neighborhood or network requires asking, if God's reign were to be more fully realized here, what would be different? This broad question helps us discover the needs of the neighborhood or people group to which we have been sent. As we answer this question and consider the passions God has given our group, we begin to find concrete ways to show that our hearts are *for* them.

N. T. Wright helps us understand how to be for a neighborhood or network of people.

The mission of the church must therefore reflect, and be shaped by, the future hope as the New Testament

> In order to live incarnationally we needed to go on the missional-incarnational journey as a community. We needed to move from being *for* the neighborhood and *with* the neighborhood to being *of* the neighborhood and *in* the neighborhood.

presents it. I believe that if we take these three areas—justice, beauty and evangelism—in terms of anticipation of God's eventual setting to rights of the world, we will find that they dovetail together and in fact that they are all part of the same larger whole, which is the message of hope and new life that comes with the good news of Jesus' resurrection.[10]

As you think about what it means to be *for* the people you are sent to as a community, consider what acts of justice and beauty you can participate in. This will give you opportunity to meaningfully engage in evangelism.

In East Hollywood we did this in part by teaming up with Hope International to start the Manna Room. It was called this because we would visit local grocery stores and pick up food that was close to being thrown out (a day from going bad), and together with those in need we distributed it to those in need.

If we want to imitate Jesus, we need to be *with* our neighbors, *with* the network of people we feel called to as a community on mission. Being *with* people is about hanging out *with* them in their apartments or at work, at the coffee shop, at an art show or a party. Being *with* our neighbor is learning about their dreams and desires, their hurts and their hopes. We need to become a character in the community.[11] To do this we need to create a rule and rhythm of life that allows us to build meaningful relationships *with* others. Being with them means walking with them in acts of justice and beauty.

The LA government divided the city into seven sections, and they encouraged neigh-borhoods to form neighborhood councils. As the neighborhood councils got certified, they received $50,000 a year for neighborhood development. I (JR) was able to help establish the East Hollywood Neighborhood Council and was elected to serve in the section of the neighborhood I lived in.

After I was elected, the council appointed me to be co-outreach coordinator. Because the council was new, the majority of the budget was given to us because we first needed to get people in the neighborhood to participate. We planted trees, made reusable shopping bags with our neighborhood name on them and held street fairs. The cool thing is that the city paid for the street fairs, and I invited the church to the party.

As we live *with* people, we start to be *of* them. Just as Paul became a Jew to the Jews and a Greek to the Greeks, we become one *of* the neighbors. God called us *out of* the world and sent us back *into the* world. Yet, as we live *in the* world, we are to be different from the world. We weren't sent to judge people but to love people. Just as Jesus became one *of* us, we participate in the movement of God's love toward people as we live in him and become one *of* them. The cultural distance between our group and theirs will likely affect the time it takes to move from *with* to *of* them. We often need to step outside our comfort zone and die to ourselves if we want to move forward in the missional-incarnational journey.

As we take the time to become one *of* them by walking in their shoes, they start to identify us as being *in* the group. No longer does the group consider us immigrants or aliens, they consider us part of the family, part of the community.

Imitating God. As we remember that God is *for* us (blessing us as he blessed Abraham so that we might be a blessing to the world), *with* us (Emmanuel, God with us), *of* us (through incarnation) and *in* us (through the Holy Spirit) we are able to embrace our sentness. If God is *in* us, then we must be *for* our neighbors, *with* our neighbors and become one *of* our neighbors. And as Christ lives in us, others will desire that he lives in them. When he lives in them, the whole journey is repeated, and the seeds of movement and multiplication grow.

FORMATIONAL LEARNING

 Meta-Learning

- What is the difference between being attractional, incarnational and extractional, and why does it matter?

 Reflective Learning

- What neighborhood or network has God sent your missional community to, and where are you on the missional-incarnational journey? Are you *for*, *with*, *of* or *in* them?

- What acts of justice, beauty or healing is God calling your missional community to bring to your neighborhood or network?

 Experiential Learning

- Map out where you are at in the missional-incarnational journey, and consider the next step that God would have you take to move forward in mission.

8.3 The Person of Peace

The following are a couple of the journal entries of Jared and Mary Beth Dragoun, church planters in the NoHo Arts District of Los Angeles who are taking the missional-incarnational journey seriously.

Update: June 6, 2015—Taking a Turn

For the last ten months we have been getting to know our neighbors. We've continually invited them into our home to join us in whatever we're doing in the community. The month of May took an exciting turn as we began receiving invitations to their homes and to join in on their parties. These new friends are wanting to include us into their lives. It may sound small, but this was a big deal in our minds. We hope that this relational reciprocation is a sign that people not only appreciate being around us, but trust us!

Update: July 8, 2015—A New Board Game, but Real Life Isn't a Game

There's a new board game in town that has our friends and neighbors begging for us to host more get-togethers. They are beginning to invite their neighbors and friends to join us. It's a blast. Sometimes I think we're having too much fun! We are truly becoming friends. With this comes great responsibility and opportunity. We have hours of fun and moments of seriousness (often afterwards) to talk "real life." . . . People are hurting (real life is definitely not fun and games) and they're looking for a listening ear. They want counsel. They're testing the water to see what we can "handle" hearing. Sometimes we feel like they're just waiting to become a victim and hope our words lead them further down a hopeless road.[12]

Jared and Mary Beth have found some *people of peace* in their neighborhood. And through those people of peace, they have met dozens of people. Most of the people they have met would never set foot in a church service, but they are now Jared and Mary Beth's friends.

The person of peace. One way to start on the missional-incarnational journey is to find *persons of peace* and enter into the community through them. The person-of-peace concept is found throughout Scripture, has been used by missionaries and was put on the map in North America by Thom Wolf, a professor who founded the Church on Brady, currently named Mosaic, in Los Angeles. Mosaic is led by Erwin McManus. The person-of-peace concept has been popularized since by a number of people, including Mike Breen and Bob and Mary Hopkins.

Thom Wolf gives us a sticky way to remember the nature of persons of peace: they are *receptive*, they have a *reputation* and they *refer* us to people in their web of relationships. One place we see the person of peace concept in action is in Luke 10:1-12, the story of Jesus sending out the Seventy-Two. As we read this story and other Scriptures

> Most of the people Jared and Mary Beth have met would never set foot in a church service, but they are now their friends.

we discover three ways to recognize a person of peace.

Receptivity. God has been working in the lives of people of peace before we even meet them (Lk 10:5-6). Thus they are receptive to our initiatives. On the missional-incarnational journey we must recognize where God is at work and join him in the process. This is based on the missionary nature of God. Cornelius (Acts 10) and Lydia (Acts 16) are other New Testament examples.

> Thom Wolf gives us a sticky way to remember the nature of persons of peace: they are *receptive,* they have a *reputation* and they *refer* us to people in their web of relationships.

Reputation. Second, they have a reputation, whether good or bad. The demoniac is an example (Mk 5). He asks Jesus if he can join him, but Jesus sends him back to share with others. Well-known drug dealers or gangsters fit in this category, as well as reputable business people.

Referral. Finally, the person of peace readily refers us to others (Acts 16:6-34). This person has a web of relationships they invite us into. As you take the missional-incarnational journey with your community, the person of peace will be a key person who will help you move forward. As you journey with the person of peace and seek to be and share the good news, consider how the Spirit is working in their extended relationships. In the New Testament it wasn't unusual to see persons of peace and their entire households come to faith (e.g., Acts 16:31-34).

Embracing the person-of-peace concept makes life exciting. Kevin and Christine Sweeney, church planters in Honolulu, can attest to this. They meaningfully connect with fashion designers, photographers and models in the art district where they live. Their people of peace are well-known artists who have invited them into their social world. They have learned to accept all invitations, whether it is to a 2 a.m. fashion show, a special party or event. Having become characters in that world, they are developing community and are being and sharing the good news as the Spirit prompts them.

The octagon. Bob and Mary Hopkins use an octagon to illustrate how to walk alongside people of peace and their *oikos* (extended social network).[13] The following is a summary of their work and a few reflections on how I (JR) have lived into this.

As we take the missional-incarnational journey with our community, we already are living the good news. The person-of-peace concept gives us wisdom about *how* and *when* to share the good news (see fig. 8.1).

Perception. When walking with a person of peace and their *oikos*, we first want to

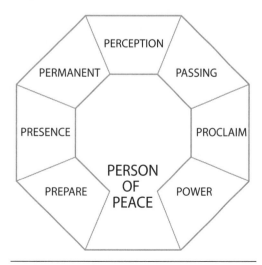

Figure 8.1. Person of peace octagon

perceive where the person and their relationships are spiritually. How close or far away are they from God? How hungry or thirsty are they? How fast or slow are they moving toward the Lord? These questions help us understand how God is at work. It's not our job to convert people; that is the work of the Holy Spirit. We are called to love and discern the proper time to share the life-giving story. If people aren't thirsty, they need salt. If they are thirsty, give them some living water.[14]

Passing or permanent. Next we want to consider whether this is a *passing* relationship or a more *permanent* one. I (JR) once met a person of peace on a trip. Initially this was someone I had a passing relationship with. But upon further conversation I discovered he was from northern Virginia, close to Washington, DC, where I was living. We exchanged numbers, and it became possible that we might become more permanent friends. The nature of the relationship we have with a person of peace and their *oikos* will shape our missional approach.

Proclaiming and presence. Depending on the guidance of the Spirit, we might be more forward in passing relationships than with our permanent relationships. God has likely put this person in our life in order for us to plant some seeds of truth; that is, we might *proclaim* the good news to them. On the other hand, more permanent relationships usually require our *presence* and actions. In this approach we love them till they ask us why.

Power and preparation. In passing relationships we ought to be open to what John Wimber calls "power evangelism." This occurs when we ask God to intervene in a dramatic way through healing prayer, a prophetic word or a Spirit-inspired dream. We should seek God's power within our permanent relationships as well, but in passing relationships, we want to leave people with a sign of God's desire to bless them and to be known by him. Our approach to our permanent relationships is to partner with God: till the soil, plant seeds and *prepare* the person of peace and their *oikos* to hear the good news at the proper time. This is more of a process.

The octagon can be used as a guide. There are no hard and fast rules. The Spirit always trumps a general approach. Just remember that faith comes by hearing the Word of God.

Take some time to not only think about these concepts but practice them, for they are at the core of the church as movement.

FORMATIONAL LEARNING

 Meta-Learning

- How do you recognize a person of peace, and why does it matter?

Reflective Learning

• How can your community on the missional-incarnational journey join persons of peace in their web of relationships?

• The Scriptures tell us to share the gospel at the proper time. How do you discern the proper time?

Experiential Learning

• Take some time in your discipleship core to identify people of peace in your life. Then discern the next step God would have you take in your relationship with your people of peace.

8.4 Presence in the Neighborhood

In Christ, God is local. His passions and plans for people become concrete when they are localized. Whether it is in a barren wilderness or a bustling city, God has always drawn his people into local places. Starting with the Garden, God gives the first human community a definitive identity, a banner for self-understanding: "Let us make human beings in our image, make them reflecting our nature / So they can be responsible for [everything here]" (Gen 1:27 *The Message*).

It's as if God builds a beautiful housing development and tells the first humans, "Take care of the place." The Trinity also gives the first human community boundaries; laying out their neighborhood:

A river flows out of Eden to water the garden and from there divides into four rivers. The first is named Pishon; it flows through Havilah where there is gold. The gold of this land is good. The land is also known for a sweet-scented resin and the onyx stone. The second river is named Gihon; it flows through the land of Cush. The third river is named Hiddekel and flows east of Assyria. The fourth river is the Euphrates. (Gen 2:14-16 *The Message*)

God limits their responsibility by framing the scope of the Garden. They are called to a certain sized place and a particular location, what we would consider a neighborhood.

In believing that God is over all and through all, we should also be jolted by the fact that God limited himself to a place two thousand years ago. Jesus moved unassumingly into Nazareth. Before Jesus died on a cross he was present for thirty years in a neighborhood. This is the good news the Scriptures portrays, a God who personally goes on mission to a certain place.

Certainly the truth of God is universal, but it first must become local. Our tendency away from local embodiment to abstract truth leads us to church forms that lean toward the attractive personalities rather than faithfulness to a place.

The church is not a commodity—a style of music, a celebrity pastor and a logo—to be franchised in a new city. The greatest gift the church can offer the world is *not* a highlight reel of our best preaching and worship performances. Technology has cultivated a church experience that falsely transcends place.

In order to partake in better spiritual programming, too many people attend a Sunday service that is not in their neighborhood. The church as industrial complex often draws people to consume "quality programming" rather than into *being* the church where they live. Missional drift occurs when the church moves away from a radical local orientation. Place-based commitment humbly embraces limits in order to stay faithful to a location.

There is no greater pursuit than cultivating a flourishing missional-incarnational community for the renewal of a neighborhood. The kingdom of God invites us to faithfully embrace a place. The local space is where all our wishes and dreams work with the people and resources of a neighborhood. Based in a particular place, we are called us to open our eyes to what is present there, to behold the weight of our neighbors' glory, as C. S. Lewis has so eloquently stated.[15] We must acknowledge that God's dwelling is already tied to the neighborhood, the streets connecting us to each other, the homes we eat in and the parks that we play in.[16] Our first orientation as a place-based community must be to look, listen and learn.[17] *What is here? Who is here? What is God doing in this place?*

Discipling out of displacement. A place-based community will crash into a nasty case of displacement in the West. Coming to terms with our displacement is imperative for the future of mission. Given our postmodern and poststructuralist turn, we see ourselves as more connected globally and less saturated locally. This cultural force has made us less emotionally present to our neighborhoods.

Six out of ten people interviewed by the Pew Research Center said they may move in the next five years.[18] Asked why they live where they do, people most often cite the pull of economic opportunity. The call to

> Certainly the truth of God is universal, but it first must become local.

stability and intentional rooting in a place is countercultural. Choosing to settle deeply, fending off transience, might seem archaic, yet the church must model being the people of God in a place.

Our *lifeworld*, a term coined by David Seamon, is the place our bodies dwell; it is a human-scaled environment we are integrally limited to.[19] Our bodies—our senses, touch, church does not happen haphazardly. How can our presence have a sense of purpose? How can it live out the truth that God's kingdom is breaking in among us? What follows is a tool for a discipleship core or a missional-incarnational community to reflect on four place-based connectors in all our lives (see fig. 8.2).

Porch: From independence to interdepen-

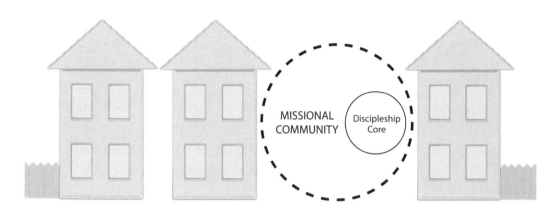

Figure 8.2. The place-based church

eyesight, footprint and our abode making—can only be in one place. We are increasingly taking this smaller world for granted, allowing it to go unnoticed and neglected. If we desire the church as movement, we are tasked with reversing this trend of displacement in the way we express being the body of Christ.

To be a place-based community we must invite disciples on a journey that no longer sees their neighborhood as a prop. This work of discipleship calls us to unlearn displacement and relearn how to be in a place, moving from haphazardness to intentionality. *How do we shift our churches toward being place-based communities?*

Being place-based. Being a place-based

dence. In the parable of the good Samaritan Jesus asked, "'Which of the three became a neighbor to the man?' . . . 'The one who treated him kindly,' the religion scholar responded. Jesus said, 'Go and do the same'" (Lk 10:36-37 *The Message*). I (Dan) had an interesting encounter a few years back when I visited an author who has written about issues of injustice in lower-income areas. As we walked to his house, I noticed that he passed his neighbors without acknowledging them. I asked him later how he felt about the neighborhood and he said, "It's nice."

Probing, I asked about his neighbors, and he said, "They're cool. Nobody bothers anyone." I found it ironic that an author writing about real people problems in real places didn't know or have much connection with his next-door neighbors. There is a disconnect when we champion "loving like Jesus" but barely extend ourselves into the lives surrounding us.

Before we think of changing the world or our city, we need to get to know our neighbors. *Neighbor* is not an abstract, overspiritualized principle. We are linked with our next-door neighbors, and we can choose to connect or not. Many have been raised to see neighbors as strangers we feel no obligation to know. Typically our home is private, insulated from the public world. Jesus makes it clear that inviting the other into our home is also an invitation to the supernatural. "Do not forget to show hospitality to strangers, for by doing so some people have shown hospitality to angels without knowing it" (Heb 13:2). Here are some questions to ponder:

> Before we think of changing the world or our city, we need to get to know our neighbors.

- Do you know your literal neighbors?
- Do you see your home first through the lens of protective security or sacred hospitality?

I remember being overly nervous about asking to borrow my neighbor's lawn mower. How did something so normal become so unnatural? Many times I walked outside to see him working on something and I thought, *Should I offer to help? It could eat up my day.* These concerns are real, but they're boundaries that impede the movement toward trusting one another, paralyzing us and perpetuating distance. Over time we began to build an interdependence that was life giving to both of us. One way we can become loving neighbors is through sharing food. The *porch* is symbolic of being in a place.

The following are some porch questions to ask:

- Are we open to using our home for hospitality with neighbors?
- Am I open to sharing my resources with my neighbors?
- Do I know my neighbors' names?
- Have I offered to help them, shovel their driveway, help with their brakes or babysit their kids?
- Do I use holidays (Christmas, Hanukkah, birthdays, etc.) to create connecting points?

Pathways: From unconscious busyness to conscious habitation. The Gospel of John tells us: "Walking along the street, Jesus saw a man blind and stopped to attend to him" (Jn 9:1-2 The Kingdom New Testament).

In downtown New York City a heroic man was stabbed attempting to save a Queens woman from a knife-wielding attacker. He lay dying in a pool of blood for more than an hour as nearly twenty-five people indifferently strolled past him, as a surveillance video revealed. Most of the

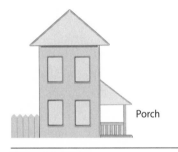

Figure 8.3. Porch

passersby moved hurriedly by without much of a pause. Not until some thirty minutes after the victim collapsed did firefighters finally arrive and discover the man, thirty-one years old, had died. Did people ignore the crime scene, or were they too busy to notice? I think they were too busy to notice. Certainly this is an exaggerated example, but often we are slaves to unconscious traveling, withdrawing into ourselves and restricting ourselves to minimal interactions with others.[20]

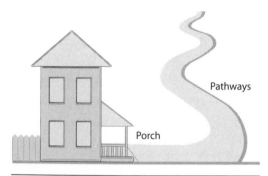

Figure 8.4. Pathways

We are often so busy that we don't see, acknowledge or engage with others on our path. We've become antisocial. The people of God must counter this modern phenomenon. *Pathways* are routes we take daily. The pathways we take shape our understanding of the city. We must gain a significant presence on our city pathways or we will be isolated from the place we belong, making people along our routes nameless and faceless. This requires a shift in behavior. How do we break this silence along our pathway? It can be simple. For example, while walking my dog I greet people and ask them questions when the opportunity arises. On my walk I always pass a bus station and stop to talk to a guy named Reggie, who has become a human to me and I to him. A re-

ciprocal relationship is sprouting. *Are we looking? Do we have eyes to see?*

Consider the following pathway questions:

- What routes do we want to take to engage our neighbors?

- Do we walk? Do we drive?

- Are there people along our pathways we've never noticed?

- Are we open to stopping along the path?

- Do we consistently take the same pathways?

Pivots: From consuming perks to beholding people. "[Jesus] had to pass through Samaria. . . . Jacob's well was still there. Jesus, worn out by the trip, sat down at the well. It was noon. A woman, a Samaritan, came to draw water. Jesus said, 'Would you give me a drink of water?'" (Jn 4:4-8 *The Message*).

A *pivot* is a spot where different sorts of people mingle, where relational intersections occur. When you pivot, there are people within arm's reach. There is a coffee shop I

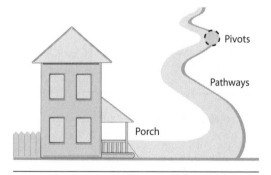

Figure 8.5. Pivots

(Dan) frequent that would be easy to hide out in as I sip on my espresso. Instead, over the years I've had to learn to make introductions, ask questions, acknowledge and engage others, and remember names. A barista once asked, "Are you a counselor or something?" It was an interesting observation, and I replied, "Not really, I just like to know who people are." His response is branded on my mind: "Well, no one likes to do that anymore, do they?" My hipster espresso artist may be right. Rootedness begins when these points of contact are nurtured. Can you imagine if beholding the people at our pivot points became Christianity 101 for disciples? Seedlings of life would be cultivated in subterranean ways without one dollar spent to launch a big church program. A convergence of people from different tribes park in that coffee shop. Recently a group of people sitting in a circle were knitting, drinking coffee and talking about politics. I couldn't help but stick my head in to find out about this quirky mix. They welcomed me in, and I made some new friends. Our pivots are vital places where the kingdom of God begins leaking into our day. Be intentional about them. Gain eyes of faith for holy interruptions and sustainable habits. The biggest temptation we face is to overlook people, seeing them as commodities to serve my needs, not people who matter to God.

The following are some pivot questions to ask:

- Are you a regular?

- Have you made introductions?

- What communities collide there?

- Where are your regular pivots (the YMCA, McDonald's, the bus stop, the park, the pub, etc.)?[21]

Parish: From indifference to responsibility. Matthew says, "Leaving Nazareth, [Jesus] went and lived in Capernaum" (Mt 4:13).

We become disoriented when our sense of location is distorted or unknown. Many people experience disorientation in relation to where they live: they don't know the emotional and physical needs, opportunities and social movements in their place. Orientation within a physical environment is essential for identity formation and for being the expression of Jesus in our place. *Parish* is the word used to describe a sphere of life in a section of a city or suburb. A parish is a smaller area within a larger area that contains an in-

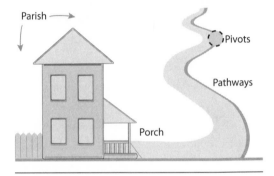

Figure 8.6. Parish

frastructure of concentrated culture, business and residence. Our ability to emotionally attach and resonate requires orientation to the scope and size of a particular place.

A parish is a manageable section of our city we feel some sense of responsibility for. When we don't understand ourselves within our neighborhood, it becomes easy to disconnect our missional actions from its welfare. How we live and how others live should matter to us.

We have a natural tendency to be myopic when we set out to do something significant in a place. We gain energy by spinning a narrative that "no one else is doing what I'm doing." In my (Dan's) section of the city diverse people have been faithfully working for the kingdom of God. We have differing theologies and personalities, but it would be quite arrogant for me to claim special status in this place.

My missional-incarnational community is in a city that resettles almost one thousand refugees each year from Burma, the Congo, Sudan, Iraq and Syria. We've felt a special burden to provide care to these strangers trying to make a new life here. Rather than starting our own program, we explored who was already pressing into this justice issue. We discovered there were others quietly tending to refugee needs. We built a partnership with an organization who could offer us training and guidance. We gleaned a world of information and experience from them, rather than trying to go it alone. We've been able to come together, despite our different beliefs, to extend peace to a people group we both care about in our parish. We still partner with this organization but have since innovated to meet some unique needs we've discovered along the way.

Our territorialism is destructive to the flourishing of the kingdom of God. The first-century disciples were as tempted by this as we are: "'Master . . . we saw someone driving out demons in your name and we tried to stop him, because he is not one of us.' 'Do not stop him,' Jesus said, 'for whoever is not against you is for you'" (Lk 9:49-50). The disciples had a strong we-they mentality even though they knew what it felt like to be outsiders in the empire. We must fight this impulse. God is doing something significant in your parish; spread out your arms to lay hold of it.

Answer the following parish questions:

- How do we fuel love for this place?

- What is beauty in our place?

- What is the brokenness in our place?

- How do we make the pains of this place our pains?[22]

Being a place-based, missional-incarnational community requires us to saturate our neighborhoods with our love-soaked presence. Our culture pulls us away from this orientation but the incarnation of God in Christ compels us to similarly embrace our neighborhoods. God became small for us, and we must become small for the life-worlds we inhabit.

FORMATIONAL LEARNING

 Meta-Learning

- Why did God make himself local?

- Why have we neglected being present in the neighborhood?

 Reflective Learning

- What fears, inadequacies or hurdles do you have to face in order to be intentionally present in your neighborhood?

 Experiential Learning

- With your discipleship core or missional community, list the people and places that fit along the four place-based connectors. Who is around your porch? Who is on your daily and weekly pathways? Who is at your pivots? Who is active in your parish?

- What step can you take in the next week or two to enhance your porch presence? What kind of help do you need to follow through?

8.5 Collaborating for the Common Good

We get a lot of snow in the Northeast. In upstate New York, where I (Dan) am from, we often get buried in it. Last winter I looked out my window and saw a small hatchback stuck on the street, spinning its tires. What caused me to look twice was that one guy was pushing from the back of the car and the other was pushing in the opposite direction from the front. No wonder they weren't moving! I put on my boots and gloves and wandered outside to help. Trying not to insult their intelligence I asked, "Are you both pushing?" They responded yes. It only took a few seconds for them to realize they were working against each other.

They hadn't communicated with each other, other than saying, "You take the front. I'll take the back." Thus a lot of energy was expended without any movement. When we all moved to the back and pushed, our combined energies solved the problem.

This reminds me of passionate churches. In our efforts to live on mission, press into injustice in our city and make an impact, we may be working against each other without knowing it. Christians tend to work with a silo mentality, rarely acknowledging that God is already active in our context. The church as movement must push the car with others rather than going it alone. My great-grandfather used to say, "Work smarter, not harder." What if we looked more carefully at mission in our neighborhoods through a lens of partnership?

Common grace. We live in a competitive age. At times people are more passionate about getting credit than doing genuine good together. Disciples must model a different way, a better and a more subservient way. A rich theology of God's grace in the world, outside of church walls, compels us to work in partnership with others. Some traditions call this "common grace." Romans 1–2 suggests that all humans possess an innate knowledge of God. Knowledge of good is inscribed by God on the heart of every human being (Rom 2:14-15), and every

person is born with a sensibility for honesty, justice and love (Rom 1:20).

Do we live up to perfection? No. But humans are endowed with the *imago Dei* (Latin for God's image). God is caring for the world through his image bearers, and we're often not even aware of it. You don't have to hang out exclusively with Christians (and you shouldn't) to see God's fingerprints in your city. God is tending to your city through those who acknowledge him and those who don't. In the book of James we see that "Every good and perfect gift is from above . . . from the Father of the heavenly lights" (Jas 1:17). This means that every act of goodness, justice and beauty—no matter who does it—is in some way enabled by God. It is a gift and therefore a form of grace.

The prophet Isaiah states,

When a farmer plows for planting. . . .
When he has leveled the surface. . . .
Does he not plant wheat in its place,
 barley in its plot,
 and spelt in its field? . . .
Grain must be ground to make
 bread. . . .
All this also comes from the LORD
 Almighty,
 whose plan is wonderful,
 whose wisdom is magnificent.
 (Is 28:24-25, 28-29)

Isaiah informs us that anyone who becomes a skillful farmer or excels in agricultural science is instructed by God. This is common grace. Artistic expressions, skillful farming, scientific discoveries, social activism,

> Christians tend to work with a silo mentality, rarely acknowledging that God is already active in our context.

and medical and technological advances are partial expressions of God's work in the world. The church needs a new imagination that is able to identify God's common grace in other organizations, activists and persons. We share far more together than has been previously acknowledged.

Common good. Disciples should be looking for God's common grace in those who care about the common good. As a missional-incarnational community becomes faithfully present in their parish, they should likewise tune into the larger work of grace God is doing for the common good. We are invited to expand our concept of church, which includes those outside our brick-and-mortar building and discover an astounding mission.

The common good is all the good we share in common in a parish, a bite-sized chunk of our city. Our focus must shift from the good happening within our own building to the good happening in our neighborhoods. God has called the local church to care for the place where they dwell, whether it is in the wilderness or the city. Hebrews 11:10 says that God is an "architect and builder." We need a thicker imagination for our neighborhoods.

T. J. Gorringe argues that theology ought to be concerned about space, architecture, design, public policy, ecological sustainability and city planning, because all of life expresses our theology. Even buildings "make moral statements." In other words, we make our space, and then our space makes us, so we ought to care about how we make our space.[23]

> Our focus must shift from the good happening within our own building to the good happening in our neighborhoods.

If our missional-incarnational communities are serious about participating in God's *common grace* for the *common good*, we must engage in meaningful, thoughtful action in the larger social, relational and financial sphere of our built environment. God in Christ wants us to have eyes to see and ears to hear what he is up to in the shared space of our city. We must look at ways to be present and partner in all the dimensions of city and town. Our good friends at the Parish Collective have crafted a helpful way to understand these dimensions (see fig. 8.7).[24] Let's unpack what they have to say.

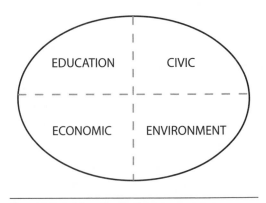

Figure 8.7. Collaborating for the common good

Economy. We all share in the economy because we care that everyone has what they need in order to flourish. There are people in your city who care deeply about food, shelter and employment being available to all, not just to the wealthy. How might you partner with others who are seeking economic common good?

I (Dan) visited a missional community recently in Harrisburg, Pennsylvania. They had observed that it was difficult for those living in the nearby homeless shelter to transition to apartment living once they found a job. The price of apartment rentals was astronomical, so homeless men and women with newfound jobs couldn't afford adequate housing.

This missional community lobbied city officials to release a nearby abandoned building into their care, and they did. They then convinced some local entrepreneurial nonprofits to rent out the bottom floor of the building. This allowed them to cover the cost of maintaining the building, which in turn freed them up to offer inexpensive rental apartments on the second and third floors to the transitional homeless population.

The journey to provide economic stability to the homeless was a long one. Significant networking and collaboration had to occur. They responded to God's act of moving deeper into the world by moving deeper into their own neighborhood. While in the neighborhood, they discovered creative solutions and possibilities already in existence.

Environment. The environment affects us in overt and covert ways. God's people should care about clean air, good soil, sidewalks and safe communal places to play and to participate in God's creation. How might you partner with others who care about this?

My (Dan's) own missional community is in the southwest side of Syracuse. The snow of Syracuse creates all sorts of issues for people. A young woman in our neighborhood observed that some landlords did not shovel the sidewalks and steps to elderly residents' apartments. This passionate woman organized an initiative called Westside Walks, which invites people to join

her in regularly shoveling out those who need help.

This is an example of environmental common good in our neighborhood. Even though we didn't have too many elderly people in our own missional community, we realized that their flourishing should be an issue for us. Some would say snowy sidewalks are a small problem, but a small problem for some is significant for others. So we joined them. Together we've experienced God's grace in partnering with Westside Walks, which has pulled our neighbors together in mutual care for one another.

Civic. Local governance and leadership are civil matters. This includes the way citizens make decisions about their city. Do those who live in the city have power to shape their city? Are those with less resources able to express their concerns about how governing decisions affect them? How is power used in the city?

Six years ago Hillary and her husband, Ryan, moved their family into southwest Detroit to join a culturally rich neighborhood and be a living manifestation of the gospel of Jesus. They enrolled their children in the local elementary school. Shortly after Hillary began volunteering in the school's library, she discovered the school would be closing the following year. Hillary's heart was grieved knowing that losing this bilingual school would be a devastating blow to the many monolingual Latino families living there.

Compelled by her calling to be present to the in-breaking kingdom, Hillary began to organize for civic engagement. She understood that many parents feared speaking up due to the risk of having their undocumented status discovered and being deported. She started by gathering parents and recording their stories so their concerns could be heard. After a long battle with civic officials, the school was taken off the list of schools to be closed.

A vital and necessary school was kept open for children in Hillary's neighborhood. With no experience in civic advocacy, Hillary is now a connecting point between her neighborhood and her missional community as she has recently been elected to a local board to help guide education at the city and state level. Her missional community has been faithfully present in the neighborhood, which has prepared them for beautiful moments in some difficult circumstances. Hillary and Ryan have been pulled into God's renewing work in ways they could have never predicted.

Education. Education is about the formation of young people and their access to society's accumulated wisdom. Do people have access to growing, maturing and developing knowledge? How can the church participate on this ground-level issue?

People and powers certainly abuse these four dimensions. Since the fall (Gen 3) people have been exploiting each other in all of these realms. Followers of Christ are called to live out an alternative story in the local neighborhood. There is a counterstory we are to play out under the nose of those who exploit and subject. This counterstory looks for ways to invigorate these dimensions with the presence of Jesus.

We're not talking missions projects here. Church mission projects are so much smaller than what is possible. The common space we indwell requires faithful presence, not one-off projects. An individual church should have no illusions that it can do all the kingdom work that needs to be done. So we need to be intentional about finding ways to partner across faith boundaries, political boundaries, denominational boundaries, class boundaries and race boundaries.

It is never easy crossing boundaries to cultivate partnerships, but it is important to God because our neighborhoods are important to God. When we, along with others, seek the restoration of our neighborhoods, we open up space for God's Spirit to meet us in surprising ways. God's Spirit hovers at those intersections of human interactions. We discover that God is not locked up in a building, but the Father, Son and Spirit are present where we are challenged to serve others and seek shalom.

FORMATIONAL LEARNING

 Meta-Learning

- How is being a disciple connected to the built environment?

- How is the built environment related to mission?

 Reflective Learning

- Which realm do you sense a passion for economic, environmental, civic and educational dimensions of life? Why?

- What part of missional partnerships are you uncertain about and feel some conflict over?

 Experiential Learning

- Seek a leader or organization in the next few weeks that cares about one or more of the economic, environmental, civic and educational realms. Discover what they are doing for your city. Who is the leader or organization? How can you partner with them? Report back what you learned from this conversation.

Epilogue

· ·

Living in Light of God's Future

We have journeyed together, learning to look through the lens of the church as movement as opposed to the church as industrial complex. We've learned the eight competencies required for starting and sustaining missional-incarnational communities, which are the core element of any church-planting movement. We've learned the importance of being place based, discipleship focused and community forming.

Along the way we have placed various tools in our backpacks, but if we are going to be faithful to the mission, we must be enveloped by sustained *faith*, stubborn *hope* and sacrificial *love*. These three marks indicate we are kingdom oriented. We cannot start and sustain missional-incarnational communities that are a sign, foretaste and instrument of God's kingdom without these marks. As Paul has said, "Three things will last forever—faith, hope, and love—and the greatest of these is love" (1 Cor 13:13 NLT).

Sustained Faith

We all start our journey with God by faith in the life, death and resurrection of Jesus. We not only start our journey with faith, but we continue to be people who live by faith. We need to have a sustained faith.

Living by faith means learning to trust God for everything in life. God calls us to do something, and we experience fear. But if we choose to follow God, we experience his presence and see his beauty through both suffering and resurrection power.

Faith is having confidence that God wants to bless us so we might be a blessing to others. Faith is seeing the unseen and clinging to God's promises until they come to pass. Faith believes that the impossible is possible. "Faith is confidence in the kindness of God no matter the confusion of circumstances."[1] Faith moves mountains and enables us to remove obstacles the devil puts on our path.

What is the greatest need you have right now? Maybe it's a financial need, or an emotional one. Are you trusting God to meet that need? Faith trusts that as we seek first his kingdom and righteousness God will provide for all our needs (Mt 6:33).

Starting and sustaining missional-incarnational communities comes with many bumps, bruises and scars. It can often feel as if everything is hanging by a thread. What do we do when we become afraid, when things look dark and bleak?

After moving to Los Angeles, our (JR's) team of thirty-six people were in fifty car accidents within the first eighteen months. According to the Holmes and Rahe Stress Scale, a score of 250 points means you are in the overstressed zone. Over three-fourths of our team scored 300 or above, with a couple of people scoring over 600.[2] We were dealing with major stress. One couple that moved to LA with us was moving into their house. While moving boxes, the husband was reaching the door of the house and a random bullet came within a foot of his head. His wife and baby daughter were nearby. They were the first staff people to leave our church plant.

After a *Los Angeles Times* article came out about our church, someone sent me (JR) an anonymous letter, using cut up letters from a magazine, threatening to hurt me physically.

Making disciples, planting churches and growing movements is one of the toughest things we will do in life. It is spiritually, emotionally and physically wearing. As we seek to bless others, we will encounter tough times. Starting missional-incarnational communities who grow into a church does not mean amassing all the stats and machinery to guarantee success. It is a step into the unknown. God meets us in the unknown.

There is a great scene in the movie *Indiana Jones and the Holy Grail*. Indy (Harrison Ford) is journeying through a dangerous obstacle course with a hard-to-decipher map. The map only gives him clues, no answers. At one point Indy arrives at a massive chasm—a bottomless pit. He doesn't know how to get across. He can't jump it or swing across. The map says, "Take a step of faith." He is baffled, believing there must be something he's missing. If he steps out, he will plummet to his death.

He struggles, and sweats and almost turns around. Eventually, Indy clutches his chest and steps into the bottomless chasm. Suddenly a pathway appears under his feet. He could not see a way, but a way was provided only after he took a step. This is faith. Along the way we will have to dig deep and lean hard into the Trinity with trust. In the midst of our suffering, our failure, we will see very little of our pathway. God will ask us to step forward into his arms.

Stubborn Hope

In addition to living by faith, we need to hold on to hope. We need stubborn hope. In starting missional communities we have to endure many emotional hits. For example, too often our expectations of what can happen in the first year are too high, and what can happen in ten years is too low. Finances are an area where we can take emotional hits. We're always stretching and straining to make ends meet. Lack of money can tear away at our self-image, create tension and cripple our relationships with those we are closest to. And sometimes people on our core team turn on us and we experience the deep wounds of betrayal. Ministry crises come when we least expect it.

When life becomes difficult and our dreams fade, what helps us persevere? When we are discouraged, what lifts our spirits? When we're ready to throw in the towel, what helps us to not give up? Hope. Hope is essential to our survival. Hope is the belief that something better is around the corner. And hope pulls us through tragedies.

Harold Wilth, a physician at the medical school of Cornell University, led a study of twenty-five thousand WWII POWs. They all survived inhumane conditions—torture, mistreatment, malnourishment and distress. Wilth's conclusion was that men and women can withstand incredible pressure and stress as long as they have hope.[3] But the moment hope is gone, life is done. We can't live without hope!

Hope not only pulls us through tragedies but brings new perspective. Hope allows us to see the world through different eyes. It's like the common illustration of a girl in college who sent her parents this letter:

Dear Mom and Dad,

I have so much to tell you. Because of the fire in my dorm room set off by the student riots, I experienced temporary lung damage and had to go to the hospital. While I was there, I fell in love with an orderly. We have moved in together. I dropped out of school when I found out that I was pregnant. Then he got fired because of his drinking, so we are going to move to Alaska where we might get married after the birth of the baby.

The letter was signed: Your loving daughter. Then there was a postscript.

P.S. None of that really happened. I did flunk my chemistry class and I wanted you to keep it in perspective.

Hope helps us keep things in perspective.

Someone once said that

- If you want to be distressed—look within.
- If you want to be defeated—look back.
- If you want to be distracted—look around.
- If you want to be dismayed—look ahead.
- If you want to be delivered—look up![4]

Each of us needs to ask what we are putting our hope in. We believe that the church is the hope of the world, but sometimes I ask myself, *Is there any hope for the church?*

If I (JR) had thirty minutes with the apostle Paul, one of the things I would ask him is this: Why did you continue planting churches even though many of the churches you planted had tons of problems? I mean, look at the church in Galatia. By your own admission you thought they had totally forgotten what the good news was all about. And what about the church in Corinth? How could you even call it a church, with all the divisions, sexual immorality and drunkenness that was going on? Come on, Paul, why bother planting more churches? After all, not only were a number of your churches messy, but planting churches caused you a lot of personal pain as well. Why did you endure so much pain? You were flogged severely on five different occasions where they whipped you thirty-nine times. How did you endure all of the beatings with rods and the imprisonments? Why did you go without sleep, food and drink at times?

As I read through the New Testament with those questions in mind, I came to realize that Paul could endure all of that because his hope was in the triune God's ability to bring about new creation—the redemption of our bodies and the redemption of the world. He had confidence that because of the life, death and resurrection of Christ, the new creation would be fully realized some day.

We all live a part of some story. Because Paul lived in God's story and understood that God will eventually make all things right, it gave him hope to endure, no matter what he faced.

Paul's hope was based on the love of the Father, the faithfulness of the Son and the power of the Holy Spirit. What story are you living in? Does it give you a stubborn hope as you think about the future, or does it bring despair?

Sacrificial Love

There are three things that endure: faith, hope and love. The greatest of these is love. The love that we experience as we live into the love of the Father, Son and Spirit fills our hearts and flows from our lives to those around us. "We love because he first loved us" (1 Jn 4:19). Jesus loved us with a sacrificial love, and because he loved us this way, we can love others sacrificially.

As we are submerged in the love of God, we can't keep it to ourselves. The overwhelming sense of love we feel compels us to invite others to experience the same. As Dallas Willard says, "The aim of God in history is the creation of an all-inclusive community of loving persons with God himself at the center."[5]

Yet we have become good at building walls. We build walls between us and people that look different from us. We build walls between us and those who have fewer resources than us. We build walls to keep out people who were born in different geographic parts of the world. We build walls to protect our version of the good life. We build walls to isolate us from problems and to protect us from pain. We have become experts at building walls.[6]

But God has sent us to build bridges. Through Christ, God has destroyed the barriers we have erected, and he invites us to live *in him* and to be a part of the one new humanity. He has commissioned us to be ministers of reconciliation, bringing together what has been torn apart. These bridges are not built "by human idealism or democratic legalism but by the work of Christ."[7]

If we are true to our faith and love our neighbors as Jesus did, we'll love them no matter their country of origin, no matter the color of their skin, no matter their financial status, no matter their sexual preference. We will love people no matter what their religious or spiritual tradition may be. We will actively work for everyone's well being, not because my neighbor is or might become a Christian. If I want to faithfully follow Jesus, I will love my neighbor because I am a Christian.

One of the most provocative things about Jesus is that he broke down walls and built bridges. He redrew the boundaries of the kingdom of God to include those who previously had been excluded. He destroyed the social and geographical walls built by the religious and government authorities. Jesus' kingdom knew nothing of political, social or religious barriers.

He preached that the kingdom of God is at hand, and all who had been in exile, all who are estranged from their Creator, are welcome at the table. It didn't matter what people's spiritual, social, ethnic or economic standing was. All were welcome.

Jesus' essential message was that the kingdom of God is now available to everyone through him. And as you follow Jesus, as you follow *his ways*, his kingdom will break into your neighborhood, your city, your world.

C. S. Lewis said, "I believe in Christianity as I believe that the sun has risen. Not only because I see it, but because by it I see everything else."[8] As we live into God's future in the present, we can be the preview, "the prototype, the herald, the midwife of the new world on the way."[9]

As you seek to make disciples, start missional-incarnational communities, plant churches and grow a movement, remember that you could be more talented than Michael Jordan, more creative than da Vinci, more gifted than Beethoven, more adventurous than Columbus, more missional than Newbigin, with more tools than Tim Allen, giving away more than Mother Teresa, a greater activist than Gandhi, a better wordsmith than Shakespeare, more paradigm-breaking than Copernicus, with a greater imagination than Einstein—but *without love, you are nothing*, and you gain nothing.

Church as movement cultivates communities who live by faith, are a voice of hope and are known by their love.[10] In order to live into church as movement, you will need to change the way you look at the church. You need to ditch the church as industrial complex. If you want movement, you need to be willing to start small and focus on making disciples, remembering that discipleship is more about imitation than instruction. You need to become a master at helping your discipleship core start missional-incarnational communities who multiply across the city, into other states and countries, and even to the uttermost parts of the earth. In this way we can be faithful to the commission Jesus gave us.

Acknowledgments

· ·

We are thankful for the love of the Father, the faithfulness of the Son and fellowship of the Holy Spirit, who have enveloped us with love and sustained our faith. God has given us a stubborn hope and he is teaching us a selfless love.

God has given us a community of beautiful people who have supported us and journeyed with us, making this book possible. We are thankful for the Baptist General Association of Virginia (BGAV); John Upton (executive director) and Wayne Faison (team coordinator) of Growth-Venture Development for investing in us and giving us the freedom to cultivate the beginnings of a church-planting movement in North America, as the apostolic arm of the BGAV.

We are thankful for our V3 team which has been integral in building the ground floor of a movement: Lori Ruffin, Lisa Racek, Lauren Tom, Sang Shin, Mike Pumphrey, Matt Alexander, Ben Sternke, Joe Racek, Matthew Watson and Ron Willoughby. We want to thank Tim Catchim, who gave his brilliance and best insights into the early days of our V3 training. We have deep appreciation for the V3 church planters spread across North America who have given us on-the-ground feedback and are the first seeds of why this book was given birth.

Without the detailed and helpful critique of our IVP editor, Helen Lee, this book wouldn't be what it is today. Helen, thanks for all of your discerning comments that enabled us to produce a work that is so much better than it would have been without you. We are also thankful for the copyediting work done by Drew Blankman.

We are thankful for our anonymous readers who gave us invaluable input. We are also grateful to Ben Sternke, Chuck Harrison, Ken Kessler, Phil Meadows, Tyrone Daniel, Matt Norman, John Chandler, Tom Mauriello, Jeremy Chen, Jay Lawson, David Bailey and Bill Couchenour for pouring over our original manuscript and giving us solid input.

I (Dan) want to thank my wife, Tonya, for her support during the writing phase and for being a champion for living into the contents of this book alongside me.

I (JR) want to thank Matthew and Stephanie Yi and their children Gabby and Thaddeus, who have shown me amazing hospitality by hosting me at their house while I was in-between residencies.

Our hope is that ordinary Christians will gather a discipleship core and start missional-incarnational communities in neighborhoods around the world that are a sign, foretaste and instrument of God's in-breaking kingdom.

Notes

· ·

Foreword

[1]Alan Hirsch, *The Forgotten Ways: Reactivating the Missional Church* (Grand Rapids: Brazos, 2006); and Alan Hirsch and Dave Ferguson, *On The Verge: The Future of the Church as Apostolic Movement* (Grand Rapids: Zondervan, 2012). For the logic of my writings see www.alanhirsch.org/blog/2015/6/27/why-i-do-the-things-i-do.

Introduction

[1]This is Michael Hyatt's terminology in his blog post "The Leadership Strategy of Jesus," *Your Virtual Mentor* (blog), March 28, 2016, http://michaelhyatt.com/the-leadership-strategy-of-jesus.html.

[2]Some of the thoughts in this section come from a devotional reading of Dallas Willard's *The Great Omission: Reclaiming Jesus's Essential Teaching on Discipleship* (New York: HarperCollins, 2006).

[3]See C. Christopher Smith and John Pattison, *Slow Church* (Downers Grove, IL: InterVarsity Press, 2014), and Tim Suttle, *Shrink* (Grand Rapids: Zondervan, 2014).

[4]Robert Coleman, *The Master Plan of Evangelism* (Old Tappan, NJ: Fleming H. Revell, 1963), 19.

[5]You can find some resources in regard to public space on our website, churchasmovement.com.

[6]While the Twelve holds theological significance, representing the twelve tribes of Israel, the number also holds sociological significance.

[7]Some of this translation is from Dallas Willard in *The Great Omission.*

1 Movement Intelligence

[1]President Dwight D. Eisenhower's Farewell Address (1961), *OurDocuments.gov*, www.ourdocuments.gov/doc.php?flash=true&doc=90.

[2]Skye Jethani, "The Evangelical Industrial Complex and the Rise of Celebrity Pastors," *Skye Jethani* (blog), February 13, 2012, https://skyejethani.com/the-evangelical-industrial-complex-the-rise-of-celebrity-pastors; Scott Bessenecker, *Overturning Tables: Freeing Missions from the Christian-Industrial Complex* (Downers Grove, IL: InterVarsity Press, 2014).

[3]"Euro-tribal" is Alan Roxburgh's terminology.

[4]David J. Bosch, *Transforming Mission: Paradigm Shifts in Theology of Mission* (Maryknoll, NY: Orbis Books, 1991), 2

[5]Alan Hirsch, *The Forgotten Ways: Reactivating the Missional Church* (Grand Rapids: Brazos, 2006).

[6]See John Drane, *The McDonaldization of the Church: Consumer Culture and the Church's Future* (Macon, GA: Smyth & Helwys, 2001).

[7]Lesslie Newbigin, *The Open Secret: An Introduction to the Theology of Mission* (Grand Rapids: Eerdmans, 1978), 127.

[8]Ibid., 60.

[9]Roland Allen, *The Spontaneous Expansion of the Church: And the Causes That Hinder It* (Eugene, OR: Wipf & Stock, 1962), 8.

[10]Hirsch, *Forgotten Ways*, 19.

[11]For an excellent resource on a historical perspective of the missional church, see Craig Van Gelder and Dwight J. Zscheile, *The Missional*

Church in Perspective: Mapping Trends and Shaping the Conversation (Grand Rapids: Baker, 2011).

[12]While the Anglican five marks are the same globally, their wording may vary country to country. I am using Australia's wording, for it expresses it well.

[13]Karl Barth, *Theologische Fragen und Antworten* (1957), 183-84; quoted in R. J. Erler and R. Marquard, eds., trans. G. W. Bromiley, *A Karl Barth Reader* (Grand Rapids: Eerdmans, 1986), 8-9; emphasis added.

[14]Vincent J. Donovan Jr., *Christianity Rediscovered: An Epistle from the Masai* (Notre Dame, IN: Fides/Claretian, 1976), 140; emphasis added.

[15]This phrase was taken from Anne Rowthorn, *The Liberation of the Laity* (Eugene, OR: Wipf and Stock, 1986), 27.

[16]Hans Küng, *The Church* (New York: Burns and Oates, 1968), 383.

[17]While it is easy to find resources showing the fallacy of the clergy-laity divide, a good start would be to read Michael Kruse's excellent article, "The 'Clergy People of God' and the Myth of Laity," *Kruse Kronicle*, September 29, 2005, http://krusekronicle.typepad.com/kruse_kronicle/2005/09/klaos_the_clerg.html.

[18]Martin Kähler, *Schriftenzur Christologie und Mission*, 90, quoted in Bosch, *Transforming Mission*, 16.

[19]Lesslie Newbigin, *A Word in Season: Perspectives on Christian World Missions* (Grand Rapids: Eerdmans, 1994), 129.

[20]Dietrich Bonhoeffer, *The Cost of Discipleship* (New York: Touchstone, 1995), 59.

[21]Philip R. Meadows, "Making Disciples That Renew the Church," *Inspire*, 2013, http://inspiremovement.org/network/making-disciples. These principles are worked out more fully in Philip R. Meadows, "Wesleyan Wisdom for Mission-Shaped Discipleship," *Journal of Missional Practice* 3, January 2014.

[22]Quoted in Octavius Brooks Frothingham, *Memoir of William Henry Channing* (Boston: Houghton, Mifflin and Co., 1886), 166.

[23]Allen, *Spontaneous Expansion of the Church*, 156.

[24]Eugene Peterson, *Answering God: The Psalms as Tools for Prayer* (New York: HarperCollins, 1989), 1.

[25]While some movement and management literature use some combination of simple, sticky, sustainable and scalable, this particular combination of terms "simple, sticky and scalable" was introduced to us by Tim Catchim, and more importantly Tim influenced us to make all our tools simple, sticky and scalable.

[26]Fredrick Buechner, *Listening to Your Life: Daily Meditations with Fredrick Buechner* (New York: HarperOne, 1992), 186.

[27]*Theo-genetic codes* terminology comes from Alan Hirsch and Tim Catchim, *The Permanent Revolution: Apostolic Imagination and Practice for the 21st Century Church* (San Francisco: Jossey-Bass, 2012), 3.

[28]This is a paraphrase of a line from Parker Palmer, *Let Your Life Speak* (San Francisco: Jossey-Bass, 2000), 3.

[29]Parts of this description of the fivefold typology come from JR Woodward, *Creating a Missional Culture: Equipping the Church for the Sake of the World* (Downers Grove, IL: InterVarsity Press, 2012).

[30]Andrew C. Dowsett, "Jesus-Given: Living the Life You Were Called to Be," unpublished manuscript, 2012, 10.

[31]If you are particularly fond of assessments, see Alan Hirsch's assessment of the fivefold typology at "What Is APEST?," *The Forgotten Ways*, www.theforgottenways.org/what-is-apest.aspx.

[32]This is an adaptation of Walter Brueggemann, quoted in Tim Suttle, *Shrink* (Grand Rapids: Zondervan, 2014), 64.

[33]For a fuller definition of each of these people gifts, go to "Equippers," *JR Woodward* (blog), accessed February 22, 2016, http://jrwoodward.net/equippers.

[34]Base and phase language was developed by Mike Breen and Steve Cockram, *Building a Discipleship Culture* (Pawleys Island, SC: 3DM, 2011), chap. 10.

2 Polycentric Leadership

[1]Some content in this section is taken or adapted from JR Woodward, *Creating a Missional Culture:*

Equipping the Church for the Sake of the World (Downers Grove, IL: InterVarsity Press, 2012).

[2]Marva Dawn, *Powers, Weakness, and the Tabernacling of God* (Grand Rapids: Eerdmans, 2001).

[3]Stanley Hauerwas, *Against the Nations: War and Survival in a Liberal Society* (Notre Dame, IN: University of Notre Dame Press, 1992), 118.

[4]Suzanne W. Morse, "Five Building Blocks for Successful Leadership," in *The Community of the Future*, ed. Frances Hesselbein et al. (San Francisco: Jossey-Bass, 1998), 234.

[5]Go to churchasmovement.com to learn about how to develop a financial framework.

[6]Alan Hirsch and Tim Catchim develop this idea in *The Permanent Revolution: Apostolic Imagination and Practice for the 21st Century Church* (San Francisco: Jossey-Bass, 2012), 21-22.

[7]Figure 2.1 is adapted from Hirsch and Catchim, *The Permanent Revolution*.

[8]Abraham Maslow developed the four stages of learning, from unconscious incompetence to unconscious competence.

[9]David E. Fitch, *The Great Giveaway: Reclaiming the Mission of the Church from Big Business, Parachurch, Psychotherapy, Consumer Capitalism and Other Modern Maladies* (Grand Rapids: Baker, 2005), 80.

[10]Ibid., 81.

3 Being Disciples

[1]This is adapted from JR Woodward, *Creating a Missional Culture: Equipping the Church for the Sake of the World* (Downers Grove, IL: InterVarsity Press, 2012), 113-14.

[2]The apostle Paul recommends people follow him as he follows Christ very directly six different times in the New Testament (1 Cor 4:16; 11:1; Gal 4:12; Phil 3:17; 4:9; 2 Thess 3:7-9).

[3]David Brenner, *The Gift of Being Yourself: The Sacred Call to Self-Discovery* (Downers Grove, IL: InterVarsity Press, 2004), 19-32.

[4]This framework and language is based on my (JR) interactions with Wil Hernandez and his book *Henri Nouwen: The Spirituality of Imperfection* (Mahwah, NJ: Paulist Press, 2006).

[5]Ibid., 3.

[6]Walter Brueggemann describes these three categories as psalms of orientation, disorientation and reorientation in *The Message of the Psalms: A Theological Commentary* (Minneapolis: Augsburg, 1984).

[7]A. W. Tozer, *The Pursuit of God* (Rockville, MD: Serenity, 2009), 13.

[8]Hernandez, *Henri Nouwen*, 2.

[9]Ibid., 3.

[10]Nouwen, Henri, *Bread for the Journey: A Daybook of Wisdom and Faith.* (New York: HarperCollins, 1997), 11.

[11]Henry Nouwen, *In the Name of Jesus: Reflections on Christian Leadership* (New York: Crossroad, 1992), 16-18.

[12]Chuck Swindoll, *Growing Strong in the Seasons of Life* (Grand Rapids: Zondervan, 1983), 156.

[13]Tim Hansel, *Through the Wilderness of Loneliness* (Colorado Springs: David C. Cook, 1991), 23.

[14]Eugene Peterson, *Leap Over a Wall: Earthy Spirituality for Everyday Christians* (New York: HarperCollins, 1997), 53.

[15]John Ortberg, *Everybody's Normal Till You Get to Know Them* (Grand Rapids: Zondervan, 2003), 82.

[16]Joseph Luft, *On Human Interaction: The Johari Model* (Palo Alto, CA: Mayflower Publishing, 1969).

[17]Fredrick Buechner, *Telling Secrets: A Memoir* (New York: HarperCollins, 1991), 2.

4 Making Disciples

[1]N. T. Wright, *Paul for Everyone* (Louisville: Westminster John Knox, 2004), 22.

[2]While the Twelve obviously have symbolic significance, correlating to the twelve tribes of Israel, they also have practical significance in the Jewish tradition. A rabbi would typically take on two handfuls of apprentices for intentional shaping purposes. Too many more than that diminished the quality of Midrash, which was a conversant and questioning way of interacting with the master's teaching.

[3]"Bruce Tuckman's 1965 Forming Storming Norming Performing Team-Development Model," © Bruce Tuckman 1965, Alan Chapman 2001–2013, www .businessballs.com/tuckmanformingstorming

normingperforming.htm. While the terms and concepts of forming, storming, norming, and performing are Tuchman's, Tim Catchim developed a two-question format for each phase. We have develop our own unique version of this.

4This issue of the movement of the temple reflects the difference between a dispensational reading and a covenantal reading of the text. I read it covenantally, believing that the temple is no longer in Jerusalem but is now in the new covenant people of God.

5Having three to five Cs, including most of the ones we have listed, are a common way people discern who should be on their team, but this unique group and order of the five was developed by Tim Catchim, along with the alliterations of "theology, team, and tactics" under compatibility, and "schedule and stress" under capacity.

6JR Woodward, *Creating a Missional Culture: Equipping the Church for the Sake of the World* (Downers Grove, IL: InterVarsity Press, 2012), 233-34. (Read this portion of the book to get longer descriptions.)

7For an example of a rule of faith, visit the church as movement website: churchasmovement.com.

5 Missional Theology

1JR Woodward, *Creating a Missional Culture: Equipping the Church for the Sake of the World* (Downers Grove, IL: InterVarsity Press, 2012), 88.

2Leonardo Boff, *Holy Trinity, Perfect Community* (Maryknoll, NY: Orbis, 2000), 3.

3Stanley J. Grenz, *Rediscovering the Triune God: The Trinity in Contemporary Theology* (Minneapolis: Fortress Press, 2004), 32.

4Mike Reeves, *Delighting in the Trinity: An Introduction to the Christian Faith* (Downers Grove, IL: InterVarsity Press, 2012), 44.

5Jonathan Marlowe, "Dance of the Trinity," *The Ivy Bush* (blog), May 18, 2008, http://theivybush .blogspot.com/2008/05/dance-of-trinity.html.

6Baxter Kruger, *The Great Dance: The Christian Vision Revisited* (Jackson, MS: Perichoresis, 2005), chap. 1.

7Stanley J. Grenz, *Rediscovering the Triune God: The Trinity in Contemporary Theology* (Minneapolis: Fortress Press, 2004), 6.

8Ibid., 15.

9See Veli-Matti Kärkkäinen, *The Trinity: Global Perspectives* (Louisville, KY: Westminster John Knox, 2007).

10Craig Van Gelder and Dwight Jr. Zscheile, *The Missional Church in Perspective* (Grand Rapids: Baker, 2011), 104.

11Miroslav Volf, *After Our Likeness: The Church as the Image of the Trinity* (Grand Rapids: Eerdmans, 1998), 173; emphasis added.

12While there were differences in Jesus' approach, we can learn how to see God at work through these resources. For a resource on asset-based community development see John McKnight and Peter Block, *The Abundant Community: Awakening the Power of Families and Neighborhoods* (San Francisco: Berett-Koehler, 2010). Free resources can be found by googling "asset-based community development."

13Bryant L. Myers, *Walking with the Poor: Principles and Practices of Transformational Development* (Maryknoll, NY: Orbis, 1999), 155.

14I (JR) develop this idea more completely in *Creating a Missional Culture.*

15David Bosch, *Transforming Mission: Paradigm Shifts in Theology of Mission* (Maryknoll, NY: Orbis, 1991), 392.

16"Sign," "foretaste" and "instrument" are common ways that Lesslie Newbigin spoke about the nature and mission of the church. I (JR) talk more about what this means in *Creating a Missional Culture.*

17N. T. Wright, *Simply Good News: Why the Gospel Is News and What Makes It Good* (New York: Harper-Collins, 2015), 49.

18This language was developed by Lesslie Newbigin and used in many of his books.

19Ursula K. Le Guin, *Language of the Night* (New York: Putnam Adult, 1979), 22.

20Harrison Monarth, "The Irresistible Power of Storytelling as a Strategic Business Tool," *Harvard Business Review*, March 11, 2014, https://hbr .org/2014/03/the-irresistible-power-of-story-telling-as-a-strategic-business-tool.

21Walter Brueggemann, *Biblical Perspectives on Evangelism: Living in a Three-Storied Universe* (Nashville: Abingdon Press, 1993), 65.

22Jonathan Wilson-Hartgrove, "The Good News

for Durham, North Carolina," in *Viral Hope: Good News from the Urbs to the Burbs (and Everything in Between)*, ed. JR Woodward (Los Angeles: Ecclesia, 2010), 155-56.

[23]Graham Tomlin, cited in Woodward, *Creating a Missional Culture*, 144.

[24]Stanley Hauerwas, *A Community of Character* (Notre Dame, IN: University of Notre Dame Press, 1981), 136.

[25]Michael E. Wittmer, *Heaven Is a Place on Earth: Why Everything You Do Matters to God* (Grand Rapids: Zondervan, 2004), 16; emphasis added.

[26]See Woodward, *Creating a Missional Culture*, 115.

[27]Wittmer, *Heaven Is a Place on Earth*, 188.

[28]Figure 5.9, aside from the icons, is a slight revision of the Kairos West LA story of God developed by my friend and coworker Andy Bleyer and some of his team.

[29]Wright, *Simply Good News*, 55.

[30]Leonardo Boff expands the seven traditional sacraments of the church to such topics as "My Father's Cigarette Butt as Sacrament," "Homemade Bread as Sacrament," "A Christmas Candle as Sacrament," "Life Story as Sacrament," "A School Teacher as Sacrament" and "Home as Sacrament." See Leonardo Boff, *Sacraments of Life and Life of the Sacraments* (Portland, OR: Pastoral Press, 1987).

[31]John Howard Yoder, *Body Politics: Five Practices of the Christian Community* (Scottdale, PA: Herald, 1992).

6 Ecclesial Architecture

[1]Stanley Grenz, *Theology for the Community of God* (Grand Rapids: Eerdmans, 2000), 464.

[2]Craig Van Gelder, *The Essence of the Church: A Community Created by the Spirit* (Grand Rapids: Baker, 2000), 106.

[3]Ibid., 23.

[4]Ibid., 24.

[5]Veli-Matti Kärkkäinen, *An Introduction to Ecclesiology: Ecumenical, Historical and Global Perspectives* (Downers Grove: InterVarsity Press, 2002).

[6]A tweet of our friend Kevin Sweeney.

[7]Marjorie Thompson, *Soul Feast: An Invitation to the Christian Spiritual Life* (Louisville, KY: Westminster John Knox, 1995), 146.

[8]Allan Bloom, quoted in Graham Tomlin, *Spiritual Fitness: Christian Character in a Consumer Culture* (London: Continuum Books, 2005), 31.

[9]Philip Kenneson, *Life on the Vine: Cultivating the Fruit of the Spirit in Christian Community* (Downers Grove, IL: InterVarsity Press, 1999).

[10]See churchasmovement.com.

[11]See churchasmovement.com.

[12]Eugene Peterson, *Working the Angles: The Shape of Pastoral Integrity* (Grand Rapids: Eerdmans, 1987), 72-73; emphasis added.

[13]Marva Dawn, *Keeping Sabbath Wholly: Ceasing, Resting, Embracing, Feasting* (Grand Rapids: Eerdmans, 1989). This is simply an overview of what she covers in her book.

[14]Diane Ackerman, "The Brain on Love," *Opinionator* (blog), *The New York Times*, February 24, 2012, www.opinionator.blogs.nytimes.com/2012/03/24/the-brain-on.love.

[15]Joseph Myers, The *Search to Belong: Rethinking Intimacy, Community, and Small Groups* (Grand Rapids: Zondervan, 2003), 22-24.

[16]While you can find some ways we start to do this at churchasmovement.com, it would require a whole book to tease this out well.

[17]Neil Cole, *Organic Church: Growing Faith Where Life Happens* (San Francisco: Jossey-Bass 2005).

[18]Lesslie Newbigin, *Foolishness to the Greeks: The Gospel and Western Culture* (London: SPCK, 1986), 3; emphasis added.

[19]JR Woodward, *Creating a Missional Culture: Equipping the Church for the Sake of the World* (Downers Grove, IL: InterVarsity Press, 2012), 36.

[20]Shelly Trebesch, *Made to Flourish: Beyond Quick Fixes to a Thriving Organization* (Downers Grove, IL: InterVarsity Press, 2015), 13.

[21]Joseph Myers, *Organic Community: Creating a Place Where People Naturally Connect* (Grand Rapids: Baker, 2007), 59.

7 Community Formation

[1]Adapted from Dan White Jr., *Subterranean: Why the Future of the Church Is Rootedness* (Eugene, OR: Cascade Books, 2015), 122.

[2]Robert J. Banks, *Paul's Idea of Community* (Grand

Rapids: Baker, 1994), 57-58.

[3]Henri Nouwen, *In the Name of Jesus: Reflections on Christian Leadership* (New York: Crossroad, 1992), 52-53.

[4]Jean Vanier, *Community and Growth* (Mahwah, NJ: Paulist Press, 1989), 110-11.

[5]Robert Karris, *Eating Your Way Through Luke's Gospel* (Collegeville, MN: Liturgical Press, 2006), 34-35.

[6]Baltimore Lutheran Campus Ministry, "The Revolutionary Table of Jesus," ministry blog, September 2, 2013, www.baltimorelutherancampus ministry.org/apps/blog/show/32736062-the -revolutionary-table-of-jesus.

[7]Jan Michael Joncas, *Tasting the Reign of God: The Meal Ministry of Jesus* (St. Paul, MN: Center for Catholic Studies, 2000), 100-102.

[8]This section is based on chapter three of *Creating a Missional Culture: Equipping the Church for the World* (Downers Grove, IL: InterVarsity Press, 2012), applied to missional communities.

[9]Andy Stanley, "Trust vs. Suspicion," Andy Stanley Leadership Podcast, http://podbay.fm/show /290055666/e/1365185340?autostart=1.

[10]Rod Tucker, *Uncovered: The Truth About Honesty and Community* (Grand Rapids: Kregal, 2014), 44-45.

[11]Larry Crabb, *Connecting: Healing for Ourselves and Our Relationships* (Nashville: W Publishing Group, 1997), 67-68.

[12]Christine D. Pohl, *Living into Community: Cultivating Practices That Sustain Us* (Grand Rapids: Eerdmans, 2012), 51-52.

[13]John Howard Yoder, *Body Politics: Five Practices of the Christian Community* (Scottdale: Herald Press, 1992), 14-15.

[14]Ibid., 16.

[15]Ibid., 17.

8 Incarnational Practices

[1]René Padilla, *Mission Between the Times* (Grand Rapids: Eerdmans, 1985), 93.

[2]Gerhard Lohfink, *Does God Need the Church?*, trans. Linda M. Maroney (Collegeville, MN: Michael Glazier Book, 1999), viii.

[3]NEAR is a simplified version of the cultural web that I (JR) develop in *Creating a Missional Culture: Equipping the Church for the Sake of the World* (Downers Grove, IL: InterVarsity Press, 2012). In this case, instead of applying it to the church, I'm applying it to the neighborhood.

[4]Robert Frost, "The Road Not Taken," 1916.

[5]Jon Huckins and Rob Yackley, *Thin Places: Six Postures for Creating and Practicing Missional Community* (Kansas City: House Studio, 2012), 49-51.

[6]For an excellent article on living incarnationally, see Karen Wilks, "Postmodern, Post-Christendom . . . Postcommunter?," *V3 Movement*, http:// thev3movement.org/2015/07/postcommuter -neighbourhood-life.

[7]Simone Weil, *The Need for Roots: Prelude to a Declaration of Duties Toward Mankind* (New York: Routledge Classics 2002), 43.

[8]Andy Crouch, "Ten Most Significant Cultural Trends of the Last Decade," quoted in Leonard Hjalmarson, *No Home Like Place: A Christian Theology of Place* (Portland, OR: Urban Loft, 2014), 126.

[9]We have adapted the language of "for, with, of and in" from Alex Absalom and Greg Nettle's free ebook, *One Of: Beginning the Missional Journey*, available at alexabsalom.com/resources.

[10]N. T. Wright, *Surprised by Hope: Rethinking Heaven, the Resurrection, and the Mission of the Church* (New York: Harper Collins, 2008), 230.

[11]I picked up this phrase from Kevin and Christine Sweeney.

[12]Both of these entries are taken from Jared and Mary Beth Dragoun's newsletter, used by permission.

[13]Bob Hopkins and Mary Hopkins, *Evangelism Strategies* (Great Britain: Alderway, 2012).

[14]This analogy came from Kevin and Christine Sweeney, cofounders of Imagine in Honolulu.

[15]C. S. Lewis, *The Weight of Glory* (New York: HarperCollins, 2001), 3-19.

[16]Jonathan Wilson-Hartgrove, *The Wisdom of Stability: Rooting Faith in a Mobile Culture* (Brewster, MA: Paraclete, 2010), 32-34.

[17]Robert J. Schreiter, *Constructing Local Theologies* (Maryknoll, NY: Orbis, 1985), 88-90.

[18]Drew DeSilver, "How the Most Ideologically Polarized Americans Live Different Lives," Fact Tank, June 13, 2014, www.pewresearch.org/fact

-tank/2014/06/13/big-houses-art-museums-and-in-laws-how-the-most-ideologically-polarized-americans-live-different-lives.

[19]David Seamon, *A Geography of the Lifeworld* (New York: St. Martins, 1979), 45-47.

[20]This paragraph is adapted from Dan White Jr., *Subterranean: Why the Future of the Church Is Rootedness* (Eugene, OR: Cascade Books, 2015), 105.

[21]Adapted from White, *Subterranean*, 105.

[22]Ibid.

[23]T. J. Gorringe, *A Theology of the Built Environment: Justice, Empowerment, Redemption* (New York: Cambridge University Press, 2002).

[24]Paul Sparks, Tim Soerens and Dwight J. Friesen, *The New Parish: How Neighborhood Churches Are Transforming Mission, Discipleship and Community* (Downers Grove, IL: InterVarsity Press, 2014).

Epilogue: Living in Light of God's Future

[1]Ann Voskamp, @AnnVoskamp, August 27, 2015.

[2]The Holmes and Rahe Stress Scale can be found at the MindTools website: www.mindtools.com/pages/article/newTCS_82.htm.

[3]I (JR) heard this illustration in a message by Rick Warren (date unknown).

[4]Robert L. Wagner, *Conversations: Developing an Intimate Dialogue* (Bloomington, IN: WestBow, 2014), 74.

[5]I heard in a number of different talks by Dallas Willard.

[6]This idea came from a talk I heard by John Upton, the director of the BGAV (Praxis Gathering, September 10, 2015).

[7]John Howard Yoder, *The Royal Priesthood: Essays Ecumenical and Ecclesiological* (Scottsdale, PA: Herald, 2006), 91.

[8]Quoted in N. T. Wright, *Simply Good News: Why the Gospel Is News and What Makes It Good* (New York: HarperOne, 2015), 31.

[9]John Howard Yoder, *For the Nations: Essays Public and Evangelical* (Grand Rapids: Eerdmans, 1997), 218.

[10]This is adapted from the mission statement of Mosaic, Los Angeles (no longer available online).

Recommended Reading

Chapter 1: Movement Intelligence

The Forgotten Ways by Alan Hirsch

The Great Omission by Dallas Willard

Signs of the Spirit by Howard A. Snyder

The Spontaneous Expansion of the Church by Roland Allan

Transforming Mission by David Bosch

Chapter 2: Polycentric Leadership

Creating a Missional Culture by JR Woodward

Eldership and the Mission of God by J. R. Briggs and Bob Hyatt

Holy Trinity, Perfect Community by Leonardo Boff

The Naked Anabaptist by Stuart Murray

Pursuing God's Will Together by Ruth Haley Barton

Chapter 3: Being Disciples

Abba's Child by Brennan Manning

Emotional Healthy Spirituality by Peter Scazzero

In the Name of Jesus by Henri Nouwen

Life on the Vine by Philip Kenneson

Leading with a Limp by Dan Allender

Chapter 4: Making Disciples

Dissident Discipleship by David Augsburger

A Long Obedience in the Same Direction by Eugene Peterson

Mere Discipleship by Lee Camp

Organic Discipleship by Jessica Lowery and Dennis McCallum

A Thicker Jesus by Glen Harold Stassen

Chapter 5: Missional Theology

The Gospel in a Pluralist Society by Lesslie Newbigin

How God Became King by N. T. Wright

The Missional Church by Darrell Guder (editor)

The Mission of God's People by Christopher J. H. Wright

Theology of Mission by John Howard Yoder

Chapter 6: Ecclesial Architecture

Cultivating Missional Communities by Innagrace Dietterich

Desiring the Kingdom by James K. A. Smith

Faithful Presence by David Fitch

Practicing the Way of Jesus by Mark Scandrette

The Search to Belong by Joseph Myers

Chapter 7: Community Formation

Life Together by Dietrich Bonhoeffer

Living into Community by Christine Pohl

Slow Church by C. Christopher Smith and John Pattison

Welcoming Justice: Movement Toward Beloved Community by John Perkins and Charles Marsh

When the Church Was a Family by Joseph H. Hellerman

Chapter 8: Incarnational Practices

Incarnate by Michael Frost

Missional: Joining God in the Neighborhood by Alan Roxburgh

The New Parish by Paul Sparks, Tim Soerens and Dwight Friesen

Subterranean by Dan White Jr.

A Theology of the Built Environment by Timothy Gorringe

About the Authors

· ·

JR Woodward has been passionately planting churches that value tight-knit community, life-forming discipleship, locally-rooted presence and boundary-crossing mission for over twenty-five years. He has helped start and multiply dozens of missional-incarnational communities from Blacksburg, Virginia, to Los Angeles. He has experienced both failure and fruitfulness, suffering and good times.

JR cofounded and currently serves on the board of the Missio Alliance, a movement of hopeful, centrist evangelicals envisioning a church *reimagined* for a world *recreated*. He is an active board member of Reliant Mission (formerly called GCM), which serves over five hundred missionaries in North America and around the world.

He currently serves as the national director for the V3 Church Planting Movement, helping to train church planters across North America in movemental ways of being the church. He is the cofounder and codirector of the Praxis Gathering, an annual gathering for planters who want to grow in grounded missional practices.

JR is the author of *Creating a Missional Culture* (IVP 2012) and a regular contributor to newchurches.com, theV3movement.org and gospel-life.net. He contributes to both academic and popular journals and blogs, including *Religious Studies Review*, *Evangelical Missions Quarterly*, *Leadership Journal*, *Gospel Centered Discipleship* and the *Verge Network*. He speaks at conferences and gatherings across the country, including *Inhabit*, *Fresh Expressions*, *Missio Alliance* and the *Praxis Gathering*.

He graduated with a master of arts in global leadership from Fuller Theological Seminary and is pursuing a PhD at the University of Manchester (UK) on the topic of how a theology of the powers shapes a leadership approach to power and structure for mission.

JR loves to surf, travel, read, skateboard and meet new people. He enjoys photography and film and attends the Sundance Film Festival whenever he can.

Website and Blog: jrwoodward.me

Twitter: @dreamawakener

Facebook: www.facebook.com/jr.woodward1

Instagram: dreamawakener

Email: jr@theV3movement.org

Dan White Jr. coleads a developing network of communities in the urban neighborhoods of Syracuse, New York. After being a full-time pastor for fifteen years, his family, along with four other families, moved into the city to plant a discipleship-centered, mission-oriented, community-shaped, neighborhood-rooted approach to *being* the church.

Dan works as a consultant and missional coach with the V3 Movement. V3 trains, plants and seeds missional expressions throughout the country. He also cofounded the Praxis Gathering. Praxis is an annual gathering of more than three hundred on-the-ground missional practitioners who are living innovative and incarnational ways of being the church.

Dan is the author of *Subterranean: Why the Future of the Church is Rootedness* (Cascade Books, 2015), voted *Leadership Journal's* "Top Ten Ministry Books of the Year" for 2015.

Dan has been featured as a speaker and presenter at the *Sentralized Conference*, the *Inhabit Conference*, the *Missio Alliance Gathering,* the *Praxis Gathering* and various other conferences.

Dan loves Salt City Coffee in Syracuse, a good conversation and a slow walk in his neighborhood.

Website and Blog: danwhitejr.com

Twitter: @danwhitejr

Email: dan@theV3movement.org

CHURCH
PLANTING
MOVEMENT

The **V3 Movement** is a training network that deeply understands the terrain of mission in the West. Every year V3 coaches church planters all over North America, from places like Seattle to Miami, from Honolulu to Toronto, from L.A. to New York, and from Dallas to Atlanta in an 18-month cohort. Research shows that church planters who engage in an in-depth training experience, alongside experienced coaches, are more likely to thrive in their efforts at church planting. This is why our cohorts provide strategic coaching for planters as you journey through the formative phases of planting movemental churches. The training is holistic, communal, peer-based, practice and process oriented, and equips you in transferable tools for discipling your team. You will discover the grassroots work of movement: tight-knit community, life-forming discipleship, locally rooted presence and boundary crossing mission.

thev3movement.org

PRAXIS
GATHERING

The **Praxis Gathering** is a unique church planting conference that is passionate about the space where real-time practice collides with rich theology, followed by deep reflection. Annually 200+ practitioners from around the country gather together in Washington, DC to learn and dialogue around the hands-on work of missional presence in our neighborhoods and networks. There is a movement afoot calling us to rediscover those on-the-ground essentials for being the church. Gather with us to be equipped, nourished and sent back into the world.

thepraxisgathering.com

 **Missio Alliance**

Missio Alliance has arisen in response to the shared voice of pastors and ministry leaders from across the landscape of North American Christianity for a new "space" of togetherness and reflection amid the issues and challenges facing the church in our day. We are united by a desire for a fresh expression of evangelical faith, one significantly informed by the global evangelical family. Lausanne's Cape Town Commitment, "A Confession of Faith and a Call to Action," provides an excellent guidepost for our ethos and aims.[1]

Through partnerships with schools, denominational bodies, ministry organizations, and networks of churches and leaders, Missio Alliance addresses the most vital theological and cultural issues facing the North American Church in God's mission today. We do this primarily by convening gatherings, curating resources, and catalyzing innovation in leadership formation.

Rooted in the core convictions of evangelical orthodoxy, the ministry of Missio Alliance is animated by a strong and distinctive theological identity that emphasizes

Comprehensive Mutuality: Advancing the partnered voice and leadership of women and men among the beautiful diversity of the body of Christ across the lines of race, culture and theological heritage.

Hopeful Witness: Advancing a way of being the people of God in the world that reflects an unwavering and joyful hope in the lordship of Christ in the church and over all things.

Church in Mission: Advancing a vision of the local church in which our identity and the power of our testimony is found and expressed through our active participation in God's mission in the world.

In partnership with InterVarsity Press, we are pleased to offer a line of resources authored by a diverse range of theological practitioners. The resources in this series are selected based on the important way in which they address and embody these values, and thus, the unique contribution they offer in equipping Christian leaders for fuller and more faithful participation in God's mission.

missioalliance.org | twitter.com/missioalliance | facebook.com/missioalliance

---

[1]www.lausanne.org/content/ctc/ctcommitment

Also by JR Woodward

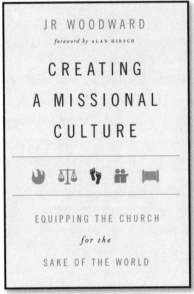

Creating a Missional Culture
978-0-8308-3653-6